Recent Research in Psychology

Ben Goertzel

The Structure of Intelligence

A New Mathematical Model of Mind

Springer-Verlag

New York Berlin Heidelberg London Paris
Tokyo Hong Kong Barcelona Budapest

Ben Goertzel, Ph.D., Department of Mathematical Sciences, University of Nevada at Las Vegas, Las Vegas, NV 89154-4020, USA

With 6 figures.

Library of Congress Cataloging-in-Publication Data
Goertzel, Ben.
    The structure of intelligence: a new mathematical model of mind
/Ben Goertzel.
        p.   cm.
    ISBN 0-387-94004-9. — ISBN 3-540-94004-9
    1. Intellect — Mathematical models.   2. Intellect — Computer
simulation.   3. Philosophy of mind.   4. Cognitive science.
    I. Title.
    BF431.G62   1993
    153 — dc20   92-44224

Printed on acid-free paper.

Production managed by Francine McNeill; manufacturing supervised by Jacqui Ashri.
Copy prepared from the author's WordPerfect file using Ventura Publisher.
Printed and bound by Edwards Brothers, Inc., Ann Arbor, MI.
Printed in the United States of America.

9 8 7 6 5 4 3 2 1

ISBN 0-387-94004-9 Springer-Verlag New York Berlin Heidelberg
ISBN 3-540-94004-9 Springer-Verlag Berlin Heidelberg New York

To
Zar and Gwumbldy

The universe is a labyrinth made of labyrinths. Each leads to another. And wherever we cannot go ourselves, we reach with mathematics.

—Stanislaw Lem, *Fiasco*

Contents

0
Introduction

0.0 Psychology versus Complex Systems Science

Over the last century, psychology has become much less of an art and much more of a science. Philosophical speculation is out; data collection is in. In many ways this has been a very positive trend. Cognitive science (Mandler, 1985) has given us scientific analyses of a variety of intelligent behaviors: short-term memory, language processing, vision processing, etc. And thanks to molecular psychology (Franklin, 1985), we now have a rudimentary understanding of the chemical processes underlying personality and mental illness. However, there is a growing feeling — particularly among non-psychologists (see e.g. Sommerhoff, 1990) — that, with the new emphasis on data collection, something important has been lost. Very little attention is paid to the question of how it all fits together. The early psychologists, and the classical philosophers of mind, were concerned with the general nature of mentality as much as with the mechanisms underlying specific phenomena. But the new, scientific psychology has made disappointingly little progress toward the resolution of these more general questions.

One way to deal with this complaint is to dismiss the questions themselves. After all, one might argue, a scientific psychology cannot be expected to deal with fuzzy philosophical questions that probably have little empirical significance. It is interesting that behaviorists and cognitive scientists tend to be in agreement regarding the question of the overall structure of the mind. Behaviorists believe that it is meaningless to speak about the structures and processes underlying behavior — on any level, general or specific. And many cognitive scientists believe that the mind is a hodge-podge of special-case algorithms, pieced together without any overarching structure. Marvin Minsky has summarized this position nicely in his *Society of Mind* (1986).

It is not a priori absurd to ask for general, philosophical ideas that interlink with experimental details. Psychologists tend to become annoyed when their discipline is compared unfavorably with physics — and indeed, the comparison

1

is unfair. Experimental physicists have many advantages over experimental psychologists. But the facts cannot be ignored. Physics talks about the properties of baseballs, semiconductors and solar systems, but also about the fundamental nature of matter and space, and about the origin of the cosmos. The physics of baseball is much more closely connected to experimental data than is the physics of the first three minutes after the Big Bang — but there is a continuum of theory between these two extremes, bound together by a common philosophy and a common set of tools.

It seems that contemporary psychology simply lacks the necessary tools to confront comprehensive questions about the nature of mind and behavior. That is why, although many of the topics considered in the following pages are classic psychological topics, ideas from the psychological literature are used only occasionally. It seems to me that the key to understanding the mind lies not in contemporary psychology, but rather in a newly emerging field which I will call — for lack of a better name — "complex systems science." Here "complex" does not mean "complicated", but rather something like "full of diverse, intricate, interacting structures". The basic idea is that complex systems are systems which — like immune systems, ecosystems, societies, bodies and minds — have the capacity to **organize themselves**. At present, complex systems science is not nearly so well developed as psychology, let alone physics. It is not a tightly-knit body of theorems, hypotheses, definitions and methods, but rather a loose collection of ideas, observations and techniques. Therefore it is not possible to "apply" complex systems science to the mind in the same way that one would apply physics or psychology to something. But complex systems science is valuable nonetheless. It provides a rudimentary language for dealing with those phenomena which are unique to complex, self-organizing systems. And I suggest that it is precisely these aspects of mentality which contemporary psychology leaves out.

More specifically, the ideas of the following chapters are connected with four "complex systems" theories, intuitively and/or in detail. These are: the theory of pattern (Goertzel, 1991), algorithmic information theory (Chaitin, 1987), the theory of multiextremal optimization (Weisbuch, 1991; Dixon and Szego, 1978; Goertzel, 1989), and the theory of automata networks (Derrida, 1987; Weisbuch, 1991).

The theory of pattern provides a general yet rigorous way of talking about concepts such as structure, intelligence, complexity and mind. But although it is mathematically precise, it is extremely abstract. By connecting the theory of pattern with algorithmic information theory one turns an abstract mathematical analysis of mind into a concrete, computational analysis of mind. This should make clear the limited sense in which the present theory of mind is computational, a point which will be elaborated below. Most of the ideas to be presented are not tied to any particular model of computation, but they are discussed in terms of Boolean automata for sake of concreteness and simplicity.

Pattern and algorithmic complexity give us a rigorous framework for discussing various aspects of intelligence. The theory of multiextremal optimization, which is closely tied to the abstract theory of evolution (Kauffman, 1969; Langton, 1988), gives us a way of understanding some of the actual processes by which intelligences recognize and manipulating patterns. Perception, control, thought and memory may all be understood as multiextremal optimization problems; and recent theoretical and computational results about multiextremal optimization may be interpreted in this context.

And, finally, the theory of automata networks — discussed in Appendix 2 — gives a context for our general model of mind, which will be called the "master network". The master network is not merely a network of simple elements, nor a computer program, but rather a network of programs: an automata network. Not much is known about automata networks, but it is known that in many circumstances they can "lock in" to complex, self-organizing states in which each component program is continually modified by its neighbors in a coherent way, and yet does its individual task effectively. This observation greatly increases the plausibility of the master network.

0.1 Mind and Computation

The analysis of mind to be given in the following chapters is expressed in computational language. It is therefore implicitly assumed that the mind can be understood, to within a high degree of accuracy, as a system of interacting algorithms or automata. However, the concept of "algorithm" need not be interpreted in a narrow sense. Penrose (1989), following Deutsch (1985), has argued on strictly physical grounds that the standard digital computer is probably not an adequate model for the brain. Deutsch (1985) has proposed the "quantum computer" as an alternative, and he has proved that — according to the known principles of quantum physics — the quantum computer is capable of simulating any finite physical system to within finite accuracy. He has proved that while a quantum computer can do everything an ordinary computer can, it cannot compute any functions besides those which an ordinary computer can compute (however, quantum computers do have certain unique properties, such as the ability to generate "truly random" numbers). Because of Deutsch's theorems, the assertion that brain function is computation is not a psychological hypothesis but a physical, mathematical fact. It follows that mind, insofar as it reduces to brain, is computational.

I suspect that most of the structures and processes of mind are indeed explicable in terms of ordinary digital computation. However, I will suggest that the mind has at least one aspect which **cannot** be explained in these terms. Chapter 11, which deals with consciousness, is the only chapter which explicitly assumes that the mind has to do with **quantum** computation rather than simply digital computation.

Many people are deeply skeptical of the idea that the mind can be understood in terms of computation. And this is understandable. The brain is the only example of intelligence that we know, and it doesn't **look** like it's executing algorithms: it is a largely incomprehensible mass of self-organizing electrochemical processes. However, assuming that these electrochemical processes obey the laws of quantum physics, they can be explained in terms of a system of differential equations derived from quantum theory. And any such system of differential equations may be approximated, to within any desired degree of accuracy, by a function that is computable on a quantum computer. Therefore, those who claim that the human mind cannot be understood in terms of computation are either 1) denying that the laws of quantum physics, or any similar mathematical laws, apply to the brain; or 2) denying that any degree of understanding of the brain will yield an understanding of the human mind. To me, neither of these alternatives seems reasonable.

Actually, there is a little more to the matter than this simple analysis admits. Quantum physics is not a comprehensive theory of the universe. It seems to be able to deal with everything **except** gravitation, for which the General Theory of Relativity is required. In fact, quantum theory and general relativity are in contradiction on several crucial points. The effect of gravity on processes occurring within individual organisms is small and easily accounted for, so these contradictions would seem to be irrelevant to the present considerations. But some scientists — for instance, Roger Penrose, in his *The Emperor's New Mind* (1989) — believe that the combination of quantum physics with general relativity will yield an entirely new understanding of the physics of the brain.

It is worth asking: if Penrose were right, what effect would this have on the present considerations? Quantum theory and general relativity would be superseded by a new Grand Unified Theory, or GUT. But presumably it would then be possible to define a GUT computer, which would be capable of approximating any system with arbitrary accuracy according to the GUT. Logically, the GUT computer would have to reduce to a quantum computer in those situations for which general relativistic and other non-quantum effects are negligible. It would probably have all the capacities of the quantum computer, and then some. And in this case, virtually none of the arguments given here would be affected by the replacement of quantum physics with the GUT.

To repeat: the assumption that brain processes are computation, if interpreted correctly, is not at all dubious. It is not a metaphor, an analogy, or a tentative hypothesis. It is a physical, mathematical fact. If one assumes — as will be done explicitly in Chapter 4 — that each mind is associated with the structure of a certain physical system, then the fact that a sufficiently powerful computer can approximate any physical system with arbitrary precision guarantees that any mind can be modeled by a computer with arbitrary precision. Whether this is a useful way to look at the mind is another question; but the validity of the computational approach to mind is not open to serious scientific dispute.

0.2 Synopsis

Since the arguments to follow are somewhat unorthodox, it seems best to state the main goals in advance:

1) To give a precise, general mathematical definition of intelligence which is "objective" in that it does not refer to any particular culture, species, etc.,

2) To outline a set of principles by which a machine (a quantum computer, not necessarily a Turing machine) fulfilling this definition could be constructed, given appropriate technology,

3) To put forth the hypothesis that these same principles are a crucial part of the structure of **any** intelligent system,

4) To elucidate the nature of and relationships between the concepts involved in these principles: induction, deduction, analogy, memory, perception, motor control, optimization, consciousness, emotion, ...

The line of argument leading up to these four goals is as follows. Chapters 1 through 4 lay the conceptual foundations for the remainder of the book. Basic mathematical concepts are reviewed: of Turing machines, algorithmic information pattern, and aspects of randomness and optimization. This theoretical framework is used to obtain precise definitions of "intelligence", "complexity", "structure", "emergence," and other crucial ideas.

For instance, the structure of an entity is defined as the set of all patterns in that entity; and the structural complexity of an entity is defined as (roughly speaking) the total algorithmic complexity of all the patterns comprising the structure of that entity. The concept of unpredictability is analyzed according to the theory of pattern, and intelligence is defined as the ability to optimize complex functions of unpredictable environments.

In Chapters 5 through 8, the framework erected in the previous chapters is applied to what Peirce called the three fundamental forms of logic: induction, deduction and analogy. Each of the forms is characterized and explored in terms of algorithmic information theory and the theory of pattern. Induction is defined as the construction, based on the patterns recognized in the past, of a coherent model of the future. It is pointed out that induction cannot be effective without a reliable pattern recognition method to provide it with data, and that induction is a necessary component of pattern recognition and motor control.

Analogy is characterized, roughly, as reasoning of the form "where one similarity has been found, look for more". Three highly general forms of analogy are isolated, analyzed in terms of the theory of pattern, and, finally, synthesized into a general framework which is philosophically similar to Gentner's (1983) "structure-mapping" theory of analogy. Edelman's theory of Neural Darwinism is used to show that the brain reasons analogically.

The structure of long-term memory is analyzed as a corollary of the nature of analogical reasoning, yielding the concept of a structurally associative memory — a memory which stores each entity near other entities with similar structures, and continually self-organizes itself so as to maintain this structure.

Finally, deduction is analyzed as a process which can only be useful to intelligence insofar as it proceeds according to an axiom system which is amenable to analogical reasoning. This analysis is introduced in the context of mathematical deduction, and then made precise and general with the help of the theory of pattern.

Chapters 9 and 10 deal with the perceptual-motor hierarchy, the network of pattern-recognition processes through which an intelligence builds a model of the world. This process makes essential use of the three forms of reasoning discussed in the previous chapters; and it is also extremely dependent on concepts from the theory of multiextremal optimization.

The perceptual hierarchy is, it is proposed, composed of a number of levels, each one recognizing patterns in the output of the level below it. This pattern recognition is executed by applying an approximation to Bayes' rule from elementary probability theory, which cannot be effective without aid from induction and deduction. The activity of the various levels is regulated according to a "multilevel methodology" (Goertzel, 1989) which integrates top-down and bottom-up control. Neurological data supports this general picture, and recent computer vision systems based on miniature "perceptual hierarchies" have been very effective.

The motor control hierarchy is closely linked with the perceptual hierarchy and operates somewhat similarly, the difference being that its task is not to recognize patterns but rather to select the actions which best fulfill the criteria assigned to it. Building on the brain model given in Chapter 6, specific model for the brain's perceptual-motor hierarchy is proposed.

Chapter 11 deals with consciousness and emotion — the two essential aspects of the construction of the subjective, interior world. Consciousness is analyzed as a process residing on the higher levels of the perceptual hierarchy, a process whose function is to make definite choices from among various possibilities. It is suggested that complex coordination of the perceptual hierarchy and the motor control hierarchy may not be possible in the absence of consciousness. And, following Goswami (1990) and others, it is argued that an ordinary computer can never be conscious — but that if a computer is built with small enough parts packed closely enough together, it automatically ceases to function as a Turing machine and becomes fundamentally a "quantum computer" with the potential for consciousness. The problem of reconciling this quantum theory of consciousness with the psychological and biological conceptions of consciousness is discussed.

Following Paulhan (1887) and Mandler (1985), emotion is characterized as something which occurs when expectations are not fulfilled. It is argued that human emotion has a "hot" and a "cold" aspect, and that whereas the "cold" aspect is a structure that may be understood in terms of digital computation, the "hot" aspect is a peculiar chemical process that is closely related to consciousness.

Finally, Chapter 12 presents the theory of the **master network:** a network of automata which achieves intelligence by the integration of induction, deduction, analogy, memory, perception, control, consciousness and emotion. It is pointed out that, according to the definition of intelligence given in Chapter 4, a sufficiently large master network will inevitably be intelligent. And it is also observed that, if one is permitted to postulate a "sufficiently large" network, nearly all of the structure of the master network is superfluous: intelligence can be achieved, albeit far less efficiently, by a much simpler structure. Finally, it is suggested that, in order to make sense of this observation, one must bring physics into the picture. It is not physically possible to build an arbitrarily large network that functions fast enough to survive in reality, because special relativity places restrictions on the speed of information transmission and quantum theory places restrictions on the minimum space required to store a given amount of information. These restrictions give rise to the hypothesis that it is not physically possible to build an intelligent machine which lacks any one of the main components of the master network.

It must be emphasized that these various processes and structures, though they are analyzed in separate chapters here, need not be **physically** separate in the body of any given intelligence. For one thing, they are intricately independent in function, so why not in implementation? And, furthermore, it seems unlikely that they are physically separate in the human brain. In the final section, I give a demonstration of how one may design an intelligent machine by combining the theory of the master network with Edelman's Neural Darwinism. In this demonstration, the various components of the master network are bound together according to an implementation-specific logic.

Finally, it must also be emphasized that the master network is not a physical structure but a **pattern**, an abstract logical structure — a pattern according to which, or so I claim, the system of patterns underlying intelligent behavior tends to organize itself. It consists of two large networks of algorithms (the structurally associative memory and the perceptual-motor hierarchy), three complex processes for transmitting information from one network to another (induction, deduction, analogy), and an array of special-purpose auxiliary optimization algorithms. Each of these networks, processes and algorithms may be realized in a variety of different ways — but each has its own distinctive structure, and the inter-connection of the five also has it own distinctive structure. Of course, an intelligence may also possess a variety of other structures — unrelated structures, or structures intricately intertwined with those described here. My hypothesis is only that the presence of the master network in the structure of an entity is a necessary and sufficient condition for that entity to be intelligent.

0.3 Mathematics, Philosophy, and Science

A scientific theory must be testable. A test can never prove a theory true, and since all but the simplest theories can be endlessly modified, a test can rarely prove a complex theory false. But, at very least, a test can indicate whether a theory is sensible or not.

I am sorry to say that I have not been able to design a "crucial experiment" — a practical test that would determine, all at once, whether the theory of the master network is sensible or not. The situation is rather similar to that found in evolutionary biology. There is no quick and easy way to test the theory of evolution by natural selection. But there are numerous pieces of evidence, widely varying in nature, reliability and relevance. How to combine and weight these various pieces of evidence is a matter of intuition and personal bias.

I certainly do not mean to imply that the theory of the master network is as well supported as the theory of evolution by natural selection — far from it. But it is not implausible that, in the near future, various sorts of evidence might combine to form a fairly convincing case for the theory. In this sense, I think the ideas proposed here are testable. Whether there will ever be a more effective way to test hypotheses about self-organizing systems such as minds and ecosystems is anybody's guess.

1
Mind and Computation

1.0 Rules

What does it mean to tell someone **exactly** what to do?

Sixty years ago no one could give this query a plausible response. Now, however, we have a generally accepted definition: a set of instructions is exact if some computer can follow them. We have a word, **algorithm**, which is intended to refer to a completely exact set of instructions. This is impressively elegant. But there's a catch — this approach is meaningful only in the context of a theory explaining exactly what a computer is. And it turns out that this problem is not so straightforward as it might seem.

Note that one cannot say "a set of instructions is exact if **every** computer can follow them." Obviously, computers come in different sizes and forms. Some are very small, with little memory or processing power. Some, like the computer chips installed in certain televisions and cars, are dedicated to one or two specific purposes. If there were little or nothing in common between the various types of computers, computer science would not deserve the label "science." But it seems that many computers are so powerful that they can simulate any other computer. This is what makes theoretical computer science possible. Computers of this sort are called "universal computers," and were first discussed by Alan Turing.

What is now called the Turing machine is the simple device consisting of:

1) a processing unit which computes according to some formula of Boolean algebra
2) a very long tape divided into squares, each square of which is marked either zero or one
3) a tape head which can move, read from and write to the tape

For instance, the processing unit might contain instructions like:

9

> If the tape reads D and -A+(B-C)(D+E)=(R-J), then move tape to
> the left, call what is read C, move the tape two to the right,
> and write (D-B)C on the tape.

The Boolean formula in the processing unit is the "program" of the Turing machine: it tells it what to do. Different programs lead to different behaviors.

Assuming that the tape head cannot move arbitrarily fast, it is clear that any specific program, running for a finite time, can only deal with a finite section of the two tapes. But theoretically, the tapes must be allowed to be as long as any program will require. Thus one often refers to an "infinitely long" tape, even though no particular program will ever require an infinitely long tape in any particular situation.

At first, Turing's colleagues were highly skeptical of his contention that this simple machine was capable of executing any exact sequence of instructions. But they were soon convinced that the behavior of any conceivable computer could be simulated by some Turing machine, and furthermore that any precise mathematical procedure could be carried out by some Turing machine. To remove all doubt, Turing proved that a certain type of Turing machine, now called a "universal Turing machine", was capable of simulating any other Turing machine. One merely had to feed the universal Turing machine a number encoding the properties of Turing machine X, and then it would act indistinguishably from Turing machine X.

PUT THE CUP ON THE TABLE

Most people who have studied the literature would concur: no one has been able to come up with a set of instructions which is obviously precise and yet cannot be programmed on a Turing machine. However, agreement is not quite universal. For instance, the philosopher Hubert Dreyfus (1978) has written extensively about the inability of existing computers to see, move around, or make practical decisions in the real world. From his point of view, it is revealing to observe that, say, no Turing machine can follow the instruction: put the cup on the table.

The problem is not, of course, that a Turing machine doesn't have any way to pick up a cup. One could easily connect a robot arm to a computer in such a way that the output of the computer determined the motions of the robot. This is the state of the art in Japanese factory design. And even if current technology were not up to the task, the fact that it **could** be done would be enough to vindicate Turing's claim.

But could it, actually, be done? What is really involved here? When I tell someone to "put the cup on the table," I am really telling them "figure out what I am talking about when I say 'the cup' and 'the table' and 'on', and then put the cup on the table." Even if we give a computer a robot eye, it is not easy to tell it how to locate a cup lying in the middle of a messy floor. And it is even harder to tell a computer how to distinguish a cup from a bowl. In fact, it is hard to tell a person how to distinguish a cup from a bowl. This is a matter of culture and language. We simply learn it from experience.

One might take all this as proof that "put the cup on the table" is not actually a precise instruction. Or, on the other hand, one might maintain that a Turing machine, provided with the proper program, could indeed follow the instruction.

But there is an element of circular reasoning in the first alternative. "Put the cup on the table" is very precise to many people in many situations. To say that it is not precise because a Turing machine cannot understand it is to **define** precision in terms of the Turing machine, in contradiction to common sense. And the second alternative presupposes a great deal of faith in the future of artificial intelligence. The hypothesis that the Turing machine can simulate any computer and execute any set of precise mathematical instructions is very well established. But the hypothesis that the Turing machine can execute any set of precise instructions is a little shakier, since it is not quite clear what "precision" is supposed to mean.[1]

In sum: there is still plenty of room for philosophical debate about the meaning of the Turing machine. In the Introduction I mentioned Deutsch's result that according to quantum theory any finite physical system can be simulated by a quantum computer. Coupled with the fact that a quantum computer cannot compute any functions besides those which a Turing machine can compute, this would seem to provide a fairly strong argument in favor of Turing's hypothesis. But, of course, physics can never truly settle a philosophical question.

---

[1]One might attempt to give an "objective" definition of precision. Perhaps one could define a set of instructions to be precise with respect to a certain set of actors (people, computers or whatever) in a certain set of situations if it yields the same results whenever it is given to one of these actors in one of these situations. If one set of instructions gets more consistent results than another (with respect to the same actors and situations), it might be said to be more precise. This could be formulated mathematically. An algorithm, a completely precise set of instructions, could then be defined as a set of instructions which is precise with respect to every intelligent actor in every possible situation.

But even this subjectivist approach would run into problems. First of all, it ignores the problem of translating a set of instructions into different languages. And, more importantly, it presupposes the solution to a very difficult question: what is intelligence? The analysis of intelligence to be given in Chapter 4 relies on the theory of computation, so to invoke it here would be circular reasoning.

BRAIN AS TURING MACHINE

In a paper of legendary difficulty, McCulloch and Pitts (1943) attempted to demonstrate that the human brain is a universal Turing machine. Toward this end, they adopted a greatly oversimplified model of the brain, ignoring the intricacies of neurochemistry, perception, localization, and the like. The McCulloch-Pitts brain is a network of dots and lines, each dot standing for a neuron and each line standing for a connection between neurons. It changes in discrete jumps: time 0, then time 1, then time 2, and so on. Each neuron operates according to "threshold logic": when the amount of charge contained in it exceeds a certain threshold T, it sends all its charge out to the neurons it is connected to. What McCulloch and Pitts proved is that a universal Turing machine can be constructed using a neural network of this sort instead of a program.

Some neuroscientists have protested that this sort of "neural network" has nothing to do with the brain. However, this is simply not the case. It is clear that the network captures one of the most prominent structures of the brain. Precisely what role this structure plays in the brain's activity remains to be seen. But it is interesting to see how tremendously powerful this one structure is, all by itself.

As mentioned above, there have been numerous efforts to form biologically realistic neural network models. One approach which has been taken is to introduce random errors into various types of simulated neural networks. This idea has led to a valuable optimization technique called "simulated annealing" (Aarts et al 1987), to be considered below.

1.1 Stochastic and Quantum Computation

When noise is added to the McCullough-Pitts network, it is no longer a Turing machine. It is a **stochastic computer** — a computer which involves chance as well as the precise following of instructions. The error-ridden neural network is merely one type of stochastic computer. Every real computer is a stochastic computer, in the sense that it is subject to random errors. In some situations, randomness is a nuisance; one hopes it will not interfere too much with computation. But in other situations, chance may be an essential part of computation. Many Turing machine algorithms, such as Monte Carlo methods in numerical analysis, use various mathematical ruses to **simulate** stochasticity.

As I will argue later, one may view randomness in the neural network as a blessing in disguise. After all, one might well wonder: if the brain is a computer, then where do new ideas come from? A deterministic function only rearranges its input. Is it not possible that innovation involves an element of chance?

One may define a stochastic Turing machine as a computer identical to a Turing machine except that its program may contain references to chance. For instance, its processing unit might contain commands like:

If the tape reads D and -A+(B-C)(D+E)=(R-J), then move tape to the left with probability 50% and move it to the right with probability 50%, call what is read C, move the tape two to the right, write (D-B)C on the tape with probability 25% and write C on the tape with probability 75%.

One may construct a theory of stochastic Turing machines parallel to the ordinary theory of computation. We have seen that a universal Turing machine can follow any precise set of instructions, at least in the sense that it can simulate any other computer. Similarly, it can be shown that there is a universal stochastic Turing machine which can simulate any precise set of instructions involving chance operations.

QUANTUM COMPUTATION

If the universe were fundamentally deterministic, the theory of stochastic computation would be superfluous, because there could never really be a stochastic computer, and any apparent randomness we perceived would be a consequence of deterministic dynamics. But it seems that the universe is not in fact deterministic. Quantum physics tells us that chance plays a major role in the evolution of the physical world. This leads us to the question: what kind of computer can simulate **any physical system**? What kind of computer can follow any precise set of physical instructions?

It turns out that neither a Turing machine nor a stochastic Turing machine has this property. This puts the theory of computation in a very uncomfortable situation. After all, the human brain is a physical system, and if computers cannot simulate any physical system, there is no reason to simply assume that they can simulate the human brain. Perhaps they can, but there is no reason to believe it. Clearly it would be desirable to design a computer which could simulate an arbitrary physical system. Then we would have a much better claim to be talking about computation in general.

As mentioned above, D. Deutsch (1985) has taken a large step toward providing such a computer. He has described the **quantum Turing machine**, which according to the laws of quantum physics can simulate the behavior of any finite physical system within an arbitrarily small degree of error. It can simulate any Turing machine, and any stochastic Turing machine, with perfect accuracy. Of course, the rules of quantum physics may be revised any day now; there are a number of pressing problems. But Deutsch's idea is a major advance.

There is much more to be said on the topic of quantum computation. But for now, let us merely observe that the question "what is a computer?" is hardly resolved. It may never be. Various abstract models may shed light on different issues, but they are never final answers. In the last analysis, "precise instructions" is just as elusive a concept as "intelligence" or "mind."

1.2 Computational Complexity

Computational complexity theory, also called algorithmic complexity theory, seeks to answer two different kinds of questions: "How hard is this problem?", and "How effective is this algorithm at solving this problem?". A number of difficult issues are involved here, and it is not possible to delve into them deeply without sophisticated mathematics. Here we shall only scratch the surface.

Questions of computational complexity are only meaningful in the context of a general theory of computation. Otherwise one can only ask "How hard is this problem for this computer?", or "How hard is this problem for this particular person?". What lets us ask "How hard is this problem?", without any reference to who is actually solving the problem, is a theory which tells us that problems are basically just as hard for one computer as for another. Here as in so many other cases, it is theory which tells us what questions to ask.

According to the theory of Turing machines, any sufficiently powerful computer can simulate any other computer. And this is not merely a theoretical illusion. In practice, computers such as PCs, mainframes and supercomputers are highly flexible. An IBM PC could be programmed to act just like a MacIntosh; in fact, there are software packages which do something very close to this. Similarly, a MacIntosh could be programmed to act just like an IBM. Turing proved that there is a program which tells a computer, given appropriate information, how to simulate any other computer. Therefore, any computer which is powerful enough to run this program can act as a universal Turing machine. If it is equipped with enough memory capacity — e.g. enough disk drives — it can impersonate any computer whatsoever.

True, this universal simulation program is very complex. But if a problem is sufficiently difficult enough, this doesn't matter. Consider the problem of sorting a list of numbers into increasing order. Suppose computer A is capable of solving this problem very fast. Then computer B, if it is sufficiently powerful, can solve the problem by simulating computer A. If the problem is sorting the list $\{2,1,3\}$, then this would be a tremendous effort, because simulating A is vastly more difficult than sorting the list $\{2,1,3\}$. But if the list in question is a billion numbers long, then it's a different story. The point is that lists of numbers can get as long as you like, but the complexity of simulating another computer remains the same.

Let us make this example more precise. Assume that both A and B have an unlimited supply of disk drives — an infinite memory tape — at their disposal. Suppose that the program for simulating computer A is so slow that it takes computer B 10 time steps to simulate one of computer A's time steps. Suppose also that computer A is capable of sorting a list of n numbers in n^2 time steps. That is, it can sort 10 numbers in 100 time steps, 100 numbers in 10000 time steps, and so on. Assume that computer B is not quite so bright, and it has a sorting program built into its hardware which takes n^3 time steps to sort a list of n numbers.

Then, if B were given a list of 3 numbers, its hardware could sort it in $3^3=27$ time steps. If it tried to sort it by simulating A, it would take $10(3^2)=90$ time steps. Clearly, it should rely on its built-in hardware. But if B were given a list of 10 numbers, it would take $10^3=1000$ steps to sort it. If it tried to sort the list by simulating A, it would take $10(10^2)$ time steps — exactly the same amount of time. And if B were given a list of 1000 numbers, it would take $1000^3=1,000,000,000$ steps to sort it using its hardware, and only $10(1000^2) =10,000,000$ steps to sort it by simulating A. The longer the list is, the more useful is the capacity for simulation, and the less useful is the built-in hardware.

The point is that as the size of the problem, n, gets bigger and bigger, the differences between computers become irrelevant. It is worth being a little more rigorous about this. Take any type of problem, and assign to each instance of it a "size" n. For example, if the problem is sorting lists of numbers, then each instance is a list of numbers, and its size is its length. Let A(n) denote the **longest** amount of time which computer A requires to solve **any** problem instance of size n. Let B(n) denote the **longest** amount of time which computer B requires to solve any problem instance of size n. Assume that the time required to solve an instance of the problem increases as n increases (just as the time required to sort a list of n numbers increases as n increases). Then it follows that the bigger n gets, the less significant is the difference between A(n) and B(n). Mathematically, we say that **as n goes to infinity**, the ratio A(n)/B(n) goes to 1.

All this follows from the assumption that any sufficiently powerful computer can simulate any other one, by running a certain "universal Turing machine" program of large but fixed size.

AVERAGE-CASE ANALYSIS

Note that the quantity A(n) is defined in terms of "worst-case" computation. It is the longest that computer A takes to solve any problem instance of size n. Any computer worth its salt can sort the list $\{1,2,3,4,5,6,7,8,9,10\}$ faster than the list $\{5,7,6,4,10,3,8,9,2,1\}$. But A(n) ignores the easy cases. Out of all the possible instances, it only asks: how hard is the hardest?

For some applications, this is a useful way to look at computation. But not always. To see why, consider the following well-known problem. A salesman, driving a jeep, must visit a number of cities in the desert. There are no mountains, rivers or other obstructions in the region. He wants to know what is the shortest route that goes through all the different cities. This is known as the Traveling Salesman Problem. Each specific instance of the problem is particular collection of cities or, mathematically speaking, a set of points in the plane. The size of an instance of the problem, n, is simply the number of cities involved.

How hard is this problem? When the data is presented pictorially, human beings can solve it pretty well. However, we must remember that even if Maria is exceptionally good at solving the problem, what Maria(n) measures is the longest it takes Maria to arrive at the correct solution for **any** collection of n cities. No human being does well according to this strict criterion. We do not always see the absolute **shortest** path between the n cities; we often identify a route which is close to correct, but not quite there. And we sometimes miss the mark entirely. So we are not very good at solving the Traveling Salesman Problem, in the sense that there are instances of the problem for which we get the answer wrong or take a long time to get to the answer. But we **are** good at it in the sense that most of the time we get reasonably close to the right answer, pretty fast. There are two different notions of proficiency involved here.

The simplest way to solve the Traveling Salesman problem is to list all the possible paths between the cities, then compare all the lengths to see which one is the shortest. The problem is that there are just too many paths. For instance, if there are 5 cities, then there are [4x3x2]/2 = 12 paths. If there are 10 cities, then there are [9x8x7x6x5x4x3x2]/2 = 181440 paths. If there are, say, 80 cities, then there are more paths than there are electrons in the universe. Using this method, the number of steps required to solve the Traveling Salesman problem increases very fast as the size of the problem increases.[2] So, given a large Traveling Salesman problem, it might be better to apply erratic human intuition than to use a computer to investigate every possible path.

Let's consider a simple analogy. Suppose you run a bank, and you have three loan officers working for you. Officer A is very methodic and meticulous. He investigates every case with the precision of a master detective, and he **never** makes a mistake. He never loans anyone more than they can afford. Everyone he approves pays back their loans, and everyone he turns down for a loan would not have paid it back anyway. The only problem is that he often takes a long time to determine his answer. Officer B, on the other hand, works entirely by intuition. He simply looks a person over, talks to them about golf or music or the weather, and then makes his decision on the spot. He rejects a some people who deserve loans, and he gives some people more or less money than they can afford to pay back. He gives loans to a few questionable characters who have neither the ability nor the inclination to pay the bank back.

Suppose that, although you really need both, you have been ordered to cut back expenses by firing one of your loan officers. Which one should go? At first

---

[2]To be precise, the number of steps required to find the shortest path between n cities with this method is (n-1)!/2.

you might think "Officer B, of course." But what if you have a lot of money to lend, and a great many people demanding loans? Then A might be a poor choice — after all, B will serve a lot more customers each month. Even though there are some cases where A is much better than B, and there are many cases where A is a little better than B, the time factor may tip the balance in B's favor.

You may be thinking "Well, a real bank executive would find someone who's both fast **and** accurate." In the case of the Traveling Salesman problem, however, no one has yet found an algorithm which finds the exact shortest path every time much faster than the simple method given above. And it seems likely that no such algorithm will ever be discovered. The Traveling Salesman problem and hundreds of other important problems have been shown to be "NP-complete", which means essentially that if there is a reasonably fast algorithm for solving any one of them, then there is a reasonably fast algorithm for solving all of them. Many mathematicians believe that the question of whether such algorithms exist is undecidable in the sense of Godel's Incompleteness Theorem: that there's no way to prove that they do, and there's no way to prove that they don't.

Now, we **have** discovered algorithms which solve the Traveling Salesman problem faster than people, and on the average come up with better answers (Peters, 1985). But there are still some collections of cities for which they give the wrong answer, or take a ridiculously long time to solve. In the case of the Traveling Salesman problem, it seems that there is no point in looking for algorithms which solve the problem exactly, every time. All the algorithms which do that are just too slow. Rather, it seems to be more intelligent to look for algorithms that solve the problem pretty well a lot of the time.

It turns out that most of the mathematical problems involved in thought and perception are a lot like the Traveling Salesman problem. They are "NP-complete". So when, in later chapters, we discuss the algorithms of thought, we shall virtually never be discussing algorithms that solve problems perfectly. The relevant concept is rather the PAC algorithm — the algorithm which is Probably Approximately Correct.

PARALLELISM

One interesting aspect of the McCullough-Pitts neural network is the way it does many things at once. At every time step, all the neurons act. The original formulation of the Turing machine was not like that; it only did one thing at a time. It moved the tapes, then looked in its memory to see what to do next. Of course, the McCullough-Pitts network and the original Turing machine are fundamentally equivalent; anything one can do, so can the other. But the McCullough-Pitts network will, in most cases, get things done faster.

The computers in popular use today are like the original Turing machine: they only do one thing at a time. This is true of everything from PCs to huge mainframe computers — Cybers, VAXs and so forth. They are **serial** computers.

Some supercomputers and special-purpose research computers, however, can work in **parallel**: they can do up to hundreds of thousands of things at once. The advantage of parallelism is obvious: speed. By using a parallel computer, one trades off space for time.

There are many different kinds of parallel computers. Some are so-called **single-instruction** machines. They can do many things at once, as long as these things are all the same. For instance, a typical single-instruction machine could multiply fifty numbers by four all at the same time. But it might not be able to multiply one number by four at the same time as it added six to another number.

Multiple-instruction machines are more interesting, but also more difficult to build and to program. A multiple-instruction parallel computer is like a bunch of serial computers connected to each other. Each one can execute a different program, and communicate the results of its computation to certain others. In a way, it is like a society of serial computers. Thinking Machines Corporation, in Cambridge, Massachusetts, has manufactured a number of powerful multiple-instruction parallel computers called Connection Machines. They are now being used in science and industry — for, among other things, modeling the behavior of fluids, analyzing visual data, and generating computer graphics.

Why is all this relevant? Some may dispute the neurophysiological relevance of the McCullough-Pitts model and its contemporary descendants. But everyone agrees that, if the brain is a computer, it must be a parallel computer. The brain contains about 100 billion neurons, all operating at once, and besides that it is continually swirling with chemical activity. The diversity of its activity leaves little doubt that, if it is indeed a computer, it is a multiple-instruction parallel computer. This is the intuition behind the recent spurt of research in parallel distributed processing.

In Chapter 11 I will take this one step further and argue that the brain should be modeled as a **multiple-instruction parallel quantum computer**. By then, it will be clear just how different such a computer is from today's serial computers. We are talking about a computer which does billions of different things at once and incorporates a huge amount of chance into its operations. As we shall see later, it is a computer whose state is not completely measurable by any sequence of physical observations. It is a computer which, in a physically precise sense, plays a significant role in the continual creation of the universe. It could be argued that a computer with all these properties should not be called a "computer". But, mathematical theories aside, the intuitive concept of computation has always been somewhat fuzzy. As warned in the Introduction, the limitations of present-day computers should not be taken as fundamental restrictions on the nature of computation.

1.3 Network, Program, or Network of Programs?

Throughout history, philosophers, scientists, and inventors have argued profusely both for and against the possibility of thinking machines. Many have also made suggestions as to what sort of general strategy one might use to actually build such a machine. Only during the last half-century, however, has it become technically possible to seriously attempt the construction of thinking machines. During this period, there have emerged two sharply divergent approaches to the problem of artificial intelligence, which may be roughly described as the "neural network approach" and the "programming approach". Cognitive science has played an important role in the development of the latter, for obvious reasons: cognitive science analyzes mental processes in terms of simple procedures, and simple procedures are easily programmable.

What I roughly label the "neural network approach" involves, more precisely, the conception, construction and study of electric circuits imitating certain aspects of the electrical structure of the brain, and the attempt to teach these circuits to display behavior similar to that of real brains. In the late 1940s and the 1950s, no other approach to AI was so actively pursued. Throughout the 1960s, it became increasingly apparent that the practical success of the neural network approach was by no means imminent — fairly large neural networks were constructed, and though the results were sometimes interesting, nothing even vaguely resembling a mind evolved. The rapid advent of the general-purpose digital computer, among other factors, led researchers in other directions. Over the past decade, however, there has been a tremendous resurgence of interest in neural networks.

The fundamental tenet of the neural network approach is that certain large, densely interconnected networks of extremely simple but highly nonlinear elements can be **trained** to demonstrate many or all of the various activities commonly referred to as intelligence. The inspiration for this philosophy was a trend in neuroscience toward the modelling of the brain as a network of neurons. The dynamics of the individual neuron was understood by Hodgkin and Huxley in 1955, although recent investigations have led to certain modifications of their analysis. Unable to mimic the incredible complexity of chemical interaction which underlies and subtly alters the operation of a biological network of neurons, and possessing few ideas as to what restrictions might be placed on the elements or structure of a network in order to encourage it to evolve intelligence, early researchers simply constructed model networks of simulated neurons and tried to teach them.

Each of the neurons of such a network is connected to a small set of other neurons in such a way that it can input charge to them. The charge which it sends to them at a given time is a function of the amount of charge which it contains as well as, possibly, other factors. Usually the function involved is a threshold function or a continuous approximation thereof. Some researchers actually built networks of simulated neurons; others merely simulated entire networks on general-purpose computers, sometimes including nontrivial physical aspects of the neural network (such as imperfect conductance of connections, and noise).

The first problem faced by neural network researchers was the fact that a simple network of neurons contains no obvious learning device. Some thought that the ability to learn would spontaneously evolve; most, however, implemented within their networks some rule for adapting the connections between neurons. The classical example is the Hebb rule (Hebb, 1949): when a connection is used, its resistance is decreased (i.e. more of the charge which is issued into it actually comes out the other end; less is lost in transit). This may be interpreted in many different ways, but it is clearly intended to serve as a primitive form of analogy; it says "this connection has been used before, so let us make it easier to use it again." Whether the brain works this way we are not yet certain. Various modifications to the Hebb rule have been proposed, mostly by researchers thinking of practical algorithmic development rather than biology (Rumelhart and McClelland, 1986).

Neither the failures nor the successes of this approach have been decisive. Various networks have been successfully trained to recognize simple patterns in character sequences or in visual data, to approximate the solutions of certain mathematical problems, and to execute a number of important practical engineering tasks. On the theoretical side, Stephen Grossberg (1987) and others have proven general theorems about the behavior of neural networks operating under a wide class of dynamics. And in various particular cases (Hopfield, 1985), it has been proved in what sense certain neural networks will converge to approximate solutions to certain problems. But it must nonetheless be said that there exists no empirical or theoretical reason to believe that neural networks similar to those hitherto designed or studied could ever be trained to possess intelligence. There is no doubt that researchers into the neural network approach have demonstrated that disordered circuits can be trained to demonstrate various types of adaptive behavior. However, it is a long way from adaptation to true intelligence.

It is clear that the "neural networks" hitherto produced involve such drastic oversimplifications of brain structure that they must be considered parallel processors of a fundamentally different nature. In fact, most contemporary practitioners of the neural network approach are quite aware of this and continue their labors regardless. Such research is important both practically and theoretically. But it is connected only indirectly with the study of the brain or the design of thinking machines. For this reason many neural network researchers prefer the term "parallel distributed processing" to "neural networks."

By the 1970s, the neural network approach had been almost entirely supplanted by what I shall call the **programming** approach: the conception, study and implementation on general-purpose computers of various "artificial intelligence" algorithms. Most such algorithms consist of clever tricks for approximating the solutions of certain mathematical problems (usually optimization problems) thought to reflect important aspects of human mental process. A few approach closer to the real world by applying similar tricks to the execution of simple tasks in computer-simulated or carefully controlled environments called "microworlds". For example, a famous program treats the problem of piling polyhedral blocks on a flat floor.

In the early days of the programming approach, AI programmers were routinely predicting that a truly intelligent computer program would be available in ten years (Dreyfus, 1978). Their optimism is quite understandable: after all, it took computers only a couple of decades to progress from arithmetic to expert chess, competent vision processing, and rudimentary theorem proving. By the late 1980s, the programming approach had succeeded in creating algorithms for the practical solution of many difficult and/or important problems — for instance, medical diagnosis and chess. However, no one had yet written an AI program applicable to two widely divergent situations, let alone to the entire range of situations to which human intelligence is applicable. Enthusiasm for AI programming declined.

Nearly all contemporary researchers have accepted this and are aware that there is no reason to believe true intelligence will ever be programmed by methods remotely resembling those currently popular. The modern practice of "artificial intelligence", has little to do with the design or construction of truly intelligent artifices — the increasingly popular term "expert systems" is far more descriptive, since the programs being created are never good at more than one thing. Feeling that the programming approach is reaching an ill-defined dead-end, many researchers have begun to look for something new. Some have seized on parallel processing as a promising possibility; partly as a result of this, the neural network approach has been rediscovered and explored far more thoroughly than it was in the early days. Some of those who found "neural networks" absurd are now entranced with "parallel distributed processing", which is essentially the same thing.

The programming approach is vulnerable to a critique which runs parallel to the standard critique of the neural network approach, on the level of mind instead of brain. The neural network approach grew out of a model of the brain as a chaotically connected network of neurons; the programming approach, on the other hand, grew out of a model of the mind as an ingenious algorithm. One oversimplifies the brain by portraying it as unrealistically unstructured, as implausibly dependent on self-organization and complexity, with little or no intrinsic order. The other oversimplifies the mind by portraying it as unrealistically orderly, as implausibly dependent upon logical reasoning, with little or no chaotic, deeply trial-and-error-based self-organization.

As you have probably guessed, I suspect that the brain is more than a randomly connected network of neurons, and that the mind is more than an assemblage of clever algorithm. I suggest that both the brain and the mind are **networks of programs.** Networks of automata.

This attitude is not exactly a negation of the neural network or programming approaches to AI. Certainly the primary aspect of structure of the brain is the neural network; and certainly the mind is proceeding according to some set of rules, some algorithm. But these assertions are insufficiently precise; they also describe many other structures besides minds and the organs which give rise to them. To deal with either the brain or the mind, additional hypotheses are required. And I suspect that neither the neural network nor the programming approach is up to the task of formulating the appropriate hypotheses.

2
Optimization

2.0 Thought as Optimization

Mental process involves a large variety of computational problems. It is not entirely implausible that the mind deals with each of them in a unique, context-specific way. But, unlike Minsky and many cognitive scientists, I do not believe this to be the case. Certainly, the mind contains a huge number of special-purpose procedures. But nearly all the computational problems associated with mental process can be formulated as optimization problems. And I propose that, by and large, there is **one general methodology** according to which these optimization problems are solved.

Optimization is simply the process of finding that entity which a certain criterion judges to be "best". Mathematically, a "criterion" is simply a function which maps a set of entities into a set of "values" which has the property that it is possible to say when one value is greater than another. So the word "optimization" encompasses a very wide range of intellectual and practical problems.

For instance, virtually all the laws of physics have been expressed as optimization problems, often with dramatic consequences. Economics, politics, and law all revolve around finding the "best" solution to various problems. Cognitive science and many forms of therapeutic psychology depend on finding the model of a person's internal state which best explains their behavior. Everyday social activity is based on maximizing the happiness and productivity of oneself and others. Hearing, seeing, walking, and virtually all other aspects of sensation and motor control may be viewed as optimization problems. The Traveling Salesman problem is an optimization problem — it involves finding the **shortest** path through n cities. And, finally, the methodological principle known as Occam's razor suggests that the best explanation of a phenomenon is the simplest one that fits all the facts. In this sense, all inquiry may be an optimization problem, the criterion being simplicity.

Some of these optimization problems have been formulated mathematically — e.g. in physics and economics. For others, such as those of politics and psychology, no useful formalization has yet been found. Nonmathematical optimization problems are usually solved by intuition, or by the application of extremely simple, rough traditional methods. And, despite a tremendous body of sophisticated theory, mathematical optimization problems are often solved in a similar manner.

Although there are dozens and dozens of mathematical optimization techniques, virtually none of these are applicable beyond a very narrow range of problems. Most of them — steepest descent, conjugate gradient, dynamic programming, linear programming, etc. etc. (Dixon and Szego, 1978; Torn et al, 1990) — rely on special properties of particular types of problems. It seems that most optimization problems are, like the Traveling Salesman problem, very hard to solve exactly. The best one can hope for is a PAC solutions. And, in the "classical" literature on mathematical optimization, there are essentially only two reasonably general approaches to finding PAC solutions: the Monte Carlo method, and the Multistart method.

After discussing these methods, and their shortcomings, I will introduce the **multilevel** philosophy of optimization, which incorporates both the Monte Carlo and the Multistart methods in a rigid yet generally applicable framework which applies to virtually any optimization problem. I will propose that **this** philosophy of optimization is essential to mentality, not least because of its essential role in the perceptual and motor hierarchies, to be discussed below.

2.1 Monte Carlo and Multistart

The Monte Carlo philosophy says: If you want to find out what's best, try out a lot of different things at random and see which one of these is best. If you try enough different things, the best you find will be almost certainly be a decent guess at the best overall. This is a common approach to both mathematical and intuitive optimization problems. Its advantages are simplicity and universal applicability. Its disadvantage is, it doesn't work very well. It is very slow. This can be proved mathematically under very broad conditions, and it is also apparent from practical experience. In general, proceeding by selecting things at random, one has to try an awful lot of things before one finds something good.

In contrast to the Monte Carlo philosophy, the Multistart philosophy depends on **local search**. It begins with a random guess x_0, and then looks at all the possibilities which are very close to x_0. The best from among these possibilities is called x_1. Then it looks at all the possibilities which are **very close** to x_1, selects the best, and calls it x_2. It continues in this manner — generating x_3, x_4, and so on — until it arrives at a guess x_n which seems to be better than anything else very close to it. This x_n is called a **local optimum** — it is not necessarily the best solution to the optimization problem, but it is better than anything in its immediate vicinity.

Local search proceeds by looking for a new answer in the immediate locality surrounding the best answer one has found so far. The goal of local search is

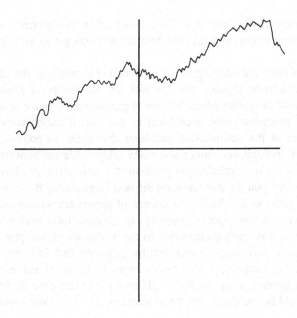

Figure 1.

to find a local optimum. But, as Figure 1 illustrates, a local optimum is not always a good answer. It could be that, although there is nothing better than x_n in the immediate vicinity of x_n, there is something much better than x_n somewhere else.

In mathematical optimization, it is usually easy to specify what "very close" means. In other domains things may be blurrier. But that doesn't mean the same ideas aren't applicable. For instance, suppose a politician is grappling with the problem of reducing carbon monoxide emissions to a safe level. Maybe the best idea she's found so far is "Pass a law requiring that all cars made after 1995 emit so little carbon monoxide that the total level of emissions is safe". Then two ideas very near this one are: "Pass a law giving tax breaks to corporations which make cars emitting safe levels of carbon monoxide", or "Pass a law requiring that all cars made after 1992 emit so little carbon monoxide that the total level of emissions is safe." And two ideas which are not very near x_0 are: "Tax automakers more and give the money to public transportation" and "Give big tax breaks to cities which outlaw driving in their downtown areas." If she decides that none of the ideas near "Pass a law requiring that all cars made after 995 emit so little carbon monoxide that the total level of emissions is safe" is as attractive as it is, then this idea is a local optimum (from her point of view). Even if she felt that taxing automakers more and giving the money to public transportation were a **better** solution, this would have no effect on the fact that giving tax breaks to corporations that make safe cars was a **local** optimum. A local optimum is only better than those things which are very similar to it.

The Multistart philosophy says: Do a bunch of local searches, from a lot f different starting points, and take the best answer you get as your guess at the overall best.

Sometimes only one starting point is needed. For many of the optimization problems that arise in physics, one can pick any starting point whatsoever and do a local search from that point, and one is guaranteed to arrive at the absolute best answer. Mathematically, a problem of this sort is called **convex**. Unfortunately, most of the optimization problems that occur in politics, sensation, motor control, biology, economics and many other fields are **nonconvex**. When dealing with a convex optimization problem, the only thing you have to worry about is how well you go about picking the best from among those entities close to your best guess so far. Each year dozens of papers are written on this topic. But convexity is a very special property. In general, local search will not be effective unless it is applied according to the Multistart philosophy.

The Multistart philosophy works well for problems that don't have too many local optima. For instance, it would take a very long time to solve the problem in Figure 1 according to the Multistart philosophy. In this case the Monte Carlo approach would be preferable; the local searches are essentially a waste of time.

2.2 Simulated Annealing

In recent years a new approach to global optimization has become popular, one which combines aspects of Monte Carlo search and local search. This method, called simulated annealing, is inspired by the behavior of physical systems. Statistical mechanics indicates that the state of many systems will tend to fluctuate in a random but directed manner.

To understand this, we must introduce the "state space" of a system, a mathematical set containing all possible states of the system. In state space, two states A and B are understood to be neighbors if there is a "simple, immediate" transition between the two. Let E(A) denote the energy of the state A.

In the particular case that the system involved is computational in nature, each of its possible states may be described by a finite sequence of zeros and ones. Then two states are neighbors if their corresponding sequences differ in exactly one place. This situation arises in "spin glass theory", a rapidly growing field which connects optimization theory and physics.

In the case of spin glasses, physics dictates that, if A and B are neighboring states, the probability of the state of the system changing from A to B is determined by 1) the quantity E(A) - E(B), and 2) the temperature, T, of the system. The schematic formula for the probability of going from state A to state B is

$$P(B \mid A) = 1/[1+\exp([E(B)-E(A)]/kT)],$$

where k is Boltzmann's constant (Mezard, 1987).

Temperature corresponds to randomness. If T=0, the system has probability one of going to a state of lower energy, and probability zero of going to a state of higher energy. So when T=0, the system will automatically settle into a local minimum of the energy function. The higher T is, the more likely it is that the law of energy minimization will be violated; that there will be a transition to a state of higher energy. The analogy with optimization is obvious. At T=0, we have local search, and at T=infinity we have P(B | A)=1/2, so we have a random search: from any state, the chance of going to either of the two neighbors is equal. At T=infinity, the system will continue to fluctuate at random forever, never expressing a preference for any particular state or set of states. This process is called **thermal annealing**.

In optimization problems, one is not concerned with energy but rather with some general function f. Let us assume that this function assigns a number to each finite string of zeros and ones. Then, in order to minimize f, one may mimic the process of thermal annealing. Starting from a random initial sequence, one may either remain there or move to one of the two neighbors; and the probability of going to a given neighbor may be determined by a formula like that involved in thermal annealing.

In practice, the spin-glass formula given above is modified slightly. Starting from a random initial guess x, one repeats the following process:

1. Randomly modify the current guess x to obtain a new guess y,
2. If f(y)<f(x) then let x=y and return to Step 1,
3. If f(y)>f(x) then let x=y with probability exp([f(y)-f(x)]/T), and return to Step 1.

The tricky part is the way the "temperature" T is varied as this process is repeated. One starts with a high temperature, and then gradually decreases it. The idea is that in the beginning one is locating the general region of the global minimum, so one does not want to be stuck in shallow local minima; but toward the end one is presumably already near the local minimum, so one simply wants to find it.

Philosophically, this is somewhat similar to the multilevel approach to be described in the following section. Both involve searches on various "levels" — but here they are levels of risk, whereas with the multilevel method they are levels of "magnification". Neither approach is perfect; both tend to be too slow in certain cases. Probably the future will yield even more effective algorithms. But it is not implausible that both simulated annealing and multilevel optimization play significant roles in the function of the mind.

2.3 Multilevel Optimization

The basic principles of multilevel optimization were enounced in my Ph.D. thesis (Goertzel, 1989). There I gave experimental and theoretical results regarding the performance of a number of specific algorithms operating according to the multilevel philosophy. Shortly after completing this research, however, I was surprised to find that the basic idea of the multilevel philosophy had been proposed by the sociologist Etzione (1968), in his *Adaptive Society*, as a method for optimizing the social structure. And a few months later I became aware of the strong similarity between multilevel optimization and the "discrete multigrid" method of Achi Brandt (1984) (who introduced the term "multilevel" into numerical analysis). Brandt's ideas were introduced in the context of spin-glass problems like those described above. These parallels indicate how extremely simple and natural the idea is.

The first key concept is that the search for an optimum is to be conducted on a finite number of "levels", each one determined by a certain characteristic distance. If the levels are denoted $1,2,...,L$, the corresponding distances will be denoted $h_1,...,h_L$, and we shall adopt the convention that $h_i<h_{i+1}$. The multilevel philosophy assumes the existence of some method of "search" which finds an optimum value "about a point x on level i." There are many ways of executing such search. For instance, one may execute Monte Carlo search over the sphere of radius h_i about x. Or one may execute Monte Carlo search over the surface of the sphere of radius h_i about x. Such choices constitute specific multilevel methods operating within the framework of the multilevel philosophy. The multilevel philosophy has to do not with the nature of the searches but with the relation between searches executed on various levels.

A method operating within the multilevel philosophy may or may not incorporate a "zero level," a local optimization method. First let us consider the case $L=1$, with a zero level. In this case the concept is as follows. Given an initial guess x_0, first execute the local optimization method is executed at this point. When the local optimization routine stops (having found a local extremum), stops proceeding fast enough (according to some preassigned threshold), or finishes a preassigned number of steps at some point w_0, then search on level 1 is executed about w_0, yielding a new point z_0. Local optimization is then executed about z_0, until it is halted by one of the three criteria, yielding a new point y_0. Next, $f(y_0)$ is compared with $f(x_0)$. If $f(y_0)$ is better than $f(x_0)$, then the entire procedure is begun from y_0; i.e. x_0 is set equal to y_0 and the algorithm is restarted. But if $f(x_0)$ is better, the program is terminated; x_0 is the "answer." The idea is to avoid getting stuck in a shallow local optimum, or getting stuck crawling up an extremely gentle slope, by "jumping" away from the optimum by the nonlocal search on level 1.

If no zero level were implemented, and the local optimization routine in the above description were replaced with the identity mapping, one would still have a viable optimization method, which we shall call the **one-level** method. If h_1 is very small, then the one-level method is a general-purpose local optimization method. In fact, in the case of a Boolean function one may take $h_1=1$ (Hamming distance) and take the level-1 search to be an exact search on the surface of the sphere of radius 1 (there is no interior but the center). One then has the standard discrete steepest-descent method. And, in the continuous case, if one takes the level-1 search method to be a Monte Carlo search on the surface of the sphere of radius h_1, then one has a simple, unoriginal approach to steepest-descent optimization which is probably as good as anything else for local optimization of functions with extremely "rugged" graphs.

Next, consider the case $L=i$, $i>1$. Here, given an initial guess x_0, we first execute the algorithm for $L=i-1$ about this point. When the $L=i-1$ routine stops (having found an "answer"), stops proceeding fast enough (according to some preassigned threshold), or finishes a preassigned number of steps at some point w_0, then search on level i is executed about w_0, yielding a new point z_0. The L=i-1 routine is then executed about z_0, until it is halted by one of the three criteria, yielding a new point y_0. Next, $f(y_0)$ is compared with $f(x_0)$. If $f(y_0)$ is better than $f(x_0)$, then the entire L=i procedure is begun from y_0; i.e. x_0 is set equal to y_0 and the algorithm is restarted. But if $f(x_0)$ is better, the program is terminated; x_0 is the "answer."

For L=2, this procedure, if it has a zero level, first seeks a local optimum, then seeks to jump out of it by searching on level 1, and then seeks to jump out of the result of this jumping-out by searching on level 2. L=2 without a zero level is the same as L=1 with the one-level method as a zero-level.

Similarly, the L=i procedure seeks to jump out of the result of jumping out of the result of jumping out of... the result of jumping out of the result of the lowest level.

The following instance may give an heuristic conception of the crux of the multilevel philosophy. For simplicity, we assume no zero level, and we assume the first of the three criteria for stopping search: search on level i is stopped only when an "answer" on level i-1 is found. The same example may just as easily be applied to the other cases.

A SIMPLE EXAMPLE

Consider a function which maps a numerical value to each house in the world, and suppose a person is trying to find the house with the highest number. If the distribution of numbers is totally random, it doesn't matter what order he checks the various houses in. But what if there   is some intrinsic, perhaps subtle, structure to it? What does the multilevel philosophy tell him to do?

Starting from a randomly selected house, he should first check all houses on that block and see which one has the highest number. Then he should check the neighboring block in the direction of this optimal house. If no house on that block is better, he should call the best house he's found so far his block-level optimum. But if some house on that block is better, then he should proceed to check the neighboring block in the direction of this new optimal house. And so on, until he finds a block-level optimum.

Once he finds a block-level optimum, he should then take a rough survey of the town in which the block sits, and make a guess as to which areas will be best (say by the Monte Carlo method). He should pick a block in one of the areas judged best and execute block-level search, as described above, from this block, and so on until he reaches a new block-level optimum. Then he should compare the two block-level optima and call the best of them his tentative town-level optimum.

Then he should proceed to the town in the direction of this optimum and there execute town-level optimization as described above. He should compare his two tentative town-level optima and, if the old one is better, call it his town-level optimum. But if the new one is better, then he should proceed to the neighboring town in its direction and locate a new tentative town-level optimum. And so on, until he obtains a town-level optimum.

Then he should make a rough survey of the county in which this town sits, and make a guess as to which areas will be best (say by the Monte Carlo method). He should pick a town in one of the areas judged best and execute town-level search, as described above, from this town, and so on until he reaches a new town-level optimum. Then he should compare the two town-level optima and call the best of them his tentative county-level optimum.

Then he should proceed to the county in the direction of this optimum and there execute county-level optimization as described above. He should compare his two tentative county-level optima and, if the old one is better, call it this county-level optimum. But if the new one is better, then he should proceed to he neighboring county in its direction and locate a new tentative county-level optimum. And so on, until he obtains a county-level optimum. Applying the same logic, he could obtain state-wide, nation-wide and global optima...

3
Quantifying Structure

3.0 Algorithmic Complexity

What does it mean to say that one thing is more complex than another? Like most words, "complexity" has many meanings. In Chapter 1 we briefly discussed the "complexity" of computation — of problems and algorithms. In this chapter we will consider several approaches to quantifying the complexity of individual entities, beginning with the simple Kolmogorov-Chaitin-Solomonoff definition.

Throughout this chapter, when I speak of computers I will mean ordinary Turing machines, not stochastic or quantum computers. As yet, no one really knows how to deal with the complexity of objects in the context of stochastic or quantum computation, not in complete generality. Since a quantum computer can compute only those functions that a Turing machine can also compute, this limitation is not fatal.

It turns out that the easiest way to approach the complexity of objects is via the complexity of sequences of numbers. In particular, I will concentrate on binary sequences: sequences of zeros and ones. As is common in mathematics, the general issue can be resolved by considering what at first sight appears to be a very special case.

The standard approach to the complexity of binary sequences was invented independently by A.N. Kolmogorov, Gregory Chaitin, and Solomonoff (Chaitin, 1987), so we shall call it the KCS complexity. In my opinion, what the KCS definition measures is not very well described by the word "complexity." **Lack of structure** would be a better term.

Given any computer A, the KCS complexity of a sequence x is defined to be the length of the shortest self-delimiting program on A which computes x. The restriction to "self-delimiting" programs is necessary for technical purposes and will not worry us much here; roughly speaking, a self-delimiting program is one which contains a segment telling the computer which runs it how long it is. In the following, I may occasionally refer to "shortest programs" instead of "shortest self-delimiting programs"; but it should be implicitly understood that all programs discussed are self-delimiting.

For instance, the KCS complexity of the sequence 10011010010010010 on an IBM PC is the length of the shortest program which, when loaded into the PC, causes it to output 10011010010010010 on the screen. In what follows, I will occasionally refer to the KCS complexity of a sequence x as KCS(x).

There is some vagueness here, as to what "length" means. For one thing, there are large differences between the various programming languages on the market today. There are a number of "high-level" languages, which allow one to type in programs vaguely resembling mathematical formulae: Fortran, Pascal, Cobol, Snobol, Ada, Prolog, C, Basic, Lisp, Forth, and so on. A program which is short in Pascal may be long in Cobol; and a program which is short in Basic may be long in Pascal. And then there is "assembly language", which refers directly to the hardware of the computer. A program in assembly language is usually very long. However, before a computer can use a program written in a high-level language, it must translate it into assembly language. (The program which does the translation is called the "compiler"). When figuring the length of a program written in Fortran, should we use the number of characters in the program as originally typed in, or the number of characters in the assembly-language translation of the program?

From the point of view of the mathematical theory of complexity, none of these issues matter. We can simply assume we are dealing with a universal Turing machine. Translating from a foreign language is essentially the same as simulating another computer. So if a sequence is long enough, its KCS complexity is essentially language-independent and computer-independent. For example, say you have a sequence x consisting of a billion 0s and 1s. Suppose it can be computed by a program of length 1,000,000 on an IBM PC. Suppose a VAX computer has been programmed to simulate a PC, and suppose this simulation program has length 200,000. Then the shortest program for computing x on the VAX cannot be any longer than 1,200,000. Because, if all else fails, one can compute x on the VAX by simulating a PC. These numbers are highly unrealistic, but the point is that as the sequences get longer and longer, the size of the simulation program remains the same. When the sequences are a trillion digits long, the 200,000 length of the simulation program will mean next to nothing.

Some of the newer programming languages are actually "universal programming languages" in a very practical sense: any contemporary programming language can be compactly written in them. For instance, one could write a C program which simulated Pascal or Lisp or Fortran, or a Lisp program that simulated Pascal or Fortran or C. (In fact, what is now known as Lisp was originally written in a simpler form of Lisp, and what is now known as C was originally written in a simpler form of C.) Let's say a certain sequence x could be computed by a very short Fortran program. Then one way to compute the sequence on a machine with a built-in Lisp compiler would be to write a Lisp program to simulate Fortran. If there were no simpler way to compute the sequence in Lisp, this might yield the shortest program for computing the sequence on that particular machine.

Again: the beauty of theoretical computer science is that, as long as we are talking about long sequences, we don't have to worry about the properties of specific machines or languages. This is what differentiates theoretical computer science from practical computer science. Naturally, the latter is more visible in the everyday world. However, both the theory and the practice of computer science are essential to the study of mind.

What is the KCS complexity of the sequence 0101010101010101 0101010101010101010101? It should be very small on any computer, because one can write a program saying "Print '01' twenty times". And what is the complexity of the sequence consisting of 01 repeated 1,000,000,000,000 times? This should still be very small on any computer, because one can write a program saying "Print '01' 1,000,000,000,000 times."

Note that this program is not quite as short as "Print 01 20 times". Our program for repeating '01' 1,000,000,000,000 times is 31 characters long, but our program for repeating '01' 20 times is only 16 characters long. The difference is, obviously, that it takes more space to write '1,000,000,000,000' than it does to write '20'. As n increases, the KCS complexity of repeating something over and over again n times increases. But it does not increase very fast. After all, 1,000,000,000,000 is 50,000,000,000 times as large as 20. But, according to the programs written above, the KCS complexity of repeating '01' 1,000,000,000,000 times is only 31/16 times the KCS complexity of repeating '01' 20 times.

The ratio of program sizes, here 31/16, may vary from computer to computer, from programming language to programming language. It would be different if this book were written in Spanish rather than English, because the equivalent of the word "print" would not have exactly five letters in it. But it is difficult to imagine a computer on which it would approach 50,000,000,000. Mathematically, we may say that as n gets bigger and bigger, the size of the shortest program for repeating something n times gets closer and closer to $\log(n)$. This is little more than common sense, because the number of digits in the decimal expansion of a large number n is always very close to $\log(n)$.

What about the KCS complexity of the sequence 010011000111000011111 00000111110000000111111000000001111111? This depends on whether it is shorter to say

Print 010011000111000011110000011111000000111111000000001111111

or to say

Do the following for k=1, then k=2, and so on up to k=7:
Print k '0's and then k '1's"

In this case the former is a bit shorter. But consider the sequence

0100110001110000111100000111111000000111111000000011111110000
000011111111100000000001111111111000000000001111111111110000000000
011111111111000000000000011111111111110000000000000011111111111
110000000000000000111111111111111?

Here there is no doubt that the latter sort of program is shorter.

Actually determining the KCS complexity of a sequence is a difficult matter. There are sequences which look completely random and can nonetheless be computed by short programs. For instance, if one printed the first ten thousand digits of the binary expansion of pi, virtually no human being would recognize any structure in it.

On the other hand, what is the complexity of a sequence x which is completely random in the sense of having no structure whatsoever? In this case the best way to compute x is to write a program saying "Print x". This program is about as long as x is. If x has n digits, this program has length n+c, for some small constant c. In the case of the program as written above, c=5. According to the KCS definition, a completely structureless sequence such as:

100101001010010000111010011010010100101100011001010100011101
1010101000100101001010010010101001010110101

is the most complex kind of sequence, with a complexity approximately equal to n. On the other hand, a sequence with a very simple structure, such as 1111111111111111111111111, is the least complex kind of sequence, with a complexity approximately equal to log(n). Sequences with more intricate structures fall somewhere in between.

It can be shown that no program can compute the KCS complexity of an arbitrary sequence. For any program P, there is some X the KCS complexity of which P cannot compute.

3.1 Randomness

It is natural to define a random sequence as one which has no statistical regularities (von Mises, 1957). For instance, one might propose that in a random binary sequence 1 should occur exactly as often as 0. Also, one might require that the four doublets 00, 01, 10 and 11 should occur equally often. And perhaps the eight triplets 000, 001, 010, 011, 100, 101, 110, and 111 should occur with equal frequency. And so on. It would clearly be desirable to define a random sequence as one in which all subsequences of length n occur with equal frequency. Let us call this the **natural definition**.

Clearly, this definition does not apply to finite sequences. Each sequence of length n contains exactly one subsequence of length n (itself), so it certainly does not contain all sequences of length n equally often. According to this definition only an **infinitely long** sequence can be random.

Early in this century it was discovered that there is a basic flaw in this approach. The restrictions imposed by the natural definition are so stringent that no sequence, finite or infinite, can possible satisfy them. However, they are not beyond repair. A **normal** sequence is defined as one in which, as you go further and further out in the sequence, the frequencies of all the subsequences of length n get closer and closer to being equal. For instance, if one took samples of a normal sequence near the beginning, one might well find a lot more 00s than 01s, 10s or 11s. But **eventually**, if one took samples far enough out, one would have to find 00s, 01s, 10s and 11s equally often.

Intuitively speaking, if you tossed a coin and recorded 0 whenever tails came up, 1 whenever heads came up, you would expect the list of 0's and 1's to be a normal sequence. Essentially, a normal sequence is a sequence in which, as you go further and further out, each digit has less and less to do with the others. Just as, in a series of coin tosses, each toss has essentially nothing to do with the others.

That is one approach to randomness. There is another approach, involving the KCS definition of complexity, which also involves infinite sequences. What is remarkable is that the two different approaches turn out to be closely related.

RANDOMNESS AND COMPLEXITY

Consider an infinitely long binary sequence x. Let x[n] denote the first n terms of x. For instance, if x = 01001101010001001010..., then x[7] = 0100110. The idea behind the KCS approach to randomness is that the complexity of the infinite sequence x can be defined in terms of the complexities of the finite sequences x[n]. The first step is to ask: as n gets bigger and bigger, what happens to the KCS complexity of x[n]? If x = 0000000..., then the question has an easy answer. The sequence x[n] consists of n zeros, and KCS(x[n]) complexity is about log(n). And, intuitively speaking, if x is totally structureless, then x[n] has a KCS complexity of about n. These considerations lead up to the crucial insight, due to Kolmogorov and Per Martin-Lof. Look at what happens to the ratio KCS(x[n])/n as n gets bigger and bigger.

If, as n gets bigger and bigger, KCS(x[n])/n gets closer and closer to 1, then it follows that for large n, KCS(x[n]) is close to n. And this means that, for large n, x[n] essentially has no structure. On the other hand, if KCS(x[n])/n gets closer and closer to zero as n increases, this means that for large n there is indeed some structure in x[n]. It means that, for large n, there is indeed a better way of computing x[n] than just saying "Print 'x[n]'".

What if x looks like this: 01010000010000010001000100 00000100010001...? Here **every other digit** is a zero: the first, the third, the fifth, and so on. But the even-numbered digits follow no apparent pattern. What if x continued this way forever? Then x[n] could be computed by a program of the form "Print this sequence, putting a '0' between every two terms: '110010...'", where '110010...' is a finite sequence consisting of the odd-numbered terms of x[n]. How long is this program? Well, the sequence consisting of the odd-numbered terms of x[n] is about n/2 digits long. So here KCS(x[n]) is about n/2. Thus KCS(x[n])/n is about 1/2.

Ignoring a number of technical issues, we may define a random infinite sequence x as a sequence for which, as n gets bigger and bigger, KCS(x[n])/n does **not** approach zero, but rather approaches some other number. A random infinite sequence x is one for which there is a fairly easy way of computing x[n], when n gets large. It can be proved that **almost all** infinitely long sequences are random in this sense — algorithmically random.

One way to understand this definition is as follows: A random sequence is an infinite sequence which cannot be summed up in any formula of finite length. For instance, 00000000... can be summed up in the formula "Repeat '0' forever". And 01001000100001000001000001... can be summed up in the formula "Repeat '0' k times and then print '1', for k=1,2,3,4,....." But a random sequence x cannot be summed up in any formula, because if it could then that formula would provide a way to compute x[n].

Clearly, every sequence which is random in this sense is not normal. Think about the sequence given three paragraphs up, whose odd-numbered digits are all zeros but whose even-numbered digits have no structure to them. No matter how far out you look, 0's and 1's are not going to occur equally often in this sequence. There will always be more 0's. The best you can say about this sequence is that it has a **subsequence** — the sequence of its even-numbered digits — which looks to be normal.

PROBLEMS WITH RANDOMNESS

The theories of randomness sketched above are not very useful in practice, for obvious reasons. It only deals with infinitely long sequences. In reality, we are always faced with finite collections of data.

This restriction to infinite sequences leads to a couple of interesting conceptual paradoxes. First of all, the very proof that random sequences exist is somewhat troublesome. We have proved that almost every infinite sequence is random, but can we prove that **any one particular sequence** is random? We cannot, because random sequences are precisely those infinite sequences which cannot be summarized in a finite formula. In fact, the set of random sequences is precisely **the set of all sequences which we cannot write down in any way.** We have proved that the set exists, but we cannot demonstrate that any particular sequence belongs to it, because in order to do so we would have to write down that particular sequence. This is not exactly a logical paradox, but it is certainly disconcerting.

G. Spencer-Brown has discovered a particularly poignant way of illustrating the implications of this logical peculiarity. Suppose, he says, that you have built a random number generator — a machine which is intended to generate numbers in such a way that each number it generates has absolutely nothing to do with the others. Then how can you test it to see if it works?

Suppose you tested it and it gave out a hundred zeros in a row. You would probably assume that it was broken. But, statistically speaking, a truly random number generator **would** generate a hundred zeros in a row sometimes. Not very often, but sometimes. There's no reason that rare occasion shouldn't come first. After all, the sequence consisting of a hundred zeros in a row is no less likely than any other sequence of a hundred numbers.

So you run it some more. And the same thing happens — it keeps giving tens. Still, you're not really justified in concluding that it doesn't work. The same argument applies. The fact is that no matter what the machine does for the first n trials, it can be argued that a true random number generator would be just as likely to generate that sequence as any other. So no matter what the machine does, you can't judge its effectiveness.

You could examine the mechanism of your random number generator to see if it **looks** as though it is operating randomly. For instance, you could supply it with a mechanical coin tosser. Then you'd probably be confident its answers were random, since you're probably confident the results of a coin toss are random. But this is nothing more or less than intuition: you're assuming something is random because you haven't seen any structure to it in the past. An intuition is not the same as a theoretical guarantee.

Essentially, this paradox arises from the assumption that a random number generator must give out every sequence of length n with equal frequency. But is there any other way to define a random number generator? One could define a random number generator as a machine which generates a normal sequence of numbers, but it is easy to see that there is no way to prove a finite sequence is part of a normal sequence. This is because the definition of normality involves going "far enough out" in a sequence. Once you go far enough out in a normal sequence, all subsequences of length n must occur equally often. But as n increases, so does the precise meaning of "far enough". Say you determine that the first million terms of a sequence present all subsequences of length 1000 or less with the appropriate frequencies. That still doesn't tell you whether or not the sequence repeats a certain subsequence of length 1,000,000,000 too often. In fact, for all you know, the sequence could consist of the same million-digit-long sequence repeated over and over and over.

And remember, normality is in a sense a weaker concept than algorithmic randomness — it says that the decimal expansion of pi is random. It is even more obvious that there is no way to tell if a finite sequence is part of an infinite (algorithmically) random sequence. After all, if we just see the fragment 01001001010011001001, how do we know it's part of a random sequence and not part of the sequence 01001001010011001001 01001001010011001001 01001001010011001001 01001001010011001001... which repeats the same fragment over and over again. This dilemma is reminiscent of the problem of induction, to be discussed in Chapter 5.

Our discussion has been phrased in terms of binary sequences, but it could be generalized to deal with any other mathematical objects in exactly the same way. The conclusions would not change a bit. The only things that are truly, mathematically random are infinitely large entities which can never even be summarized in finite formulas. And there is no practical way to tell if a given physical machine produces mathematically random sequences.

In sum: randomness is a phantom. In reality, all we can do is assume that those things we've detected no structure in are random. But this is a working assumption, not a mathematical guarantee. And therefore, the question of whether the mind and brain are stochastic or deterministic is a phantom as well. Thus there can never be an empirical reason to say that the mind or the brain is a stochastic computer rather than a deterministic computer. Because, scientifically speaking, to say that X is random is only to say that X has aspects in which we cannot detect any order. To declare that there is consequently no order there is unjustified.

3.2 Pattern

Charles S. Peirce, the turn-of-the-century American philosopher, liked to talk about the "one law of mind." He gave this law many different formulations, the most suggestive of which was only five words: "the tendency to take habits". This simple, potent idea is at the heart of the theory of mind to be presented in the following chapters. But instead, of "habits", I prefer to speak of "patterns". And rather than taking "habit" or "pattern" as a primitive undefined term, I will begin by providing a sketchy but completely rigorous mathematical theory of pattern.

As I understand it, the concept of pattern relies on two simpler ideas: combination and complexity. More precisely, in order to talk about certain entities being patterns in other entities, we must have

1) some way of combining certain pairs of entities y and z to obtain a third entity called y*z
2) some way of computing, for every entity x, a nonnegative real number $|x|$ called the complexity of x

Any set of entities which fulfills these requirements may be called a **pattern space**. Formally, we may say:

Definition 3.1: A pattern space is a set $(S,*,| \ |)$, where S is a set,* is a binary operation defined on some subset of SxS, and $| \ |$ is a map from S into the nonnegative real numbers.

Let's consider a simple example: Turing machines and finite binary sequences. If y is a Turing machine and z is a finite binary sequence, then there is a natural way of combining x and y — just put y on the input tape of the Turing machine, extending to the right of the tape head. In this case, we can define x*y to be the binary sequence which appears on the tape of the Turing machine y after, having been started with z on its tape, its program finishes running. It is true that there is no guarantee the Turing machine will ever stop running. But if it doesn't, we can simply consider x*y to be undefined, and leave it at that.

As for requirement number 2, we can define the complexity $|z|$ of a finite binary sequence z as its length. And, roughly speaking, we can define the complexity $|y|$ of a Turing machine y as the length of its program. More precisely, $|y|$ might be defined as length of the code number which, when fed into a certain universal Turing machine, enables that Turing machine to act exactly like machine y in every situation. Here $|y|$ and $|z|$ are nonnegative numbers, so the set of Turing machines and finite binary sequences is a pattern space.

Since we shall be returning to this example again and again, it is worth formulating a specific notation. Let $|z|_T$ denote the length of a finite binary sequence z, and let $|y|_T$ denote the length of the program y.

Now we are prepared to ask: what is a pattern?

First of all, a pattern is a pattern **in** something, in some entity x. Secondly, a pattern is an **ordered pair** of entities, denoted (y,z). And finally, we have what I shall call the **fundamental pattern inequality**:

Definition 3.2: Let a, b, and c denote constant, nonnegative numbers. Then an ordered pair (y,z) is a **pattern** in x if x=y*z and

$$a|y| + b|z| + cC(y,z) < |x|.$$

The only unfamiliar term here is C(y,z). This denotes the complexity of obtaining x from (y,z). If y is a Turing machine program and z is a finite binary sequence, we shall let $C_T(y,z)$ denote the number of time steps which the Turing machine takes to stop when equipped with program y and given z as initial input.

For many purposes, the numbers a, b and c are not important. Often they can all be taken to equal 1, and then they don't appear in the formula at all. But in some cases it may be useful to set a=b=1 and c=0, for instance. Then the formula reads $|y| + |z| < |x|$. The constants lend the formula an element of flexibility.

Intuitively, an ordered pair (y,z) is a pattern in x if the complexity of y, plus the complexity of z, plus the complexity of getting x out of y and z, is less than the complexity of x. In other words, an ordered pair (y,z) is a pattern in x if it is **simpler** to represent x in terms of y and z than it is to say "x". The constants a, b and c just weight things: if a=3/4 and b=5/4, for example, then the complexity of y counts less than the complexity of z.

The definition of pattern can be generalized to ordered n-tuples, and to take into account the possibility of different kinds of combination, say $*_1$ and $*_2$.

Definition 3.3: An ordered set of n entities $(x_1,x_2,...,x_n)$ is a pattern in x if $x=x_1*_1x_2*_2...*_{n-1}x_n$ and $a_1|x_1|+a_2|x_2|+...+a_n|x_n|+ a_{n+1}C(x_1,...,x_n) < |x|$, where $C(x_1,...,x_n)$ is the complexity of computing $x_1*_1x_2*_2...*_{n-1}x_n$ and $a_1,...,a_{n+1}$ are nonnegative numbers.

Also, the following concept will be of use:

Definition 3.4: The **intensity in x** of a ordered pair (y,z) such that y*z=x may be defined as

$$IN[(y,z)|x] = (|x| - [a|y| + b|z| + cC(y,z)])/|x|.$$

Obviously, this quantity is positive whenever (y,z) is a pattern in x, and negative or zero whenever it is not; and its maximum value is 1.

AN EXAMPLE: GEOMETRIC PATTERN

Most of our discussion will be devoted to Turing machines and binary sequences. However, the definition of pattern does not involve the theory of computation. Essentially, a pattern is a "representation as something simpler"; and simplicity need not necessarily be defined in terms of computation. Instead of Turing machines and binary sequences let us now consider pictures. Suppose that A is a one inch square black-and-white picture, and B is a five inch square picture made up of twenty-five non-overlapping copies of A. Intuitively, it is **simpler** to represent B as an arrangement of copies of A, than it is to simply consider B as a "thing in itself". Very roughly speaking, it would seem likely that part of the process of remembering what B looks like consists of **representing** B as an arrangement of copies of A.

This intuition may be expressed in terms of the definition of pattern. Where x and y are square regions, let:

y*$_1$z denote the region obtained by placing y to the right of z
y*$_2$z denote the region obtained by placing y to the left of z
y*$_3$z denote the region obtained by placing y below z
y*$_4$z denote the region obtained by placing y above z.

And, although this is obviously a very crude measure, let us define the complexity $|x|$ of a square region with a black-and-white picture drawn in it as the proportion of the region covered with black. Also, let us assume that two pictures are identical if one can be obtained by a rigid motion of the other.

The operations *$_1$, *$_2$, *$_3$ and *$_4$ may be called **simple** operations. **Compound** operations are, then, compositions of simple operations, such as the operation (x*$_1$w*$_2$x)*$_4$w. If y is a compound operation, let us define its complexity $|y|$ to be the length of the shortest program which computes the actual statement of the compound operation. For instance, $|(x*_1w*_2x)*_4w|$ is defined to be the length of the shortest program which outputs the sequence of symbols "(x*$_1$w*$_2$x)*$_4$w".

Where y is a simple operation and z is a square region, let y*z denote the region that results from applying y to z. A compound operation acts on a number of square regions. For instance, (x*$_1$w*$_2$x)*$_4$w acts on w and x both. We may consider it to act on the ordered pair (x,w). In general, we may consider a compound operation y to act on an ordered set of square regions $(x_1,x_2,...,x_n)$, where x_1 is the letter that occurs first in the statement of y, x_2 is the letter that occurs second, etc. And we may define $y*(x_1,...,x_n)$ to be the region that results from applying the compound operation y to the ordered set of regions $(x_1,...,x_n)$.

Let us return to the two pictures, A and B, discussed above. Let $q=A*_1A*_1A*_1A*_1A$. Then, it is easy to see that $B=q*_4q*_4q*_4q*_4q$. In other words, $B = (A*_1A*_1A*_1A*_1A)*_4(A*_1A*_1A*_1A*_1A)*_4(A*_1A*_1A*_1A*_1A)*_4$ $(A*_1A*_1A*_1A*_1A)*_4(A*_1A*_1A*_1A*_1A)$. Where y is the compound operation given in the previous sentence, we have $B=y*A$.

The complexity of that compound operation, $|y|$, is certainly very close to the length of the program "Let $q=A*_1A*_1A*_1A*_1A$; print $q*_4q*_4q*_4q*_4q$". Note that this program is shorter than the program

$$\text{"Print } (A*_1A*_1A*_1A*_1A)*_4(A*_1A*_1A*_1A*_1A)*_4 (A*_1A*_1A*_1A*_1A)*$$
$$(A*_1A*_1A*_1A*_1A)*_4(A*_1A*_1A*_1A*_1A)\text{",}$$

so it is clear that the latter should not be used in the computation of $|y|$.

We have not yet discussed the term $C(y,(B_1,...,B_n))$, which represents the amount of effort required to execute the compound operation y on the regions $(x_1,...,x_n)$. For simplicity's sake, let us simply set it equal to the number of times the symbol "*" appears in the statement of y; that is, to the number of simple operations involved in y.

So, is (y,A) a pattern in B? Let us assume that the constants a, b and c are all equal to 1. We know $y*A=B$; the question is whether $|y|+|A|+C(y,A) < |B|$.

According to the above definitions, $|y|$ is about 37 symbols long. Obviously this is a matter of the particular notation being used. For instance, it would be less if only one character were used to denote $*_1$, and it would be more if it were written in binary code.

And $C(y,z)$ is even easier to compute: there are 24 simple operations involved in the construction of B from A.

So we have, very roughly speaking, $37 + |z| + 24 < |x|$. This is the inequality that must be satisfied if (y,z) is to be considered a pattern in x. Rearranging, we find: $|z| < |x| - 61$. Recall that we defined the complexity of a region as the proportion of black which it contains. This means that (y,z) is a pattern in x if and only if it the amount of black required to draw B exceeds amount of black required to draw A by more than 61. Obviously, whether or not this is the case depends on the units of measurement.

This is a very simple example, in that the compound operation y involves only one region. In general, we may define $|(x_1,...,x_n)| = |x_1|+...+|x_n|$, assuming that the amount of black in a union of disjoint regions is the sum of the amounts of black in the individual regions. From this it follows that $(y,(x_1,...,x_n))$ is a pattern in x if and only if $a|y| + b(|x_1|+...+|x_n|) + cC(y,(x_1,...,x_n)) < |x|$.

Results similar to these could also be obtained from a different sort of analysis. In order to deal with regions other than squares, it is desirable to replace $*_1$, $*_2$, $*_3$, $*_4$ with a single "joining" operation $*$, namely the set-theoretic union $\cup$. Let $z=(x_1,...,x_n)$, let y be a Turing machine, let f be a method for converting a picture into a binary sequence, let g be a method for converting a binary sequence into a picture. Then we have

> **Definition 3.5:** If $x = x_1 \cup x_2 \cup ... \cup x_n$, then (y,z,f,g) is a pattern in x if $a|y|+b|z|+c|f|+d|g|+eC(y,z,f,g) < |x|$.

We have not said how $|f|$ and $|g|$ are to be defined. This would require a detailed consideration of the geometric space containing x, which would take us too far afield. This general approach is somewhat similar to that taken in Chaitin (1978).

ORDERS OF COMPLEXITY

It should be apparent from the foregoing that complexity and pattern are deeply interrelated. In this and the following sections, we shall explore several different approaches to measuring complexity, all of which seek to go beyond the simplistic KCS approach. Remember, according to the KCS approach, complexity means structurelessness. The most "random", least structured sequences are the most complex. The formulation of this approach was a great step forward. But the next step is to give formulas which capture more of the intuitive meaning of the word "complexity".

First, we shall consider the idea that pattern itself may be used to define complexity. Recall the geometric example of the previous section, in which the complexity of a black-and-white picture in a square region was defined as the amount of black required to draw it. This measure did not even presume to gauge the effort required to **represent** a black-and-white picture in a square region. One way to measure the effort required to represent such a picture, call it x, is to look at **all** compound operations y, and **all** sets of square black-and-white pictures $(x_1,...,x_n)$, such that $y*(x_1,...,x_n)=x$. One may then ask which y and $(x_1,...,x_n)$ give the **smallest** value of $a|y| + b(|x_1| + ... + |x_n|) + c(y,(x_1,...,x_n))$. This minimal value of $a|y| + b(|x_1|+...+|x_n|)$ may be defined to be the second-order" complexity of x. The second-order complexity is then be a measure of **how simply x can be represented** — in terms of compound operations on square regions.

In general, given any complexity measure $|\ |$, we may use this sort of reasoning to define a complexity measure $|\ |'$.

> **Definition 3.6:** If $|\ |$ is a complexity measure, $|\ |'$ is the complexity measure defined so that $|x|'$ is the smallest value that the quantity $a|y| + b|z| + cC(y,z)$ takes on, for any (y,z) such that $y*z=x$.

$|x|'$ measures how complex the simplest representation of x is, where complexity is measured by $|\ |$. Sometimes, as in our geometric example, $|\ |$ and

$|\ |'$ will measure very different things. But it is not impossible for them to be identical.

Extending this process, one can derive from $|\ |'$ a measure $|\ |''$: the smallest value that the quantity

$$a|y|' + b|z|' + cC(y,z)$$

takes on, for any (y,z) such that y*z=x. $|x|''$ measures the complexity of the simplest representation of x, where complexity is measured by $|\ |'$. It might be called **second-order complexity**. And from $|\ |''$, one may obtain a measure $|\ |'''$, third-order complexity. It is clear that this process may be continued indefinitely.

It is interesting to ask when $|\ |$ and $|\ |'$ are equivalent, or almost equivalent. For instance, assume that y is a Turing machine, and x and z are binary sequences. If, in the notation given above, we let $|\ | = |\ |_T$, then $|x|'$ is a natural measure of the complexity of a sequence x. In fact, if a=b=1 and c=0, it is exactly **the KCS complexity of x**. Without specifying a, b and c, let us nonetheless use Chaitin's notation for this complexity: I(x).

Also, let us adopt Chaitin's notation I(v|w) for the complexity of v **relative** to w.

Definition 3.7: Let y be a Turing machine program, v and w binary sequences; then I(v|w) denotes the smallest value the quantity $a|y|_T + cC_T(y,w)$ takes on for any self-delimiting program y that computes v when its input consists of w.

Intuitively, this measures how hard it is to compute v given complete knowledge of w.

Finally, it should be noted that $|\ |$ and $|\ |'$ are not always substantially different:

Theorem 3.1: If $|x|'=I(x)$, a=b=1, and c=0, then there is some K so that for all x $|\ |x|' - |x|''| < K$.

Proof: $a|y|' + b|z|' + cC(y,z) = |y|' + |z|'$. So, what is the smallest value that $|y|' + |z|'$ assumes for any (y,z) such that y*z=x? Clearly, this smallest value must be either equal to $|x|'$, or very close to it. For, what if $|y|' + |z|'$ is bigger than $|x|'$? Then it cannot be the smallest $|y|' + |z|'$, because if one took z to be the "empty sequence" (the sequence consisting of no characters) and then took y to be the shortest program for computing x, one would have $|z|'=0$ and $|y|'=|x|'$. And, on the other hand, is it possible for $|y|'+|z|'$ to be smaller than $|x|'$? If $|y|'+|z|'$ were smaller than x, then one could program a Turing machine with a program saying "Plug the sequence z into the program y," and the length of this program would be less than $|x|'$, or at least greater than $|x|'$ by no more than the length of the program P(y,z)="Plug the sequence z into the program y". This length is the constant K in the theorem.

Corollary 3.1: For a Turing machine for which the program P(y,z) mentioned in the proof is a "hardware function" which takes only one unit of length to program, $\mid \mid '' = \mid \mid '$.

Proof: Both $\mid \mid '$ and $\mid \mid ''$ are integer valued, and by the theorem, for any x, $\mid x \mid ' \leq \mid x \mid '' \leq \mid x \mid ' + 1$.

PATTERNS IN PATTERNS; SUBSTITUTION MACHINES

We have discussed pattern in sequences, and patterns in pictures. It is also possible to analyze patterns in other patterns. This is interesting for many reasons, one being that when dealing with machines more restricted than Turing machines, it may often be the case that the only way to express an intuitively simple phenomenon is as a pattern in another pattern. This situation will arise in our analysis of the perceptual hierarchy, several chapters down the road.

Let us consider a simple example. Suppose that we are not dealing with Turing machines, but rather with "substitution machines" — machines which are capable of running only programs of the form P(A,B,C)="Wherever sequence B occurs in sequence C, replace it with sequence A". Instead of writing P(A,B,C) each time, we shall denote such a program with the symbol (A,B,C). For instance, (1,10001,100011000110001100011000110001) = 11111. (A,B,C) should be read "substitute A for B in C".

We may define the complexity $\mid x \mid$ of a sequence x as the length of the sequence, i.e. $\mid x \mid = \mid x \mid _T$, and the complexity $\mid y \mid$ of a substitution program y as the number of symbols required to express y in the form (A,B,C). Then, $\mid 100011000110001100011000110001 \mid = 25$, $\mid 11111 \mid = 5$, and $\mid (10001,1,z) \mid = 11$. If z=11111, (10001,1,z)= 100011000110001100011000110001. For example, is (10001,1,z), 11111) a pattern in 100011000110001100011000110001? What is required is that

$$a(11) + b(5) + cC((10001,1,z),11111) < 25.$$

If we take a=b=1 and c=0 (thus ignoring computational complexity), this reduces to

$$11 + 5 < 25.$$

This is true, so it is indeed a pattern.

If we take c=1 instead of zero, and leave a and b equal to one, then it will still be a pattern, as long as the computational complexity of obtaining 100011000110001100011000110001 from (10001,1,11111) does not exceed 9. It would seem most intuitive to assume that this computational complexity

C((10001,1,z),11111) is equal to 5, since there are 5 1's into which 10001 must be substituted, and there is no effort involved in locating these 1's. In that case the fundamental inequality reads

$$11 + 5 + 5 < 25,$$

which verifies that a pattern is indeed present.

Now, let us look at the sequence x = 100100100100100100111001 1001001001001001001011101110100100100100100100110111 100100100100100100. Remember, we are not dealing with general Turing machines, we are only dealing with substitution machines, and the only thing a substitution machine can do is plug one sequence in for another. Anything which cannot be represented in the form (A,B,C), in the notation given above, is not a substitution machine.

There are two obvious ways to compute this sequence x on a substitution machine. First of all, one can let y=(100100100100100100,B,z), and z= B 0111001B1011101110B110111B. This amounts to recognizing that 100100100100100100 is repeated in x. Alternatively, one can let y'=(100,B,z'), and let z'= BBBBBB0111001BBBBBB1011101110BBBBBB 110111BBBBBB. This amounts to recognizing that 100 is a pattern in x. Let us assume that a=b=1, and c=0. Then in the first case $|y| + |z|$ = 24 + 27 = 51; and in the second case $|y'| + |z'|$ = 9 + 47 = 56. Since $|x|$ = 95, both (y,z) and (y',z') are patterns in x.

The problem is that, since we are only using substitution machines, there is no way to combine the two patterns. One may say that 100100100100100100 a pattern in x, that 100 is a pattern in x, that 100 is a pattern in 100100100100100100. But, using only substitution machines, there is no way to say that the simplest way to look at x is as "a form involving repetition of 100100100100100100, which is itself a repetition of 100".

Let us first consider $|x|'$. It is not hard to see that, of all (y,z) such that y is a substitution machine and z is a sequence, the minimum of $|y| + |z|$ is obtained when y=(100100100100100100,B,z), and z= B 0111001 B 1011101110 B 110111 B. Thus, assuming as we have that a=b=1 and c=0, $|x|'$=51. This is much less than $|x|$, which equals 95.

Now, let us consider this optimal y. It contains the sequence 100100100100100100. If we ignore the fact that y denotes a substitution machine, and simply consider the sequence of characters "(100100100100100100,B,z)", we can search for patterns in this sequence, just as we would in any other sequence. For instance, if we let y_1=(100,C,z_1), and z_1=CCCCCC, then y_1*z_1=y, $|y_1|$=10, and $|z_1|$=6. It is apparent that (y_1,z_1) is a pattern in y, since $|y_1| + |z_1|$ = 10 + 6 = 16, whereas $|y|$ = 18. By recognizing the pattern (y,z) in x, and then recognizing the pattern (y_1,z_1) in y, one may express both the repetition of 100100100100100100 in x and the repetition of 100 in 100100100100100100 as patterns in x, **using only substitution machines**.

Is (y_1,z_1) a pattern in x? Strictly speaking, it is not. But we might call it a **second-level** pattern in x. It is a pattern in a pattern in x. And, if there were a pattern (y_2,z_2) in the sequences of symbols representing y_1 or z_1, we could call that a **third-level** pattern in x, etc.

In general, we may make the following definition:

Definition 3.8: Let F be a map from SxS into S. Where a first-level pattern in x is simply a pattern in x, and n is an integer greater than one, we shall say that P is an n'th-level pattern in x if there is some Q so that P is an n-1'th-level pattern in x and P is a pattern in F(Q).

In the examples we have given, the map F has been the implicit map from substitution machines into their expression in (A,B,C) notation.

APPROXIMATE PATTERN

Suppose that $y_1 * z_1 = x$, whereas $y_2 * z_2$ does not equal x, but is still very close to x. Say $|x| = 1000$. Then, even if $|y_1| + |z_1| = 900$ and $|y_2| + |z_2| = 10$, (y_2,z_2) is not a pattern in x, but (y_1,z_1) is. This is not a flaw in the definition of pattern — after all, computing something near x is not the same as computing x. Indeed, it might seem that if (y_2,z_2) were really so close to computing x, it could be modified into a pattern in x without sacrificing much simplicity. However, the extent to which this is the case is unknown. In order to incorporate pairs like (y_2,z_2), we shall introduce the notion of approximate pattern.

In order to deal with approximate pattern, we must assume that it is meaningful to talk about the **distance** $d(x,y)$ between two elements of S. Let (y,z) be any ordered pair for which $y * z$ is defined. Then we have:

Definition 3.9: The ordered pair (y,z) is an **approximate pattern** in x if $[1 + d(x,y*z)][a|y| + b|z| + cC(y,z)] < |x|$, where a, b, c and C are defined as in the ordinary definition of pattern.

Obviously, when $x = y * z$, the distance $d(x,y*z)$ between x and $y*z$ is equal to zero, and the definition of approximate pattern reduces to the normal definition. And the larger $d(x,y*z)$ gets, the smaller $a|y| + b|z| + cC(y,z)$ must be in order for (y,z) to qualify as a pattern in x.

Of course, if the distance measure d is defined so that $d(a,b)$ is infinite whenever a and b are not the same, then an approximate pattern is an exact pattern. This means that when one speaks of "approximate pattern", one is also speaking of ordinary, exact pattern.

Most concepts involving ordinary or "strict" pattern may be generalized to the case of approximate pattern. For instance, we have:

Definition 3.10: The intensity of an approximate pattern (y,z) in x is
$$IN[(y,z)\,|\,x] = (\,|\,x\,|\,-[1+d(x,y*z)][a\,|\,y\,|\,+b\,|\,z\,|\,+cC(y,z)])/\,|\,x\,|.$$

Definition 3.11: Where v and w are binary sequences, the **approximate complexity** of v relative to w, $I_a(v,w)$, is the smallest value that $[1+d(v,y*w)][a\,|\,y\,|\,+cC(y,w)]$ takes on for any program y with input w.

The incorporation of inexactitude permits the definition of pattern to encompass all sorts of interesting practical problems. For example, suppose x is a curve in the plane or some other space, z is a set of points in that space, and y is some interpolation formula which assigns to each set of points a curve passing through those points. Then $I_a[(y,z)\,|\,x]$ is an indicator of how much use it is to approximate the curve x by applying the interpolation formula y to the set of points z.

3.3 Meaningful Complexity

Koppel [8] has recently proposed an alternative to the KCS complexity measure. According to Koppel's measure, the sequences which are most complex are not the structureless ones. Neither, of course, are they the ones with very simple structures, like 00000000000.... Rather, the more complex sequences are the ones with more "sophisticated" structures.

The basic idea [10] is that a sequence with a sophisticated structure is part of a **natural class** of sequences, all of which are computed by the same program. The program produces different sequences depending on the data it is given, but these sequences all possess the same underlying structure. Essentially, the program represents the structured part of the sequence, and the data the random part. Therefore, the "sophistication" of a sequence x should be defined as the size of the program defining the "natural class" containing x.

But how is this "natural" program to be found? As above, where y is a program and z is a binary sequence, let $|y|$ and $|z|$ denote the length of y and z respectively. Koppel proposes the following algorithm, defined with respect to a Turing machine that has two tapes instead of just one, a program tape and a data tape:

1) search over all pairs of binary sequences (y,z) for which the two-tape tape Turing machine with program y and data z computes x, and find those pairs for which $|y| + |z|$ is smallest,
2) search over all pairs found in Step 1, and find the one for which $|y|$ is biggest. This value of $|z|$ is the "sophistication" of x.

All the pairs found in Step 1 are "best" representations of x. Step 2 searches all the "best" representations of x, and find the one with the most program (as opposed to data). This program is assumed to be the natural structure of x, and its length is therefore taken as a measure of the sophistication of the structure of x.

There is no doubt that the decomposition of a sequence into a structured part and a random part is an important and useful idea. But Koppel's algorithm for achieving it is conceptually problematic. Suppose the program/data pairs (y_1, z_1) and (y_2, z_2) both cause a Turing machine to output x, but whereas $|y_1|$=50 and $|z_1|$=300, $|y_2|$=250 and $|z_2|$=110. Since $|y_1|+|z_1|$=350, whereas $|y_2|+|z_2|$=360, (y_2, z_2) will not be selected in Step 1, which searches for those pairs (y,z) that minimize $|y|+|z|$. What if, in Step 2, (y_1, z_1) is chosen as the pair with maximum $|y|$? Then the sophistication of x will be set at $|y_1|$=50. Does it not seem that the intuitively much more sophisticated program y_2, which computes x **almost** as well as y_1, should count toward the sophistication of x?

In the language of pattern, what Koppel's algorithm does is:

1) Locate the pairs (y,z) that are the most intense patterns in x according to the definition of pattern with $|\ |$, a=b=1, c=0.

2) Among these pairs, select the one which is the most intense pattern in x according to the definition of pattern with $|\ |$, a=1, b=c=0.

It applies two different special cases of the definition of pattern, one after the other.

How can all this be modified to accommodate examples like the pairs (y_1, z_1), (y_2, z_2) given above? One approach is to look at some sort of combination of $|y|+|z|$ with $|y|$. $|y|+|z|$ measures the combined length of program and data, and $|y|$ measures the length of the program. What is desired is a small $|y|+|z|$ but a large $|y|$. This is some motivation for looking at $(|y|+|z|)/|y|$. The smaller $|y|+|z|$ gets, the smaller this quantity gets; and the bigger $|y|$ gets, the smaller it gets. One approach to measuring complexity, then, is to search all (y,z) such that x=y*z, and pick the one which makes $(|y|+|z|)/|y|$ smallest. Of course, $(|y|+|z|)/|y| = 1 + |z|/|y|$, so whatever makes $(|y|+|z|)/|y|$ smallest also makes $|z|/|y|$ smallest. Hence, in this context, the following is natural:

Definition 3.12: The **crudity** of a **pattern** (y,z) is $|z|/|y|$.

The crudity is simply the ratio of data to program. The cruder a pattern is, the greater the proportion of data to program. A very crude pattern is mostly data; and a pattern which is mostly program is not very crude. Obviously, "crudity" is intended as an intuitive opposite to "sophistication"; however, it is not exactly the opposite of "sophistication" as Koppel defined it.

This approach can also be interpreted to assign each x a "natural program" and hence a "natural class". One must simply look at the pattern (y,z) in x whose crudity is the smallest. The program y associated with this pattern is, in a sense, the most natural program for x.

LOGICAL DEPTH

Bennett [9], as mentioned above, has proposed a complexity measure called "logical depth", which incorporates the time factor in an interesting way. The

KCS complexity of x measures only the length of the shortest program required for computing x — it says nothing about how long this program takes to run. Is it really correct to call a sequence of length 1000 simple if it can be computed by a short program which takes a thousand years to run? Bennett's idea is to look at the **running time** of the shortest program for computing a sequence x. This quantity he calls the **logical depth** of the sequence.

One of the motivations for this approach was a desire to capture the sense in which a biological organism is more complex than a random sequence. Indeed, it is easy to see that a sequence x with no patterns in it has the smallest logical depth of any sequence. The shortest program for computing it is "Print x", which obviously runs faster than any other program computing a sequence of the same length as x. And there is no reason to doubt the hypothesis that biological organisms have a high logical depth. But it seems to us that, in some ways, Bennett's definition is nearly as counterintuitive as the KCS approach.

Suppose there are two competing programs for computing x, program y and program y'. What if y has a length of 1000 and a running time of 10 minutes, but y' has a length of 999 and a running time of 10 years. Then if y' is the shortest program for computing x, the logical depth of x is ten years. Intuitively, this doesn't seem quite right: it is not the case that x fundamentally requires ten years to compute.

At the core of Bennett's measure is the idea that the shortest program for computing x is the most natural representation of x. Otherwise why would the running time of this particular program be a meaningful measure of the amount of time x requires to evolve naturally? But one may define the "most natural representation" of a given entity in many different ways. Bennett's is only the simplest. For instance, one may study the quantity $dC(y,z) + e|z|/|y| + f(|y|+|z|)$, where d, e and f are positive constants defined so that $d+e+f=3$. The motivation for this is as follows. The smaller $|z|/|y|$ is, the less crude is the pattern (y,z). And, as indicated above, the crudity of a pattern (y,z) may be interpreted as a measure of how natural a representation it is. The smaller $C(y,z)$ is, the less time it takes to get x out of (y,z). And, finally, the smaller $|y|+|z|$ is, the more intense a pattern (y,z) is. All these facts suggest the following:

Definition 3.13: Let m denote the smallest value that the quantity $dC(y,z) + e|z|/|y| + f(|y|+|z|)$ assumes for any pair (y,z) such that $x=y*z$ (assuming there is such a minimum value). The **meaningful complexity** of x may then be defined as the time complexity $C(y,z)$ of the pattern (y,z) at which this minimum m is attained.

Setting $d=e=0$ reduces the depth complexity to the logical depth as Bennett defined it. Setting $e=0$ means that everything is as Bennett's definition would have it, except that cases such as the patterns (y_1,z_1), (y_2,z_2) described above are resolved in a more intuitive matter. Setting $f=0$ means that one is considering the time complexity of the **most sophisticated** — least crude, most structured — representation of x, rather than merely the shortest. And keeping all the constants nonzero ensures a balance between time, space, and sophistication.

Admittedly, this approach is not nearly so tidy as Bennett's. Its key shortcoming is its failure to yield any particular number of crucial significance — everything depends on various factors which may be given various weights. But there is something to be said for considering all the relevant factors.

3.4 Structural Complexity

We have discussed several different measures of static complexity, which measure rather different things. But all these measures have one thing in common: they work by singling out the **one** pattern which minimizes some quantity. It is equally interesting to study the **total amount** of structure in an entity. For instance, suppose x and x' both have KCS complexity A, but whereas x can only be computed by one program of length A, x' can be computed by a hundred totally different programs of length A. Does it not seem that x' is in some sense more complex than x, that there is more to x' than to x?

Let us define the **structure** of x as the set of all (y,z) which are approximate patterns in x^1, and denote it St(x). Then the question is: what is a meaningful way to measure the size of P(x). At first one might think to add up the intensities $[1+d(y*z,x)][a|y|+b|z|+cC(y,z)]$ of all the elements in P(x). But this approach has one crucial flaw, revealed by the following example.

Say x is a sequence of 10,000 characters, and (y_1,z_1) is a pattern in x with $|z_1|=70$, $|y_1|=1000$, and $C(y_1,z_1)=2000$. Suppose that y_1 computes the first 1000 digits of x from the first 7 digits of z_1, according to a certain algorithm A. And suppose it computes the second 1000 digits of x from the next 7 digits of z_1, according to the same algorithm A. And so on for the third 1000 digits of z_2, etc. — always using the same algorithm A.

Next, consider the pair (y_1,z_1) which computes the first 9000 digits of x in the same manner as (y_2,z_2), but computes the **last** 1000 digits of x by storing them in z_1 and printing them after the rest of its program finishes. We have $|z_2|=1063$, and surely $|y_2|$ is not much larger than $|y_1|$. Let's say $|y_2|=150$. Furthermore, $C(y_2,z_2)$ is certainly no greater than $C(y_1,z_1)$: after all, the change from (y_1,z_1) to (y_2,z_2) involved the replacement of serious computation with simple storage and printing.

The point is that both (y_1,z_1) and (y_2,z_2) are patterns in x, but in computing the total amount of structure in x, it would be foolish to count both of them. In general, the problem is that different patterns may share similar components, and it is unacceptable to count each of these components several times. In the present example the solution is easy: don't count (y_2,z_2). But one may also construct examples of very different patterns which have a significant, sophisticated component in common. Clearly, what is needed is a general method of dealing with similarities between patterns.

---

[1] Assuming the constants a, b, and c, and the metric d(v,w), have previously been set.

Recall that $I_a(v \mid w)$ was defined as the approximate version of the effort required to compute v **from w**, so that if v and w have nothing in common, $I_a(v,w)=I_a(v)$. And, on the other hand, if v and w have a large common component, then both $I_a(v,w)$ and $I_a(w,v)$ are very small. $I_a(v \mid w)$ is defined only when v and w are sequences. But we shall also need to talk about one **program** being similar to another. In order to do this, it suffices to assume some standard "programming language" L, which assigns to each program y a certain binary sequence $L(y)$. The specifics of L are irrelevant, so long as it is computable on a Turing machine, and it does not assign the same sequence to any two different programs.

The introduction of a programming language L permits us to define the complexity of a program y as $I_a(L(y))$, and to define the complexity of one program y_1 relative to another program y_2, as $I_a(L(y_1) \mid L(y_2))$. As the lengths of the programs involved increase, the differences between programming languages matter less and less. To be precise, let L and L_1 be any two programming languages, computable on Turing machines. Then it can be shown that, as $L(y_1)$ and $L(y_2)$ approach infinity, the ratios $I_a(L(y_1))/I_a(L_1(y_1))$ and $I_a(L(y_1) \mid L(y_2))/I_a(L_1(y_1) \mid L_1(y_2))$ both approach 1.

Where z is any binary sequence of length n, let $D(z)$ be the binary sequence of length 2n obtained by replacing each 1 in z with 01, and each 0 in z with 10. Where w and z are any two binary sequences, let wz denote the sequence obtained by placing the sequence 111 at the end of $D(w)$, and placing $D(z)$ at the end of this composite sequence. The point, as usual, is that 111 cannot occur in either $D(z)$ or $D(w)$, so that wz is essentially w juxtaposed with z, with 111 as a marker in between.

Now, we may define the complexity of a program-data pair (y,z) as $I_a(L(y)z)$, and we may define the complexity of (y,z) relative to (y_1,z_1) as $I_a(L(y)z \mid L(y_1)z_1)$. And, finally, we may define the complexity of (y,z) relative to a **set** of pairs $\{(y_1,z_1),(y_2,z_2),...,(y_k,z_k)\}$ to be $I_a(L(y)z \mid L(y_1)z_1L(y_2)z_2...L(y_k)z_k)$. This is the tool we need to make sense of the phrase "the total amount of structure of x".

Let S be any set of program-data pairs (x,y). Then we may define the **size** $\mid S \mid$ of S as the result of the following process:

Algorithm 3.1:

Step 0. Make a list of all the patterns in S, and label them (y_1,z_1), (y_2,z_2), ..., (y_N,z_N).[2]

Step 1. Let $s_1(x)=I_a(L(y_1)z_1)$.

Step 2. Let $s_2(x)=s_1(x)+I_a(L(y_2)z_2)I(L(y_1)z_1)$.

Step 3. Let $s_3(x)=s_2(x)+I_a(L(y_3)z_3 \mid L(y_1)z_1L(y_2)z_2))$

Step 4. Let $s_4(x)=s_3(x)+I_a(L(y_4)z_4 \mid L(y_1)z_1L(y_2)z_2L(y_3)z_3))$

...

Step N. Let $\mid S \mid =s_N(x)=s_{N-1}(x)+$
$I_a(L(y_N)z_N \mid L(y_1)z_1L(y_2)z_2)...L(y_{N-1})z_{N-1})$

---

[2] It should be clear that in the present context there cannot not possibly be an infinite number of patterns in x.

At the k'th step, **only** that portion of (y_k, z_k) which is independent of $\{(y_1, z_1), ..., (y_{k-1}, z_{k-1})\}$ is added onto the current estimate of $|S|$. For instance, in Step 2, if (y_2, z_2) is independent of (y_1, z_1), then this step increases the initial estimate of $|S|$ by the complexity of (y_2, z_2). But if (y_2, z_2) is highly dependent on (y_1, z_1), not much will be added onto the first estimate.

The size $|S|$ is defined as the average of the estimates obtained in this manner from all possible orderings of the (y_i, z_i).

Where $St(x)$ is the set of all patterns in x, we may now define the **structural complexity** of x to be the quantity $|St(x)|$. This is, I suggest, the sense of the word "complexity" that one uses when one says that a person is more complex than a tree, which is more complex than a bacterium. In a way, structural complexity measures how many insightful statements can possibly be made about something. There is much more to say about a person than about a tree, and much more to say about a tree than about a bacterium.

ALGEBRA AND TOPOLOGY OF PATTERN SPACE

From the definition of structural complexity we may obtain the extremely useful notion of **structural similarity**, which we shall also refer to as **pattern-distance**. As the name suggests, this is a measure of how "close" two entities are, structurally speaking. We denote the structural similarity of x and y by $d_\#(x,y)$, and define it as the structural complexity of the symmetric difference of $St(x)$ and $St(y)$. It measures the amount of pattern in x but not y, or in y but not x. This concept will play a central role in our treatment of memory and analogy.

The following concept, though it refers only to structure, not structural complexity, is equally essential.

Definition 3.14: The emergence between x and y is defined as
$$Em(x,y) = St(xUy) - St(y) - St(y).$$

The intuitive meaning of emergence should be clear: it is what is present in the whole but not the parts. In the realm of pattern, the whole is in general more than the sum of the parts, in the sense that not all the patterns in the whole are patterns in the parts.

Finally, the following idea, though not so crucial, sheds some light into certain matters.

Definition 3.15: (y_1, z_1) is said to be complementary to (y_2, z_2) in x to the following extent: $1 - IN(x, y_1, z_1)/[IN(L(y_1), y_2, z_2) + IN(z_1, y_2, z_2)]$. If y_1 is complementary to y_2 in x and y_2 is complementary to y_1 in x, then y_1 and y_2 are said to be complementary in x.

Complementarity, intuitively, is a very weak form of negation. If y_1 is highly complementary to y_2 in x, that means that although one can effectively represent x in terms of either y_1 or y_2, once one has represented x in terms of y_1, one cannot effectively represent the elements of this representation in terms of y_2. If y_1 and y_2 are both entirely "independent" in St(x), this will usually be the case.

Crude intuitive examples of this phenomenon may be drawn from nearly any field of study. For instance, in quantum mechanics one may represent an electron as a wave or as a particle, but once one has represented it as either one cannot interpret one's representation in terms of the other one. Or: one may view the American economy as a battleground of class struggle, or as an arena of gradual evolution by natural selection through competition — but once one has diagrammed the economy in terms of conflicting classes, one cannot analyze the diagram in Social Darwinist terms; and vice versa. Of course, these are little more than analogies; in order to make such applications at all precise one would have to provide exact definitions of the terms involved.

COMPUTABLE APPROXIMATIONS

The structural complexity of x is a measure of the total size of the set of all regularities in x. Unfortunately, as I noted above, it is uncomputable. Step 0 of Algorithm 3.1, in its full generality, is not programmable. Therefore, in order to apply the notion of structural complexity to real-world problems, it is necessary to restrict oneself to some particular class of patterns. One way to do this is via **schematic structural complexity** (SSC), a simple notion that will lead us naturally to more interesting complexity measures such as the Lempel-Ziv complexity and the n'th order Boolean complexities.

In the theory of genetic classifier systems (Goldberg, 1989), a schema is a sequence such as 1001**1011101010*1**111, where * is a "don't care" symbol signifying that either a 0 or a 1 may occupy the indicated place. Let us consider a slightly more general notion of schema, in which each "don't care" symbol has a tag ($*_1, *_2$, etc.), and each "don't care" symbol may stand for a binary sequence of any length. And let us define a **schematizer** as a function which maps schema into binary sequences, by inserting in place of each occurence of the "don't care" symbol $*_i$ some binary sequence w_i. Each pair (schematizer, schema) is a **schematic program**; it defines a unique binary sequence.

The schematic structural complexity (from here on, SSC) of a binary sequence may be described in terms of Algorithm 3.1 with a modified initial step.

Algorithm 3.2:
    Step 0'. Make a list of all schematic programs that are patterns in x, and
    label them $y_1,...,y_N$
    Steps 1-N. As in Algorithm 3.1

The result of this algorithm may be called the **schematic size** of x, the well-definition of which follows from the following generalization of Theorem 2.1.

Theorem 3.2. The result of Algorithm 4.1 is invariant with respect to permutation of the y_i.

In analogy to structural complexity, the SSC of a sequence x may be defined as the schematic size of the set of all patterns in x, $S(x)$.

A schematic program represents the simplest sort of compression: it compresses an image or sequence by abstracting repeated figures. A more flexible approach may be obtained by considering more general programs. For instance, one might define a **metaschematizer** as a map from schema to schema, which takes in a schema and replaces each occurence of the "don't care" symbol $*_i$ with some schema S_i. A metaschematic program is then any program whose action may be represented in the form schematizer($m_1(m_2(...(m_k(\text{schema}))...))$), where the m_i are metaschematizers.

Given this, one may define the "metaschematic structural complexity" of a sequence in an obvious way. This complexity measure recognizes not only repeated figures, but repeated figures within repeated figures and so on. It is new in detail but not in concept — it is a very close approximation to the Lempel-Ziv complexity (Lempel and Ziv, 1978).

The Lempel-Ziv complexity misses a great deal of structure. By definition, no computable approximation to the structural complexity can capture **every** type of structure. However, there is a large gap between repetitions and completely general patterns. One way to fill this gap is with the **n'th order Boolean structural complexity**. This complexity measure may be developed by analogy to the schematic and metaschematic structural complexities.

We will need to use **vector** Boolean operations, which act coordinatewise on Boolean sequences. For example the vector negation of 1010110 is 0101001; the vector conjunction of 11010 and 01011 is 11011. And we will say that a Boolean function (of an arbitrary number of variables) is of order n if it can be written using less than n+1 disjunctions and conjunctions.

An **n'th order Boolean schematic program** for computing an array x may be defined as a pair (schema, schematizer), where the schema is a sequence composed of of 0's, 1's, unlabeled "don't care" symbols *, and k different labeled "don't care" symbols $*_1,...,*_k$. The schematizer consists of: 1) a **memory**, which consists of a set of l binary sequences, and 2) a collection of k vector Boolean functions $f_1,...,f_k$ of order n, each of which takes exactly l sequences as arguments. The k'th array Boolean function computes the array to be substituted for the "don't care" symbol $*_i$.

From the n'th order Boolean schematic programs one may obtain **n'th order Boolean metaschematic programs** in a natural way. The n'th order Boolean structural complexity is then defined in terms of these programs, just as the metaschematic structural complexity is defined in terms of ordinary metaschematic programs. It should be clear that any pattern can be expressed as an n'th order Boolean schematic program for some n. Therefore, the n'th order Boolean programs are one way of forming a bridge between Lempel-Ziv complexity and general structural complexity.

These approximations are rather technical; they are not as conceptually elegant as the structural complexity itself. However, it is clear that at least the n'th order Boolean complexity is relevant to mentality, because no brain can compute Boolean functions of arbitrarily high order.

4
Intelligence and Mind

4.0 The Triarchic Theory of Intelligence

Though there is a vast psychological literature on intelligence, it contains surprisingly few insights into the foundational questions which interest us here: what is intelligence, and how can it, practically or theoretically, be quantified? The problem is that, as Robert Sternberg has observed, theories of intelligence are not all theories of the same thing. Rather, they tend to be theories of different aspects of intelligence. To make matters worse, the theorists who propose these theories rarely make it clear just what aspects of intelligence their theories embrace (1987, p.141).

The psychology of intelligence has dwelled on the context-specific and the easily measurable. But transcending the bounds of particular contexts is what intelligence is all about; and there is no reason to expect this ability to be easy to gauge.

The confusion may be traced back to the turn of the century. First, Galton (1883) analyzed intelligence as a combination of various psychophysical abilities, everything from strength of grip to reaction time. And then, not too much later, Binet and Simon (1916) proposed that intelligence is a matter of problem solving, logical reasoning and spatial judgement. Binet's approach was of more immediate practical use — it led to the I.Q. test, which is fairly good at predicting certain aspects of behavior; e.g. at predicting which children are capable of benefiting from schooling. But aspects of Galton's theory have recently been revived (Carroll, 1976; Jensen, 1982). It is now clear that mental speed is closely connected with intelligence; and some modern psychologists (Hunt, 1978; Jensen, 1979) have advocated studying intelligence in terms of quantities such as speed of lexical access. Now it is recognized that the ideas of Galton and Binet, though at first glance contradictory, are on most important points complementary: they refer to different aspects of intelligence.

Just as modern psychology has integrated the ideas of Galton and Binet, Sternberg's "triarchic theory" proposes to synthesize several apparently contradictory currents in the contemporary psychology of intelligence. It seeks to understand the interconnections between: 1) the structures and processes underlying intelligent behavior, 2) the application of these structures to the problem of attaining goals in the external world, and 3) the role of experience in molding intelligence and its application. Sternberg's triarchic theory is useful here, not because its details are particularly similar to those of the mathematical theory to be presented below, but rather because it provides a convenient context for relating this abstract mathematics with contemporary psychological research. The triarchic theory begins with mainstream psychology and arrives at the somewhat radical hypothesis that, although intelligence can be defined only relative to a certain context, there are certain universal structures underlying all intelligent behavior.

STRUCTURES AND PROCESSES

In the triarchic theory, the structures and processes underlying intelligence are divided into three different categories: metacomponents, performance components, and knowledge-acquisition components. From the point of view of internal structure, intelligence is understood as a problem-solving activity which is allocated specific problems from some external source.

Metacomponents have to do with the high-level management of problem-solving: deciding on the nature of the problem with which one is confronted, selecting a problem-solving strategy, selecting a mental representation of the problem, allocating mental resources to the solution of the problem, monitoring problem-solving progress, and so on.Studies show that all of these factors are essential to intelligent performance at practical tasks (MacLeod, Hunt and Mathews, 1978; Kosslyn, 1980; Hunt and Lansman, 1982).

Metacomponents direct the search for solutions; but they do not actually provide answers to problems. The mental structures which do **this** are called performance components. These are of less philosophical interest than metacomponents, because the human mind probably contains thousands of different special-case problem-solving algorithms, and there is no reason to suppose that every intelligent entity must employ the same ones. Most likely, the essential thing is to have a very wide array of performance components with varying degrees of specialization.

For example, consider a standard analogy problem: "lawyer is to client as doctor is to a) patient b) medicine". Solving this problem is a routine exercise in induction. Given three entities W, X and Y:

1) the memory is searched for two entities W and X,
2) a relation R(W,X) between the two entities is inferred from the memory,
3) the memory is searched for some Z so that R(Y,Z) holds.

This process is a performance component, to be considered in much more detail in the following chapter. It is not "low-level" in the physiological sense; it requires the coordination of three difficult tasks: locating entities in memory based on names, inference of relations between entities, and locating entities in memory based on abstract properties. But it is clearly on a lower level than the metacomponents mentioned above.

Neisser (1983), among others, believes that the number of performance components is essentially unlimited, with new performance components being generated for every new context. In this point of view, it is futile to attempt to list the five or ten or one hundred most important problem solving algorithms; the important thing is to understand how the mind generates new algorithms. There is certainly some truth to this view. However, it may be argued that there are some relatively high-level performance components which are of universal significance — for instance, the three forms of analogy to be discussed in the following chapter. These general algorithms may be used on their own, or in connection with the more specific procedures in which Neisser, Hunt (1980), Jensen (1980) and others are interested.

This brings us to the knowledge acquisition components of intelligence: those structures and processes by which performance components and metacomponents are learned. For example, three essential knowledge acquisition components are: sifting out relevant from irrelevant information, detecting significant coincidences (Barlow, 1985), and fusing various bits of information into a coherent model of a situation. These three abilities will be considered in detail in later chapters.

The importance of effective knowledge acquisition for intelligence is obvious. The ability to speed-read will help one perform "intelligently" on an I.Q. test; and the ability to immediately detect anomalous features of the physical environment will help one perform intelligently as a detective. One might argue that factors such as this do not really affect intelligence, but only the ability to put intelligence to practical use. However, intelligence which is not used at all cannot be measured; it is hard to see how it could even be studied theoretically. The mathematical theory of intelligence to be given below provides a partial way around this dilemma by admitting that one part of a mind can be intelligent with respect to another part of the mind even if it displays no intelligent behavior with respect to the external environment.

INTELLIGENCE AND EXPERIENCE

The experiential approach to intelligence begins with the idea that most behavior is "scripted" (Schank and Abelson, 1977). Most actions are executed according to unconscious routine; and strict adherence to routine, though certainly the intelligent thing to do in many circumstances, can hardly be called the essence of intelligence. It would rather seem that the core of intelligence is to be found in the **learning** of new scripts or routines.

For instance, one might focus on the rate at which newly learned scripts are "automatized". The faster a behavior is made automatic, the faster the mind will be free to focus on learning other things. Or one could study the ability to deal with novel situations, for which no script yet exists. Insight, the ability to synthesize appropriate new metacomponents, performance components and even knowledge acquisition components, is essential to intelligence. It has been extensively studied under the label "fluid intelligence" (Snow and Lohman, 1984).

The relevance of insight to tests such as the I.Q. test is a controversial matter (Sternberg, 1985). It would seem that most I.Q. test problems involve a fixed set of high-level metacomponents, as well as a fixed set of performance components: analogical, spatial and logical reasoning procedures. In other words, in order to do well on an I.Q. test, one must know how to manage one's mind in such a way as to solve puzzles fast, and one must also have a mastery of a certain array of specialized problem-solving skills. However, in this example one sees that the dichotomy between metacomponents and performance components is rather coarse. It would seem that, to do well on an I.Q. test, one has to have a great deal of insight on an **intermediate** plane: on a level between that of specific problem-solving methods and that of overall management strategies. One must have a mastery of appropriate high-level and low-level scripts, and an ability to improvise intermediate-level behavior.

INTELLIGENCE AND CONTEXT

One may look at intelligence as an array of structures and processes directed toward the solution of specific, externally given problems. One may understand intelligence as the **learning** of new structures and processes. Or — third in Sternberg's triarchy — one may hypothesize that

> intelligent thought is directed toward one or more of three behavioral goals: **adaptation to an environment, shaping of an environment, or selection of an environment.** These three goals may be viewed as the functions toward which intelligence is directed: Intelligence is not aimless or random mental activity that happens to involve certain components of information processing at certain levels of experience. Rather, it is purposefully directed toward the pursuit of these three global goals, all of which have more specific and concrete instantiations in people's lives. (1987, p. 158)

This contextual approach to intelligence has the advantage that it is not biased toward any particular culture or species.

For instance, Cole, Gay and Sharp (1971) asked adult Kpelle tribesmen to sort twenty familiar objects, putting each object in a group with those objects that "belonged" with it. Western adults tend to sort by commonality of attributes: e.g. knives, forks and spoons together. But Western children tend to sort by function: e.g. a knife together with an orange. The Kpelle sorted like Western children — but the punchline is, when asked to sort the way a stupid person would, they sorted like Western adults. According to their culture, what we consider intelligent is stupid; and vice versa. By asking how well a person has adapted to their environment, rather than how well a person does a certain task, one can to some extent overcome such cultural biases.

Sternberg distinguishes adaptation to an environment from shaping an environment and selecting an environment. In the general framework to be presented below, these three abilities will be synthesized under one definition. These technicalities aside, however, there is a serious problem with defining intelligence as adaptation. The problem is that the cockroach is very well adapted to its environment — probably better adapted than we are. Therefore, the fact that an entity is well adapted to its environment does **not** imply that it is intelligent. It is true that different cultures may value different qualities, but the fact that a certain culture values physical strength over the ability to reason logically does not imply that physical strength is a valid measure of intelligence.

Sternberg dismisses this objection by postulating that

> the components of intelligence are manifested at different levels of experience with tasks and in situations of varying degrees of contextual relevance to a person's life. The components of intelligence are... universal to intelligence: thus, the components that contribute to intelligence in one culture do so in all other cultures as well. Moreover, the importance of dealing with novelty and automatization of information processing to intelligence are... universal. But the manifestations of these components in experience are... relative to cultural contexts. (1987, p. 168)

This is a powerful statement, very similar to one of the hypotheses of this book: that there is a **universal structure of intelligence**. However, psychology brings us only this far. Its conceptual tools are not adequate for the problem of characterizing this structure in a general, rigorous way.

4.1 Intelligence as Flexible Optimization

Having just reviewed certain aspects of the psychological perspective on intelligence, it is worth observing how different the engineering perspective is. As one might expect, engineers have a much simpler and much more practical definition of intelligence.

Control theory deals with ways to cause complex machines to yield desired behaviors. Adaptive control theory deals with the design of machines which respond to external and internal stimuli and, on this basis, modify their behavior appropriately. And the theory of **intelligent control** simply takes this one step further. To quote a textbook of automata theory (Aleksander and Hanna, 1976)

> [An] automaton is said to behave "intelligently" if, on the basis of its "training" data which is provided within some context together with information regarding the desired action, it takes the correct action on other data within the same context not seen during training.

This is the sense in which contemporary "artificial intelligence" programs are intelligent. They can generalize within their limited context: they can follow the one script which they are programmed to follow.

Of course, this is not really intelligence, not in the psychological sense. It is true that modern "intelligent" machines can play championship chess and diagnose diseases from symptoms — things which the common person would classify as intelligent behavior. On the other hand, virtually no one would say that walking through the streets of New York requires much intelligence, and yet not only human beings but rats do it with little difficulty, but no machine yet can. Existing intelligent machines can "think" within their one context — chess, medical diagnosis, circuit design — but they cannot deal with situations in which the context continually shifts, not even as well as a rodent can.

The above quote defines an intelligent machine as one which displays "correct" behavior in any situation **within one context**. This is not psychologically adequate, but it is on the right track. To obtain an accurate characterization of intelligence in the psychological sense, one must merely modify their wording. In their intriguing book *Robots on Your Doorstep*, Winkless and Browning (1975) have done so in a very elegant way:

> Intelligence is the ability to behave appropriately under unpredictable conditions.

Despite its vagueness, this criterion does serve to point out the problem with ascribing intelligence to chess programs and the like: compared to our environment, at least, the environment within which they are capable of behaving appropriately is very predictable indeed, in that it consists only of certain (simple or complex) patterns of arrangement of a very small number of specifically structured entities.

Of course, the concept of appropriateness is intrinsically subjective. And unpredictability is relative as well — to a creature accustomed to living in interstellar space and inside stars and planets as well as on the surfaces of planets, or to a creature capable of living in 77 dimensions, our environment might seem just as predictable as the universe of chess seems to us. In order to make this folklore definition precise, we must first of all confront the vagueness inherent in the terms "appropriate" and "unpredictable."

Toward this end, let us construct a simple mathematical model. Consider two computers: S (the system) and E (the environment), interconnected in an adaptive manner. That is, let S^t denote the state of the system at time t, and let E^t denote the state of the environment at time t. Assume that $S^t=f(S^{t-1},E^{t-1})$, and $E^t=g(S^{t-1},E^{t-1})$, where f and g are (possibly nondeterministic) functions characterizing S and E. What we have, then, is a discrete dynamical system on the set of all possible states SxE: an apparatus which, given a (system state, environment state) pair, yields the (system state, environment state) pair which is its natural successor. We need to say what it means for S to behave "appropriately", and what it means for E to be "unpredictable".

4.2 Unpredictability

Intuitively, a system is unpredictable if a lot of information about its past state tends to yield only a little information about its future state. There are many different ways to make this precise. Here we shall consider four different definitions of unpredictability, three of them original.

Let us consider a discrete dynamical system (f,X), which consists of a "state space" X and a function f mapping X into X. For the details to follow, it should be assumed that X is a finite space, so that concepts of algorithmic complexity may be easily applied. But in fact, the ideas are much more general; they apply to any metric space X. A **trajectory** of the system (f,X) is a sequence $(x,f(x),f^2(x),...)$, where $f^n(x)=f(f(...f(x)...))$, the n'th iterate of f applied to x.

In this notation, we may define the **Liapunov sensitivity**, or L.-sensitivity, of a dynamical system as follows:

> **Definition 4.1:** The L.-sensitivity K(a,n) of a dynamical system (f,X) at a point x in X is defined as the average over all y so that $d(x,y)<a$ of $d(f^n(x),f^n(y))$.

The function K tells you, if you know x to within accuracy a, how well you can estimate $f^n(x)$.

Different choices of "averaging" function yield different definitions. The most common way of averaging two entities A and B is the arithmetic mean $(A+B)/2$, but there are other common formulas. For positive numbers such as we have here, there is the geometric mean $(AB)^{1/2}$ and the power mean $(A^p + B^p)^{1/p}$. In general, a function A which takes in n real numbers and puts out another is said to be an average if $min(x_1,...,x_n) \leq A(x_1,...,x_n) \leq max(x_1,...,x_n)$ for all n-tuples of numbers $x_1,...,x_n$.

If the average of a set of n numbers is defined as the maximum element of the set, and X is not a discrete space but a space of real numbers or vectors, then in many cases it is known that K(a,n) is equal to a $exp(L(x)n)$, where L(x) is called the "Liapunov exponent" of the dynamical system (Collet and Eckmann, 1980). Often the Liapunov exponent is independent of x, i.e. L(x)=L. This exponent has the advantage of being easily computable. But the maximum function is not always a reasonable choice of average: if one is interested in making a guess as to what $f^n(x)$ is **probably** going to be, then one wants an average which (like, say, the arithmetic mean) does not give undue emphasis to unlikely situations.

To measure the sensitivity of a system, one merely averages the sensitivities at all points x in X. Here again, there is a choice to be made: what sort of average? But since we are speaking conceptually and not making explicit calculations, this need not bother us.

Next, let us consider a form of unpredictability which has not previously been identified: structural sensitivity, or **S-sensitivity**.

Definition 4.2: The S-sensitivity K(a,n) of a dynamical system (f,X) at a point x in X is defined as the average over all y so that d(x,y)<a of $d_\#(xf(x)...f^n(x),xf(x)...f^n(x))$.[1]

This measures how sensitively the structure of a trajectory depends on its initial point.

Conversely, one may also consider reverse structural sensitivity, or **R.S.-sensitivity** — roughly, how sensitively the point a trajectory passes through at time n depends on the structure of the trajectory up to that point. To be precise:

Definition 4.3: The R.S.-sensitivity K of a dynamical system (f,X) at a point x in X is defined as the average over all y so that
$$d_\#(xf(x)...f^n(x),xf(x)...f^n(x))<a \text{ of } d(f^n(x),f^n(y)).$$

This is not so similar to L-sensitivity, but it has a simple intuitive interpretation: it measures how well, from observing patterns in the behavior of a system, one can determine its immediately future state.

Finally, let us define what might be called structural-structural sensitivity, or **S.S.-sensitivity**.

Definition 4.4: The S.S.-sensitivity K(a,n,m) of a dynamical system (f,X) at a point x in X is defined as the average, over all y so that
$$d_\#(xf(x)...f^n(x),xf(x)...f^n(x))< a, \text{ of}$$
$$d_\#(xf(x)...f^n(x),xf(x)...f^n(x)).$$

This measures how difficult it is to ascertain the future structure of the system from its past structure.

What is essential here is that we are talking about the unpredictability of structure rather than the unpredictability of specific values. It doesn't matter how different two states are if they lead to similar structures, since (or so I will hypothesize) what the mind perceives is structure.

Theoretically, to measure the L.-, S.-, R.S.- or S.S.-sensitivity of a system, one merely averages the respective sensitivities at all points x in X. But of course, the word "measure" must be taken with a grain of salt.

The metric $d_\#$ is, in general, an uncomputable quantity. For practical purposes, we must work instead with d_C, the distance which considers only patterns in the computable set C. For example, C could be the set of all n'th order Boolean patterns, as discussed at the end of Chapter 3. If one replaces $d_\#$ with d_C in the above definitions, one obtains L.-, S.-, R.S.- and S.S.-sensitivities **relative to C**.

Estimation of the sensitivity of a system in these various senses could potentially be quite valuable. For instance, if a system were highly sensitive to

---

[1]Juxtaposition is used here in the sense of Section 3.4.

initial conditions, but not highly structurally sensitive, then although one could not reasonably predict the exact future condition of the system, one would be able to predict the general structure of the future of the system. If a system were highly structurally sensitive but not highly S.S.-sensitive, then, although knowledge of the present state would tell little about the future structure, knowledge of the past structure would tell a lot. If a system were highly R.S.-sensitive but not highly S.S.-sensitive, then by studying the structure of a system one could reasonably predict the future structure but not the exact future state. The precise relation between the various forms of unpredictability has yet to be explored, but it seems likely that all these combinations are possible.

It seems to me that the new sensitivity measures defined here possess a very direct relation to unpredictability as it occurs in real social, psychological and biological situations — they speak of what studying a system, recognizing patterns in it, can tell about its future. L.-sensitivity, on the other hand, has no such connection. L.-sensitivity — in particular, the Liapunov exponent — is profoundly incisive in the analysis of intricate feedback systems such as turbulent flow. However, speaking philosophically, it seems that when studying a system containing feedback on the level of structure as well as the level of physical parameters, one should consider unpredictability on the level of structure as well as the level of numerical parameters.

In conclusion, I would like to make the following conjecture: that when the logic relating self-organization with unpredictability is untangled, it will turn out that real highly self-organizing systems (society, the brain, the ecosystem, etc.) are highly Liapunov sensitive, structurally sensitive and R.S.-sensitive, but are not nearly so highly S.S.-sensitive. That is: roughly speaking, it should turn out that by studying the structure of the past, one can tell something about the structure of the future, but by tracking or attempting to predict specific events one will get nowhere.

4.3 Intelligence as Flexible Optimization, Revisited

As above, let us consider dynamical systems on spaces SxE, where S is the state space of a system and E is the set of states of its environment. Such dynamical systems represent **coevolving** systems and environments.

We shall say that such a dynamical system contains an **S.-sensitive** environment to extent e if it is S.-sensitive to degree at least e for every system S; and so forth for L., R.S. and S.S.-sensitivity. One could modify this approach in several ways, for instance to read "for almost any system S," but at this stage such embellishments seem unnecessary. This concept addresses the "unpredictable conditions" part of our definition of intelligence: it says what it means for a system/environment dynamic to present a system with unpredictable conditions.

Next we must deal with "appropriateness". Denote the appropriateness of a state S^t in a situation E^{t-1} by $A(S^t, E^{t-1})$. I see no reason not to assume that the range of A is a subset of the real number line. Some would say that A should measure the "survival value" of the system state in the environment; or, say, the amount of power that S obtains from the execution of a given action. In any case, what is trivially clear is that the determination of appropriate actions may be understood as an optimization problem.

One might argue that it is unfair to assume that A is given; that each system may evolve its own A over the course of its existence. But then one is faced with the question: what does it mean for the system to act intelligently in the evolution of a measure A? In the end, on some level, one inevitably arrives at a value judgement.

Now we are ready to formulate the concept of intelligence in abstract terms, as "the ability to maximize A under unpredictable conditions". To be more precise, one might define a system to possess S-intelligence with respect to A to degree $||h||$ if it has "the ability to maximize A with accuracy g in proportion b of all environments with S-sensitivity $h(a,b,c)=abc$ and $||\ ||$ is some measure of size, some norm. And, of course, one might define L.-, R.S.- and S.S.-intelligence with respect to A similarly.

But there is a problem here. Some functions A may be trivially simple to optimize. If A were constant then all actions would be equally appropriate in all situations, and intelligence would be a moot point. One may avoid this problem as follows:

Definition 4.5: Relative to some computable set of patterns C, a system S possesses S.-intelligence to a degree equal to the maximum over all A of the product [S.-intelligence of S with respect to A, relative to C]*[computational complexity of optimizing A]. L., R.S., and S.S.-intelligence may be defined similarly.

This, finally, is our working definition of intelligence. In terms of Sternberg's triarchic theory, it is essentially a **contextual** definition. It characterizes the intelligence of a given entity in terms of its interactions with its particular environment; and what is intelligent in one environment may be unintelligent in another. Unfortunately, at present there is no apparent means of estimating the intelligence of any given entity according to this definition.

For simplicity's sake, in the following discussion I will often omit explicit reference to the computable set C. However, it is essential in order that intelligence be possible, and we will return to it in the final chapter. Anything that is done with $d_\#$ can also be done with d_C.

I believe that high S.S. intelligence is, in general, impossible. The reason for this is that, as will become clear in the Chapter 9, perception works by recognizing patterns; so that if patterns in the past are no use in predicting patterns in the future, mind has no chance of predicting anything. I suggest that intelligence works by exploiting the fact that, while the environment is highly L., S.- and R.S.-sensitive, it is **not** highly S.S.-sensitive, so that pattern recognition does have predictive value.

The master network, described in Chapter 12, is a system S which is intended to produce a decent approximation to appropriate behavior only in environments

E for which the relevant dynamical system on SxE is **not** extremely S.S.-sensitive — and not even in all such environments. It is hypothesized to be a universal structure among **a certain subset** of L., S.- and R.S.-intelligent systems, to be specified below. Thus, a more accurate title for this book would be *The Structure of Certain Liapunov, Structural and Reverse Structural Intelligent Systems*.

In other words: roughly speaking, the main goal of the following chapters is to explore the consequences of the contextual definition of intelligence just given — to see what it implies about the structure and experiential dynamics of intelligence. To be more precise about this, we shall require a bit more formalism.

4.4 Mind and Behavior

Let S be any system, as above. Let i_t and o_t denote the input to and output of S at time t, respectively. That is, o_t is that part of S_t which, if it were changed, could in certain circumstances cause an immediate change in E_{t+1}; and i_t is that part of E_t which, if it were changed, could in certain circumstances cause an immediate change in S_{t+1}.

Then we may define the **behavioral structure** of an entity S over the interval (r,s) as the fuzzy set $B[S;(i_r,...,i_s)] = \{Em(i_r,o_{r+1}),Em(i_{r+1},o_{r+2}),...,Em(i_s,o_{s+1}),$ $St[Em(i_r,o_{r+1}),Em(i_{r+1},o_{r+2}),...,Em(i_s,o_{s+1})]\}.$[2] This is a complete record of all the patterns in the behavior of S over the interval (r,s).

Then what is a model of S, on the interval (r,s)? It is a function M_S so that $B[M_S;(i_r,...,i_s)]$ is as close to $B(S;(i_r,...,i_s))$ as possible. In other words, a good model is a simple function of which one can say "If S worked like this, it would have behaved very much the same as it actually did."

In order to specify what is meant by "close", one might define the **magnitude** of a fuzzy set Z, $||Z||$, as the sum over all z of the degree to which z is an element of z. Then, $||Y-Z||$ will be a measure of the size of the total difference between two fuzzy sets Y and Z.

For instance, assume M_S is a Turing machine program; then the best model of S might be defined as the function M_S which minimized $|M_S| * ||B[M_S;(i_r,...,i_s)]-B[S,(i_r,...,i_s)]||$, where $|M_S|$ denotes the size of M_S (perhaps $(M_s)=|L(M_s)|_T$).

In general, one good way to go about finding models is to look for functions Y so that $|Y| * ||[Y(S(i_p)),...,Y(S(i_q))]-[S(o_{p+1}),...,S(o_{q+1})]||$ is small on some interval (p,q). Such functions — simple models of the structures of particular

---

[2]The notation $St[Em(i_r,o_{r+1}),...,Em(i_s,o_{s+1})]$ could be further formalized using the notion of juxtaposition developed in Section 3.4 It is shorthand for $w_1w_2...w_N$, where $\{w_i\}$ is the set of all elements contained in $\{Em(i_r,o_{r+1}),...,Em(i_s,o_{s+1})\}$.

behaviors — are the building blocks out of which models are made. Combining various such functions can be a serious problem, so that it may not be easy to find the best model, but it is a well-defined problem.

That takes care of behavior. Now, what about mind? Let us define the **structure** St[S;(r,s)] of a system S on the interval (r,s) as the set of patterns in the ordered set $[S_r,...,S_s]^3$, where S_t, as above, denotes the **state of S** at time t. This is the actual structure **of the system**, as opposed to B[S;(r,s)], which is the structure of the system's behavior. In the case where S is a human or some other organism, through psychology we only have access to B[S;(r,s)], but through biology we can also study St[S;(r,s)].

We may define a **mind** as the structure of an intelligent system. This means that a mind is not a physical entity but rather a Platonic, mathematical form: a system of functions. Mind is made of patterns rather than particles.

The central claim of this book is that a certain structure, the master network, is part of the mind of every intelligent entity. One might make this more precise in many ways. For instance, define the **general intelligence** of a system to be the average of its R.S.-intelligence, its S.-intelligence, and its L.-intelligence. Then I propose that:

Hypothesis 4.1: There is a high correlation coefficient between 1) the degree with which the master network is an element of St[S;(r,s)], and 2) general intelligence.

If this is too much to believe, the reader may prefer a weaker statement:

Hypothesis 4.2: If A is more L.-, S.- and R.S.-intelligent than B, the master network is almost never less prominent in A than in B.

These hypotheses will be considered again in Chapter 12, once the master network has been described in detail.

---

[3] A remark similar to the previous footnote applies here.

5
Induction

5.0 Justifying Induction

After reading a certain amount of philosophy, it is easy to become confused as to exactly what the problem of induction is. For our purposes, however, the problem of induction is very simple and straightforward. Why is it justified for a system to assume that a pattern it has observed in its environment or itself will continue to be a pattern in its environment or itself in the future?

Leibniz (1704) was the first major philosopher to comprehend the seriousness of the problem of induction. He did not presume to have solved it, but rather claimed to have a research programme which would eventually lead to its solution. His "Universal Characteristic" was to be a systematization of all human knowledge in mathematical form, in such a way that the various possible answers to any given question could be assigned precise probabilities based on the background knowledge available.[1]

But although Leibniz made important advances, Hume (1739) was the first to give the problem of induction its modern form. He gave a sequence of brilliant arguments to the effect that human knowledge is, in fact, induction. For instance, he spent a great deal of effort demonstrating that the "fact" that one thing causes another, say that fire causes smoke, is "known" to us only in the sense that we have seen it do so consistently in the past, and therefore assume it will continue to do so in the future. At the time this was an largely novel insight into the nature of human knowledge. The crux of his analysis of induction was his argument that it is fundamentally **unjustifiable**; however, without the conception

---

[1] It is often assumed that this programme was intended to be purely deductive in the sense of symbolic logic (which Leibniz originated); that it was intended to provide the absolutely correct answer to any question. But this is erroneous; Leibniz's intention was actually rather similar to that of modern Bayesians (Hacking, 1978).

of knowledge as inductive, his clever insight in this regard would have been meaningless.

After all — to summarize and simplify Hume's argument — how do we know induction works? Either we know it by "divine revelation" or "deduction" or some other principle which has nothing to do with the specific properties of the real world, or we know it because of some reasoning as to specific properties of the real world. If the latter, then how do we know these specific properties will continue into the future? This assumption is itself an act of inductive reasoning! So the two alternatives are: justify induction by some a priori principle unconnected with the real world, or justify induction by induction. And the latter is inadmissible, for it is circular reasoning. So induction is just another form of dogmatism.

I take it for granted that Hume was right — induction is **unjustifiable**. But nonetheless, we execute inductions every day. As I see it, the practical problem of induction is the problem of coming up with a simple, general, useful model of the universe according to which induction is indeed possible. This is quite distinct from the philosophical problem of induction. In solving the practical problem, we are permitted to justify induction in terms of some principle divorced from observable reality. The objective is to find the best way of doing so.

A SIMPLE EXAMPLE

Consider the sequence 1010101010.... Given no background knowledge except that there will indeed be a next term, and that it will be either 0 or 1, simple intuitive inductive reasoning indicates that the next term should be a 1. One reasons: "Every time a 0 has occurred, it has been followed by a 1; hence with probability 1 this 0 is followed by a 1."

Similarly, given the sequence 010101001010101010... and the same minimal background information, one could reason: "Eight out of the nine times a 0 has occurred, it has been followed by a 1; hence with probability 8/9 this zero is followed by a 1."

But this sort of reasoning is, of course, plagued by serious problems. It makes the implicit assumption that the **probability distribution** of 0's and 1's will be the same in the future as it was in the past. So it makes an inductive assumption, an assumption as to the "regularity" of the world. There is no "a priori" reason that such assumptions should be justified — but we intuitively make them, and they seem to work fairly well.

INDUCTION AND DEDUCTION

Many people would be willing to accept logical deduction on faith, and justify induction in terms of deduction. This would be one way of solving the practical problem of induction; unfortunately, however, it doesn't seem to work. Even if one **does** take it on faith that the universe is constituted so that the familiar rules of deductive logic are valid, there is no apparent way of solving the practical problem of induction. The rules of deductive logic give no reason to assume that the regularities of the past will continue into the future.

In one sense this is a technical point, regarding the specific forms of deductive logic now known. It might be argued that we simply don't know the **true** deductive logic, which **would** justify induction. But that is not a very convincing argument; it is certainly not something on which to base a theory of mind.

And modern physics has added a new wrinkle to this controversy. In 1936, Von Neumann and Birkhoff proposed that a special non-classical "quantum logic" is required for the analysis of microscopic phenomena. Over the past few decades this suggestion has evolved into a flourishing research programme. Mittelstaedt (1978) and other quantum logicians contend that the choice of a deductive system must be made inductively, on the basis of what seems to work best for describing reality — that what we call logic is not absolute but rather a product of our particular physical experience. If one accepts this postulate, then clearly there is no point in trying to justify induction deductively, for this would be just as circular as justifying induction inductively.

5.1 The Tendency to Take Habits

The American philosopher Charles S. Peirce founded a vast philosophical system on the principle of "the tendency to take habits." By this he meant, roughly, the following:

> **Peirce's Principle:** Unless restrained by the extension of another habit, a habit will tend to extend itself.

Here "extend" is taken to refer to both space and time, and "habit" is essentially synonymous with "pattern." In a way this is a distant relative of Newton's First Law of Motion: unless somehow obstructed, an object will travel in a straight line.

Peirce never seriously sought a proof of this principle; he considered it primary and irreducible. He did, however, provide an amusing cosmogonic argument, which begins with the assumption that, out of the primordial void, various habits emerged at random, with extremely small intensities. Once the tendency to take habits comes into existence to an indefinitely small degree, he argued, then by the tendency to take habits the particular habit which is the tendency to take habits is extended — et cetera. Hence the tendency to take habits is strengthened, and hence more and more habits which emerge to a miniscule degree will be extended, and this constitutes an extension of the tendency to take habits, and hence the tendency to take habits will be further extended — et cetera.

Clearly, this sort of reasoning — though intriguing — contains all sorts of hidden assumptions; and there is not much point in debating whether or not it is really a "justification" of Peirce's principle. It is best to take the simpler path and assume Peirce's principle outright.

I will assume, first of all, that "a pattern tends to extend itself through time". This does not imply that **all** patterns continue indefinitely through time; this is obviously absurd. Merely a **tendency** is posited: merely that, given that a pattern X has occurred in the past, the probability that X occurs in the future is greater than it would be if the events at each time were determined with no reference whatsoever to previous events. Roughly speaking, this is equivalent to the hypothesis that the environment is **self-organizing**.

Clearly, this assumption requires that the world, considered as a dynamical system, is not highly S.S.-sensitive. If the world were highly S.S.-sensitive, then one would need essentially complete knowledge regarding the structure of the past world in order to predict the structure of the future world. But if the world possessed the tendency to take habits, then there would be a good chance the patterns one recognized would be continued to the future, thus limiting the possible degree of S.S.-sensitivity. This relationship can be spelled out in a precise inequality; but there seems little point. The basic idea should be clear.

Conversely, one might wonder: does low S.S.-sensitivity inherently imply low tendency to take habits? It seems not. After all, low S.S.-sensitivity implies that it is possible to compute future structure from past structure, not that future structure is similar to past structure.

It may be worth phrasing this distinction more precisely. The structure of a dynamical system over an immediately past interval of time (the "past structure") does not, in general, determine the structure of the system over an immediately future interval of time (the "future structure"). But the past structure does place certain constraints upon the future structure; it enforces a certain probability distribution on the set of all future structures. That is to say, future structure is dependent upon past structure according to some stochastic function F. Then, all low S.S.-sensitivity says is that, if X and Y are close, F(X) and F(Y) are reasonably close (here X and Y are structures, i.e. sets of patterns). But what the tendency to take habits says is that X and F(X) are reasonably close. From this it is apparent that the tendency to take habits implies low S.S.-sensitivity, but not vice-versa.

Let us return to our previous example. In the case of 0101010101010..., the tendency to take habits translates the assumption that the next term will be a 0 into the assumption that the pattern x=y*z will be continued, where x is the sequence involved, y is the function $f(A)=AAA...A$ which juxtaposes A n times, * is function evaluation, and z=01. Clearly $|y|$, $|z|$ and $C(y,z)$ are rather small, so that this will be a pattern in reasonably short sequences of the form 0101010101010.... It is also important to note that, in the case 0101010010101010..., the most natural application of the tendency to take habits involves the same y and z as above, but in this case as an **approximate** pattern. One might consider $d(y*z,x)=1$, since y*z may be changed into x by one insertion.

I have not yet been any more specific than Peirce as to what "the tendency to take habits" actually is. Clearly, if one saw the sequence 0101010101010... in reality, one might or might not assume that, by induction, the next term was a 1. It would depend on context. For instance, if one were receiving such numbers as output from a computer program, and the last twelve outputs one had received were all either 0101010101000 or 1010101010111, then having seen 01010101010 one would probably assume the next term was going to be a 0. Obviously, this is also induction; one is merely inducing relative to a larger data set. What the tendency to take habits, properly formulated, should tell us is that given no other relevant knowledge, one should assume a given pattern will **continue, because there is a certain** tendency for patterns to continue, and if one does not assume this there is nothing to do but assume a uniform distribution on the set of possible outcomes. When two patterns are in competition — when they cannot both continue — then one must make a decision as to which one to assume will continue.

This example might be taken to suggest that the pattern based on the largest data set is always the best bet. But this is not the case. For what if one's computer outputs the following five sequences: 9834750940, 2345848530, 0000000000, 9875473890, 1010101010. Then when one sees for the sixth output 010101010, what is one to assume will be the last term? Does one follow the pattern extending over all five of the prior inputs, that all sequences end in 0? Or is one to obey the internal logic of the sequence, bolstered by the fact that the fifth sequence, with a very similar structure, and the third sequence, with a fairly similar structure, were each continued in a way which obeyed their internal logic? According to my intuition, this is a borderline case.

One could concoct a similar example in which the clear best choice is to obey the structure of the individual sequence. Indeed, if one simply replaced the final digit of the first sequence with a 1, then ending in 0 might still be an approximate pattern, but according to my intuition the best guess for the next term of the sixth sequence would definitely be 1.

If nothing else, the examples of the previous paragraph demonstrate that the choice of pattern is a matter of intuition. The tendency to take habits is a powerful, but it doesn't tell you what to assume when experience or logic tells you that two patterns, both historically prominent, cannot **both** occur. And the case of two contradictory patterns is a relatively simple one: in reality, every mind has recognized a huge set of patterns, each one contradicting numerous others.

In order to resolve this dilemma, I will propose a strengthening of Peirce's formulation of the tendency to take habits. I suggest that, when it possesses little or no information indicating the contrary, an intelligence should assume that the most intense of a group of contradictory patterns will continue. This strategy can only work, of course, if the universe operates according to the following special principle:

Strengthened Peirce's Principle: A pattern tends to continue, and the more intense a pattern it is, the more likely it is to continue.

This principle does not say **how much** more likely. But in general, a mind may want to consider the **probability** of a given pattern occurring in the future. In that case, it would need to know the exact nature of the relation between intensity and chance of continuance. One might think that this relation could be determined by induction, but this would lead to circular reasoning, for the execution of this induction would require some assumption as to the nature of this induction. At some level one must make an a priori assumption.

In sum: I have not attempted to "justify" induction; I have rather placed a condition on the universe under which a certain form of induction will generally be effective. This condition — the strengthened Peirce's principle — rules out high S.S.-sensitivity but not high L.- S.- and R.S.-sensitivity, and it is not implied by low S.S.-sensitivity. It is clear that, in a universe obeying the strengthened Peirce's principle, a system can achieve a degree of intelligence by **recognizing patterns** and assuming that they will continue.

This idea makes sense no matter how complexity is defined; it relies solely on the definition of pattern. But if one restricts attention to Turing machines, and considers complexity to mean KCS complexity, then the present approach to induction becomes extremely similar to the "classical" proposal of Solomonoff (1964). His paper, "A Formal Theory of Induction," was one of the three original sources of the KCS complexity. His essential idea was a mathematical form of Occam's razor: **the simplest explanation is the one most likely to be correct.** He took this as a given, defined an explanation of a binary sequence as a program computing it, and went on to construct the KCS complexity as a measure of simplicity.

5.2 Toward a General Induction Algorithm

The strengthened Peirce's principle is only a beginning. It is a basic philosophical assumption which ensures the possibility of intelligence through pattern recognition. All the standard mathematical methods for predicting the future are based on probability theory. In this section I will show that it is indeed possible to combine prediction based on pattern with prediction based on probability. Most of the ideas here are completely straightforward, and the reader who prefers to avoid mathematical formalism will lose little by skimming over this section.

From the abstract philosophical point of view, this approach may be controversial; it assumes that elementary probability theory works, and probability is a troublesome concept. This difficulty will be discussed in Chapter 9, in a different context. For now, let us simply apply the theory of probability without worrying about justifications.

Let $P(X)$ denote the probability that the proposition X is true; let $P(X|E)$ denote the probability that X is true given that the proposition E is true. Recall that $P(X|E)=P(XE)/P(E)$, unless $P(E)=0$. Let us consider events Y_i of the form "Pattern P_j is present in the environment to intensity Kl over time period (t,v)", where j and K are integers, and set $p_i=P(Y_i)$. If there are n patterns and $0 \leq K < M$, then there will be $N=nM$ events Y_i. Essentially, the task of making a coherent model may be summarized as follows. Where t denotes the present time, let Q_s denote the proposition "Patterns Q_{s1}, Q_{s2},..., Q_{sn} have been observed during the interval $[t-s,t]$ with respective intensities K_{s1},...,K_{sn}". The question is: what is $P(Y_i|Q_s)$, for each s? Strictly speaking, this is a different problem for each s. However, the knowledge generated in solving it for, say, s=1000, would obviously be useful in solving it for s=1100, 2000, or 10000. In general, the larger s is, the harder the problem is, since there will be more Q_j.

The estimation of the probabilities $P(Y_i|Q_s)$ is a very difficult problem. Probably there will always be a need for rough heuristics. But still, a more detailed analysis can lend some insight into what is involved. $\{Q_{sj}\}$ is the set of patterns observed in the time interval $[t-s,t]$. Let us assume that all the possible combinations of elements of $\{Q_{sj}\}$ have been listed in some specified order, and that $\{Q_{sj(k,1)}, Q_{sj(k,2)},....\}$ refers to the k'th one. Then for any v, and any u between s+v and t, we may introduce a set of propositions, $\{R_{uvk}\}$, which includes all propositions of the form "$Q_{sj(k,1)}$ and $Q_{sj(k,2)}$ and ... have been observed during (u-v,u) with respective intensities $K_{sj(k,1)}$, $K_{sj(k,2)}$,....." And, finally, we may define $P_s(R_{uvk})$ as the result of applying Algorithm 3.1 to the set of patterns referred to by R_{uvk} [in the notation of that algorithm, let $Q_{sj(k,1)}=(y_1,z_1)$, etc.]. According to the strengthened Peirce's principle, this indicates how likely it is for the k'th conjunction of patterns to occur.

So, in this framework, estimating $P(Y_i|Q_s)$ comes down to **first** using the $P_s(R_{uvk})$ to estimate a set of **most likely** future scenarios, a set of subsets of $\{Q_{si}\}$ which are intense enough and mutually consistent enough to be plausible; and **second**, using the $P_s(R_{uvk})$ to estimate the $P(Y_i|Q_{sj})$ for those Q_{sj} in this future scenario.

The second part, estimating the $P(Y_i|Q_{sj})$, is relatively tractable; it doesn't require all the $P_s(R_{uvk})$, but only the relatively miniscule subset involving conjunctions of the form P_jQ_l, where Q_l is an element of some Q_{sj} and P_j is the pattern to which the proposition Y_i refers. In practice an intelligent system would probably have to forego the testing of all the Y_i, and for those Y_i which it selected to test it would have to ignore some of the conjunctions P_jQ_l. For those Y_i and Q_{sj} selected, it would simply have to use the formula $P(Y_i|Q_{sj})=P(Y_iQ_{sj})/P(Q_{sj})$.

Unfortunately, the task of choosing a set of most likely futures, is far, far less palatable. This is a very difficult optimization problem, and what's worse, in general it refers to the entire set of $P_s(R_{uvk})$. The array $\{R_{uvk}\}$ is so large that no conceivable intelligence could ever compute it for a situation involving a realistic number of patterns. So in order for intelligent prediction to be possible, some sort of very rough approximation method is required.

Let's assume — for reasons that will become clear in later chapters — that certain patterns in Q_s have been labeled as **important**. By what process doesn't matter right now. Define the **prominence** of a pattern as the product of its intensity with its importance. Then one rough approximation algorithm is as follows. Consider perhaps seven different values of s — e.g. a second, a minute, an hour, a day, a week, a year, a lifetime — and seven different values of v. For each of these values of s, start with, say, the seven most prominent patterns, and consider all the various combinations of them. Estimate for each of these 896 combinations the appropriate **average over all u** of $P_s(R_{uvk})$, where v runs through all seven values. For each v retain the seven which yield the highest numbers (there could be some repetition in this set if the same pattern were prominent on two different time scales). Then, for each v, for each of these seven patterns P, consider all the combinations of P with the six next most prominent patterns in Q_s (where s corresponds to the time scale on which P was selected as prominent). For each of these combinations, compute the appropriate average over all u of $P_s(R_{uvk})$ (where v corresponds to the time scale according to which the initial element of R_{uvk} was retained). Select the seven which yield the highest numbers. Then, for each v, for each of these seven patterns P, consider all the combinations of P with the **next** most prominent patterns in Q_s....

Obviously, the numbers could be tinkered with. Perhaps they could be selected more intelligently. But the basic idea should be clear: with luck, you can **accrete** a reasonably likely projection on any future time scale v by starting with an intense, important pattern and progressively adding less and less intense and important patterns onto it. At each stage a number of possible additions are considered, and those which contradict least are retained. This is a very crude methodology. It relies essentially on the precept that more intense habits can be expected to continue with greater certainty — without this assumption, one might as well start with randomly selected "important" patterns as with intense ones.

The moral of all this is that if the **philosophical** problem of induction is unsolvable, the **general practical** problem of induction is formidable. By proposing the tendency to take habits as a fundamental law, we have analyzed induction in terms of pattern recognition. By proposing that more intense patterns have more propensity to continue we have given a clue as to how to go about resolving the contradictory predictions which the tendency to take habits inevitably gives rise to. But this is nothing more than a general precept, a hint as to how to go about doing things: even if, on average, the more intense of a set of contradictory patterns prevails, it is folly to invariably assume that the more intense pattern one has perceived will prevail. To go beyond mere philosophical maxims requires a general framework for talking about the probabilities of various combinations of patterns, and this leads into a maze of sets and indices. It is extremely difficult to use past experience to tell which of two contradictory patterns will prevail.

But this task is necessary for intelligence: what we are talking about is no less than building a plausible model of the future on the basis of the past. Hopefully the homeliness of the necessary formalism does not obscure the very basic nature of the questions being addressed. Although induction is generally recognized to be essential to mentality, there has been very little work done on the general practical problem of induction. Philosophers have tirelessly debated the fine points of arguments for and against the justifiability and possibility of induction; and computer scientists have made a great deal of progress studying induction in limited contexts (Blum and Blum, 1975; Daley and Smith, 1986). But, cumbersome as the ideas of this section imply a hybrid pattern-theoretic/probabilistic method of predicting, on the basis of patterns recognized in the world in the past, the probability that a given pattern X will occur with intensity K in the future on a time scale [t,t+v], where t is the present.

5.3 Induction, Probability, and Intelligence

In conclusion, let us now return to the question of intelligence. Assuming that the world is unpredictable and yet possesses the tendency to take habits to a significant degree, let us ask: how should a system act in order to approximately maximize the given "appropriateness" function A? In other words, let us ask the Kantian question: how is intelligence possible? One reasonable answer is, by repeating the following schematic steps:

1. **Recognize patterns** in the environment.
2. **Construct a model** of what the future will be like, based on reasoning by induction, assuming the strengthened Peirce's principle and using probability theory. That is, where t denotes the present time, construct a set of statements of the form "according to my best guess, the probability that the environment will exhibit pattern X, with intensity K, over time interval [t,t+v], is P(X,K,v)", where P(X,K,v) is as high as possible.
3. **Estimate** what strategy will maximize A according to such an assumption.

In later chapters it will be proposed that this three-step process is applied recursively — that each of the three steps will often involve the application of all three steps to certain subproblems. And the process will be embedded in a larger, subtler web of structures and processes. But nonetheless, these three steps form the core about which the ideas of the following chapters will be arranged.

6
Analogy

6.0 The Structure-Mapping Theory of Analogy

Induction, as we have analyzed it, requires a store of patterns on which to operate. We have not said how these patterns are to be obtained. Any general global optimization algorithm could be applied to the problem of recognizing patterns in an environment. But pattern recognition is a difficult problem, and a mind needs rapid, reasonably accurate solutions. Not just any algorithm will do.

One might propose to determine, by induction, an effective pattern recognition algorithm. But although this might be possible, it would be very slow. Such a process probably occurred during the evolution of intelligent species, but within the lifespan of one organism there is simply not time.

In Chapter 9, I will propose that intelligent entities solve pattern recognition problems with a "perceptual hierarchy" that applies the multilevel philosophy of global optimization sketched in Chapter 2. Among other things, this perceptual hierarchy makes continual use of two processes: analogy and deduction. And deduction, it will be argued in Chapter 8, is also essentially dependent on analogy. Hence analogical reasoning is an essential part of the picture of intelligence drawn at the end of the previous chapter.

WHAT IS ANALOGY

What I mean by analogy is, roughly, reasoning of the form "A is similar to B in respect X, therefore A is also similar to B in respect Y." As with induction, it is difficult to say exactly why analogy works as well as it does. But there is no disputing its effectiveness. Bronowski (1956) has driven the point home so forcefully that an extended quote seems appropriate:

> Man has only one means to discovery, and that is to find *likeness* between things. To him, two trees are like two shouts and like two parents, and on

this likeness he has built all mathematics. A lizard is like a bat and like a man, and on such likenesses he has built the theory of evolution and all biology. A gas behaves like a jostle of billiard balls, and on this and kindred likenesses rests much of our atomic picture of matter.

In looking for intelligibility in the world, we look for unity; and we find this (in the arts as well as in science) in its unexpected likenesses. This indeed is man's creative gift, to find or make a likeness where none was seen before — a likeness between mass and energy, a link between time and space, an echo of all our fears in the passion of Othello.

So, when we say that we can explain a process, we mean that we have mapped it in the likeness of another process which we know to work. We say that a metal crystal stretches because its layers slide over one another like cards in a pack, and then that some polyester yarns stretch and harden like a metal crystal. That is, we take from the world round us a few models of structure and process (the particle, the wave, and so on), and when we research into nature, we try to fit her with these models.

Even more intriguingly, Bronowski goes on to relate **analogy** with **structure**:

Yet one powerful procedure in research, we know, is to break down complex events into simpler parts. Are we not looking for the understanding of nature in these? When we probe below the surface of things, are we not trying, step by step, to reach her ultimate and fundamental constituents?

We do indeed find it helpful to work piecemeal. We take a sequence of events or an assembly to pieces: we look for the steps in a chemical reaction, we carve up the study of an animal into organs and cells and smaller units within a cell. This is our atomic approach, which tries always to see in the variety of nature different assemblies from a few basic units. Our search is for simplicity, in that the distinct units shall be few, and all units of one kind identical.

And what distinguishes one assembly of these units from another? the elephant from the giraffe, or the right-handed molecule of sugar from the left-handed? The difference is in the organization of the units into the whole; the difference is in the structure. And the likenesses for which we look are also likenesses of structure.

This is the true purpose of the analytic method in science: to shift our gaze from the thing or event to its structure. We understand a process, we explain it, when we lay bare in it a structure which is like one we have met elsewhere.

What Bronowski observed in the history and psychology of science, Gentner and Gentner (1983) have phrased in a more precise and general way. They speak of the "Generative Analogy Hypothesis" — the hypothesis that analogies are used in generating inferences. And in order to test this hypothesis, they set forth a specific theoretical framework for analogical processing, called "structure-mapping." According to this framework, analogical reasoning is concerned with deriving statements about a **target** domain T from statements about a **base** domain B. Each domain is understood to consist of a number of "nodes" and a collection of relations between these nodes. Essentially, a node may be any sort of entity — an object, a color, etc. A structure-mapping begins with a relation which takes certain base nodes into certain target nodes: if the source nodes are $(b_1,...,b_n)$ and the target nodes are $(t_1,...,t_n)$, it is a map $M(b_i)=t_j$, where i ranges over some subset of $(1,...,n)$. Analogy occurs when it is assumed that a relation which holds between b_i and b_k also holds between $M(b_i)$ and $M(b_k)$.

The theory of structure-mapping analogy states that reasoning of this form is both common and useful. This hypothesis has been verified empirically — e.g. by studying the way people reason about electricity by analogy to water and other familiar "base" domains. Furthermore, the evidence indicates that, as Gentner and Gentner put it, relations "are more likely to be imported into the target if they belong to a system of coherent, mutually constraining relationships, the others of which map into the target." If a relation is part of a larger pattern of relationships which have led to useful analogies, people estimate that it is likely to lead to a useful analogy.

The structure-mapping theory of analogy — sketched by Bronowski and many others and formalized by Gentner and Gentner — clearly captures the essence of analogical reasoning. But it is not sufficiently explanatory — it does not tell us, except in a very sketchy way, why certain relations are better candidates for analogy than others. One may approach this difficult problem by augmenting the structure-mapping concept with a more finely-grained pattern-theoretic approach.

INDUCTION, DEDUCTION, ANALOGY

Peirce proclaimed the tendency to take habits to be the "one law of mind", and he divided this law into three parts: deduction, induction, and abduction or analogy. The approach of computer science and mathematical logic, on the other hand, is to take deductive reasoning as primary, and then analyze induction and analogy as deviations from deduction. The subtext is that deduction, being infallible, is the best of the three. The present approach is closer to Peirce than it is to the standard contemporary point of view. When speaking in terms of pattern, induction and analogy are more elementary than deduction. And I will argue that deduction cannot be understood except in the context of a comprehensive understanding of induction and analogy.

STRUCTURAL SIMILARITY

As in Chapter 3, define the distance between two sequences f and g as $d_\#(f,g)=|(P(f)-P(g))U(P(g)-P(f)|_\#$. And define the approximation to d#(f,g) with respect to a given set of functions S as

$$d_S(f,g)=\left|\,[(S\cap P(f))-(S\cap P(g))]U[(S\cap P(g))-(S\cap P(f))]\,\right|_{\#}.$$

This definition is the key to our analysis of analogy.

A metric is conventionally defined as a function d which satisfies the following axioms:

1. $d(f,g) \le d(g,h) + d(f,h)$.
2. $d(f,g) = d(g,f)$.
3. $d(f,g) \ge 0$.
4. $d(f,g)=0$ if and only if f=g.

Note that $d_\#$ is not a metric, because it would be possible for P(f) to equal P(g) even if f and g were nonidentical. And it would not be wise to consider equivalence classes such that f and g are in the same class if and only if $d_\#(f,g)=0$, because even if $d_\#(f,g)=0$, there might exist some h such that $d_\#(Em(f,h),Em(g,h))$ is nonzero. That is, just because $d_\#(f,g)=0$, f and g are not for all practical purposes equivalent. And the same argument holds for d_S — for $d_S(f,g)=0$ does not in general imply $d_S(Em(f,h),Em(g,h))$, and hence there is little sense in identifying f and g. A function d which satisfies the first three axioms given above might be called a pseudometric; that is how $d_\#$ and d_S should be considered.

TRANSITIVE REASONING

To understand the significance of this pseudometric, let us pause to consider a "toy version" of analogy that might be called transitive reasoning. Namely, if we reason that "f is similar to g, and g is similar to h, so f is similar to h," then we are reasoning that "d(f,g) is small, and d(g,h) is small, so d(f,h) is small." Obviously, the accuracy of this reasoning is circumstance-dependent. Speaking intuitively, in the following situation it works very well:

g   f
h

But, of course, one may also concoct an opposite case:

f   g   h

Since our measure of distance, $d_\#$, satisfies the triangle inequality, it is always the case that $d_\#(f,h) \le d_\#(g,h) + d_\#(f,g)$. This puts a theoretical bound on the possible error of the associated form of transitive reasoning. In actual circumstances where transitive reasoning is utilized, some approximation to $d_\#$ will usually be assumed, and thus the relevant observation is that $d_S(f,h) \le d_S(g,h) + d_S(f,g)$ for any S. The fact that $d_S(f,h)$ is small, however, may say as much about S as about the relation between f and h. The triangle inequality is merely the final phase of transitive reasoning; equally essential is to the process is the pattern recognition involved in approximating $d_#$.

6.1 A Typology of Analogy

Analogy is far more powerful than transitive reasoning; nonetheless, according to the present analysis it is nothing more than a subtler way of manipulating the pattern distance. I will introduce three forms of analogical reasoning — **structural analogy, modeling,** and **contextual analogy** — and propose a unified structure for analogical reasoning which encompasses all of them. It is perhaps not obvious that all conceivable cases of analogical reasoning are included in this formulation — but I have been unable to find a counterexample. What I am attempting here is vaguely similar to Aristotle's list of the seventeen forms of syllogistic logic. He did not **prove** his list exhaustive, but it nonetheless served well for a long time.

STRUCTURAL ANALOGY

Consider the following approach to recognizing patterns in an entity x.

1. $d_S(x',x)$ is small.
2. (y,z) is, approximately, a pattern in x'.
3. Thus something near (y,z) is, approximately, a pattern in x.

The justification of the process is obvious: d_S is an approximation of $d_#$, and $d_#$ is a measure of difference in pattern. In general, if $d_#(A,B)$ is small, then most of the patterns in A are also patterns in B, and vice versa. And as this distance gets smaller, the reasoning gets more certain.

This process I will call **structural analogy**; it is the simplest of the three forms. Quite simply, X is structurally analogous to x' if x and x' have similar structure. Roughly speaking, structural analogy is the assumption that if x and x' have some similar structures, then they have other similar structures.

For a less formal example, consider the following experiment, described by Ornstein (1986, p.159):

> A man comes in to give a lecture to students. Afterward, the students are told that he is either a student or a professor and are asked to rate the lecture. Not surprisingly, they rate the lecture as being better if a professor has given it, but what is surprising is that they rate the lecturer as **taller** if he was identified as a professor.

It would appear that what is happening here is an unconscious, erroneous structural analogy. The students observe that the lecturer has something in common with the loose collection of patterns that might be called "high status" or "superiority". Therefore they assume, unconsciously, that he is likely to have **other** patterns in common with this same collection. This assumption is not overpoweringly strong, but it is enough to bias their perceptions.

MODELING

Let us begin with a rough example. Suppose one seeks a method of making housing less expensive (i.e. one seeks a certain pattern in the domain of knowledge about housing, which domain we may call x). Then one might decide to reason by analogy to the automobile industry. Automobiles bear some similarity to houses — both are designed to contain humans, both are manufactured in great number throughout the developed world, both represent fairly major investments for the average person, etc. There are obviously significant differences also, but the association is by no means arbitrary. One might reasonably ask: how does one make inexpensive cars?

In reasoning thus, one would be beginning (Step 1 in the process of structural analogy) with the observation that the entity "housing" is in some measure similar to the entity "cars". In the notation given above, if the domain of knowledge about housing is x, then the domain of knowledge about cars is x'.

Cars, one might then observe, are much less expensive when mass-produced than when custom-built and custom-designed. And cars are being made cheaper and cheaper by more and more efficient methods of mass production. This is Step 2 in the process of structural analogy: one is recognizing a pattern in x'.

Finally, one might map this reasoning back to the domain of houses, searching in the vicinity of "cars are made less expensive through mass production" and finding "houses are made less expensive through mass production" (Step 3). The validity of this hypothesis could then be tested by exploring whether it is in fact possible to make the production of housing less expensive through mass production — by exploring the feasibility of trucking or air-lifting a pre-assembled house to a given location, etc.

This may be interpreted as an illustration of structural analogy: the structure of the housing industry is somewhat similar to the structure of the auto industry, so further similarities are assumed to exist. But it also suggests a slightly different form of analogical reasoning, which I shall call **modeling**. For in this example the relation between x' and x was exactly the same as the relation between (y,z) and the pattern finally found in x. That is, if we define a function f by f(g(cars))= g(housing), then f(inexpensive cars) = inexpensive housing, and also f(mass-produced cars) = mass-produced housing. This suggests the following general form of reasoning:

1. $d_S(f(x),x)$ is small.
2. (y,z) is, approximately, a pattern in $f(x)$.
3. Thus something near $(f^{-1}(y),f^{-1}(z))$ is, approximately, a pattern in x.

In general, f^{-1} may be multivalued; it may be a relation rather than a function. This poses a moderate computational difficulty (Grandy, 1985), which may be dealt with by maximum-entropy methods like those discussed in Chapter 9.

BRAINSTORMING

Why would modeling analogy work? If f(w) is always structurally similar to w, for any w, then it is just a special form of structural analogy, and it is justified whenever structural analogy is justified. Otherwise, however, it is a question of whether the function f "preserves patterns". There might be some functions f for which Steps 2 and 3 taken exclusively of Step 1 would be a plausible form of reasoning. In such cases it would follow from "(y,z) is a pattern in x" that "something near (f(y),f(z)) is probably a pattern in f(x)." But, on the other hand, there are certainly many functions which do not preserve patterns in this sense.

In some cases, the choice of a function f which does **not** generally tend to preserve patterns may be highly valuable. This is one way of understanding the process of "brainstorming": one transforms a problem x into a context f(x) which is fairly unlikely to have much to do with the original context, seeks an answer in this context, and then tries to map the answer back. For instance, in thinking about international combat, one might say to oneself "now, pretend each country is a little boy, and the various parties of the war are just little boys squabbling." In this case we would be selecting f so that f(g(nations))=g(boys).

Let us assume that one has mapped the particularities of a war into the particularities of a squabble, and then thought of a way to resolve the squabble. Then in order to get anything useful one would have to map one's answer back into the domain of nations, i.e. one would have to take f^{-1} of one's answer. In this case it would seem that f is only moderately pattern-preserving, and such an experiment would have a fair but not excellent chance of yielding a relevant suggestion.

Mathematically this form of reasoning may be viewed as the attempt to find a function f, mapping a given domain D into a given range R, that is approximately "topologically semiconjugate" to the structure operator S(x). That is, f maps D to R and, ideally, S(f(x))=f(S(x)). Often R may be understood as a model of D, in the sense that each element x of D may be associated with an element of R in such a way that the relation of x to other elements y of D is similar to the relation of f(x) to the elements f(y) of R.

CONTEXTUAL ANALOGY

Only one form of analogy remains. What if x and x' have no inherent structural commonality, but are related to other patterns in similar ways? One might still reason analogically that x and x' are similar. Or one might reason analogically from the observation that x and x' are related to **different** patterns in similar ways. Let us call this **contextual analogy**. Such reasoning is not encompassed under structural analogy or modeling — a new formula is required.

To say that x and x' are related to other patterns in similar ways, is to say that $d_\#(Em(x',w'),Em(x,w))$ is small.[1] Thus contextual analogy rests on those aspects of x which do not manifest themselves in the internal structure of x, but which nonetheless emerge when x is conjoined with other entities.

For instance, suppose w=w' is a codebook which contains several different codes, including Code A and Code B. Suppose x is a message in Code A, and x' is a message in Code B — and suppose x and x' both convey the same message. Then x and x' may not appear similar; they may have no virtually no patterns in common.

To see this, observe that the meaning conveyed by a coded message, say x, is not generally a pattern in that coded message. If the meaning of the message x is called M_x, and the function (contained in the codebook) which translates x into M_x is called F, then we may write $F(x)=M_x$. But (F,M_x) is a pattern in X only if $a|F| + b|M_x| + cC(F,M_x) < |x|$, and this is not at all inevitable. Perhaps $|M_x|$ is less than $|x|$, but if the codebook is large or difficult to use, then $|F|$ or $C(F,M_x)$ may be sizeable. And the same could be said for x'.

So in this example, $d_\#(x,x')$ may be small, but what about $d_\#[Em(x',w), Em(x,w)]$? Clearly, M_x is an element of $Em(x',w)$, and $M_{x'}$ is an element of $Em(x',w)$, so that if M_x and $M_{x'}$ are equal, this distance is small. Contextual analogy would occur, for instance, if one reasoned that, because the messages x and x' have similar meanings, they may have come from the same person.

This example is not at all artificial; in fact it may turn out to be central to mental function. The mind works in terms of symbol systems, which may be considered as highly sophisticated codebooks. Street signs are coded messages, as are sentences. Suppose one reasons that sentence A has a similar meaning to sentence B, another, and therefore that the person uttering sentence A may have a similar attitude to the person uttering sentence B. This is contextual analogy, because the meaning of a sentence is not actually a pattern in that sentence, but rather a pattern emergent between that sentence and the "codebook" of language.

A GENERAL ANALOGY ALGORITHM

One may incorporate all three forms of analogy in one general process:

1. $d_S(St(f(x')\cup w')-St(w'),St(x\cup w)-St(w))$ is small.
2. (y,z) is, approximately, an element of $St(f(x')\cup v')-St(v')$.
3. Thus something near $(f^{-1}(y),f^{-1}(z))$ is, approximately, an element of $St(x\cup v)-St(v)$, where $v=f^{-1}(v')$ is perhaps a good guess.

---

[1] As usual, this statement and similar ones to follow may be further formalized in terms of the notion of juxtaposition introduced in Section 3.4.

In the case of structural analogy, f is the identity mapping, and w', v and v' are the empty set, but x' is different from x.

In the case of modeling, x=x' and w', v and v' are the empty set, but f is not the identity mapping.

In the case of contextual analogy, f is the identity mapping but w' is not the empty pattern; v and v' may or may not be the empty set. If v and v' are the empty set, then one has the form of reasoning "x and x' have similar relations to y and y' respectively; therefore x and x' may be structurally similar." And if neither v nor v' is the empty set, one has the form of reasoning "x and x' have similar relations to y and y'; therefore they may also have similar relations to v and v'."

The reason for expressions such as $St(x \cup v)-St(v)$ is to specify that, for instance, either patterns in x or patterns in $Em(x,v)$ are desirable, but not patterns in v alone.

The general algorithm — which I will call, simply, **analogy** — hence includes the three forms of analogy discussed above. It also encompasses hybrid forms. For instance, if x=x', but f is not the identity and neither v, v' nor w' are the empty set, then one is mapping x to a model range via f and executing contextual rather than structural analogy in this range.

This general idea could be implemented in many different ways. For instance, consider the following hybridization of structural and modeling analogy:

1. $d_S(x',x)$ is small.
2. Select (y,z) which is, approximately, a pattern in f(x).
3. Check if something near $(f^{-1}(y),f^{-1}(z))$ is, approximately, a pattern in x'. If this doesn't turn out to be the case, and f is reasonably near the identity, then check if something near (y,z) is, approximately, a pattern in x'.

In this implementation, modeling is considered partly as a tool for searching the space near (y,z).

Each step of the process of analogy involves a significant effort: first, to pick x' or f; second, to recognize a pattern in f(x'); third, searching in a certain vicinity for a pattern in x, and fourth, inverting f. It would be possible to execute the latter three tasks by some general optimization algorithm, and to pick x' or f at random. But in order to reap the full power of analogical reasoning, it is necessary to have access to an intelligently structured database. In the next section, we shall consider the hypothesis that memory is structured specifically so as to efficiently supply the process of analogy with the data it requires.

ANALOGIES AMONG DIGRAPHS

It should be noted that an entity which characteristically seeks certain types of patterns will therefore characteristically make certain types of analogies. In other words, different analogies may occur to different entities, depending on the idiosyncracies of the pattern recognition algorithms involved. This point of view may be helpful in relating the present approach to other analyses of analogy.

For instance, Poetzsche's (1988) theory of analogy deals only with structural analogy and applies to precisely those entities which:

1. recognize patterns only in digraphs.
2. compute structural similarity using only patterns (x,y) of the form $y=\{v,w\}$, where v = "construct x by connecting node n_1 of z to node m_1 of w, node n_2 of z to node m_2 of w,..." and * is defined accordingly.

In other words, according to Poetszche's definitions, two digraphs are structurally similar if they have a common subgraph.

This scheme deals well with processes that can be easily decomposed into subprocesses. In particular, Poetszche is concerned with robot motion: his goal is to construct a robot which can figure out how to complete a task based on knowledge of how to complete similar tasks. Toward this end, he has designed a robot which internally expresses each task as a digraph of "elementary tasks". Given a new task, the robot searches its memory for a task with a structurally similar digraph and then (by structural analogy) uses this as the starting point for figuring out how to do the task at hand.

6.2 Analogy and Induction

Induction and analogy are obviously closely related. In induction one assumes the future will be similar to the past, and tries to guess which of a set of past patterns will continue into the future. In analogy one assumes that similar entities will have similar patterns, and directs pattern recognition on this basis. The difference is that in analogy, one is merely trying to locate patterns in some entity x, by analogy to some entity x'. In induction, on the other hand, one assumes that a complete catalogue of patterns has already been recognized, and one tries to make a coherent model out of these patterns. The two processes complement each other.

BACKGROUND KNOWLEDGE

Many AI researchers view analogical reasoning with a great deal of skepticism. For instance, Bipin Indurkhya has argued that

> One naturally asks: Given some state of background knowledge, what justification is there, if any, that similarities in certain respects determine similarities in other respects? ...an inference from analogy cannot be justified on the basis of existing similarity between the source and the target alone. The justification, if any, must come from the background

knowledge in some other form.... Once it is realized that an inference based only on some existing similarity between the source and the target — and nothing else — is about as justified as a random inference, one learns to exercise extreme caution in deriving an inference from analogy. One seeks justification in other places; it must be some other piece of knowledge, some piece of fact, which "justifies" why the existing similarities determine the inferred ones. And if no such justification can be found, the so-called analogical inference is to be properly discarded. (1988, pp. 224-25)

In the notation introduced above, the "source" is x' and the "target" is x. The point is that, in general, there is no reason to believe that the existence of some similarities between x and x' implies the existence of other similarities. Indurkhya thinks this implication must be drawn from "facts" and "background information."

Really, there are two questions here. The first is, when is it justifiable to assume that the existence of a degree D_1 of similarity between x and x' implies a degree D_2 of similarity between x and x'. In other words, how can one tell when reasoning by analogy is justifiable at all; and when is it justifiable, how can one tell to what extent? The other is, how is it possible to tell, based on the **type** of similarity between x and x', what kinds of further similarities to look for. That is: in Step 2 of the analogy algorithm, is there some way to determine what sorts of patterns (y,z) should be looked at on the basis of the similarities used for the computation? Indurkhya, expressing a view which is widespread in the AI community, states that both of these questions should be answered by reference to "background knowledge".

Does this requisite background knowledge perhaps come from deduction? This may be true in certain instances. But, as we shall see, deductive reasoning is only useful when it is paired with analogical reasoning. The analogies used in executing deductive reasoning cannot **all** be executed on the basis of background information obtained by deduction.

Does the background knowledge come from experience? If so, it does not come directly from raw, unprocessed sense perception; it comes out of the process of induction. Induction requires pattern recognition. And I suggest that effective general pattern recognition requires analogy. From this it follows that the background information Indurkha requires cannot come entirely from experience: either it comes from some other source or it is not always necessary.

However, although induction may not be used to justify every particular analogy, it may still be used to justify analogy in general. This may sound contradictory, but the paradox is only apparent. Not all the analogies used in inductive reasoning can be justified inductively. However, if analogies that are **not justified** by induction are used anyway, and they happen to work, then the tendency to take habits implies that analogy can be expected to work in the future.

I find this argument rather convincing. On the basis of ample real-world experience, we know that analogy has often worked in the past. We have obtained useful results from it so often that its effectiveness must be considered a very intense pattern in the past. Therefore, by the tendency to take habits — by induction — it is relatively likely that analogy will work in the future. Hence it is advisable to reason by analogy.

Another way to phrase this is to postulate a "spatial" tendency to take habits, to the effect that analogy does in fact tend to work more often than it would in a randomly selected universe obeying the temporal tendency to take habits. This strategy seems much less elegant than in the temporal, inductive tendency to take habits; it has more of an ad hoc flavor. But it does yield the desired result.

6.3 Hierarchical Analogy

We have not yet discussed the possibility that analogies might be justified by analogy. Obviously, analogy as a general mode of thought cannot be justified by analogy; that would be circular reasoning. But, just as particular analogies can be justified by inductive or deductive background knowledge, so can particular analogies be justified by analogical background knowledge. In some cases, the mind may use analogical reasoning to determine how probable it is that similarity A between x and x' will imply similarity B between x and x' by observing which similarities have, in similar situations, led to which other similarities. Actually, this sort of analogical background information is a special kind of inductive background information, but it is worth distinguishing.

Let us be more precise. Assume that processor P_1 executes a long sequence of analogical reasoning processes, and processor P_2 observes this sequence, recording for each instance a vector of the form (w,w',f,w,w',v,v',R,r), where r is a number measuring the total prominence of the patterns recognized in that instance, and R is the set of patterns located.

The prominence of a pattern may — as in the previous chapter — be defined as the product of its intensity with its importance. The prominence of a set of patterns S may be crudely defined as $|S|K$, where S is the structural complexity $|S|$ of the set and K is some number representing the prominence of the set. A very crude way to define K is as the average over all (y,z) in S of the importance of (y,z). A more accurate definition could be formulated by a procedure similar to Algorithm 3.1.

Then processor P_2 can seek to recognize patterns (y,z) with the property that when x is a pattern in (w,w',f,w,w',v,v',R), r tends to be large. This is an optimization problem: maximize the correlation of r with the intensity of x, over the space of patterns in the first six components of the vector. But it is a particularly difficult optimization problem in the following sense: determining what entities lie in the space over which optimization is taking place is, in itself, a very difficult optimization problem. In other words, it is a constrained optimization problem with very unpleasant constraints. One very simple approach would be the following:

1. Using straightforward optimization or analogy, seek to recognize patterns in (x,x',f,w,w',v,v',R).
2. Over the space of patterns recognized, see which ones correlate best with large r.
3. Seek to recognize new patterns in (x,x',f,w,w',v,v',R) in the vicinity of the answer(s) obtained in Step 2.

Perhaps some other approach would be superior, but the difficulty is that one cannot expect to find patterns in a given narrow vicinity merely because functions in that region correlate well with r. The focus must be on the location of patterns, not the search for large correlation with r.

In this way analogy could be used to determine which analogies are likely to pay off. This might be called second-level analogy, or "learning by analogy about how to learn by analogy." And the same approach could be applied to the analogies involved in analyzing analogies, yielding third-level analogy, or "learning by analogy how to learn by analogy how to learn by analogy." Et cetera. These are tremendously difficult optimization problems, so that learning on these levels is likely to be rather slow. On the other hand, each insight on such a high level will probably have a great impact on the effectiveness of lower-level analogies.

Let us be more precise about these higher levels of learning. A processor which learns by second level analogy must be connected to a processor which learns by analogy, in such a way that is has access to the inputs and the outputs of this processor. Similarly, a processor which learns by third level analogy must be connected to a processor which learns on the second level in such a way that it has access to the inputs and the outputs of this second-level processor — and the inputs and outputs of this second-level processor include all the inputs and outputs of at least one first-level processor. In general, the absolute minimum number of inputs required for an n'th-level analogy processor is proportional to n: this is the case, for instance, if every n'th level processor is connected to exactly one (n-1)'th level processor. If each n-level processor is connected to k (n-1)'th level processors for some k>1, then the number of inputs required for an n'th level processor is $[1-k^{n+1}]/[1-k]$.

In general, if a set of analogical reasoning processors — N_k learning on level k, k≤n — is arranged such that each processor learning on level k is connected to all the inputs and outputs of some set of n_k processors on level k-1, then the question of network architecture is the question of the relation between the N_k and the n_k. For instance, if $N_k n_k = 8 N_{k-1}$, then each (k-1)-level processor is being analyzed by eight different k-level processors; but if $N_k n_k = N_{k-1}$, then each (k-1)-level processor is being analyzed by only one k-level processor.

This is an hierarchical analogy network: a hierarchy of processors learning by analogy how to best learn by analogy how to best learn by analogy how to best learn by analogy... how to best learn by analogy. As will be explained in later chapters, in order to be effective it must be coupled with a structurally associative memory network, which provides a knowledge base according to which the process of analogy can be executed.

6.4 Structural Analogy in the Brain

The neurons of the cortex are organized in clusters, each containing 50 to 10,000 neurons. The neurons of each cluster are connected primarily to other neurons in the same cluster. Edelman (1988) has proposed that it makes sense to think of connections between clusters, not just individual neurons, as being reinforced or inhibited; and he has backed this up with a detailed mathematical model of neural behavior. Following this line of thought, it is the nature of the interaction between neural clusters which interests us here. We shall show that, according to a simple model inspired by Edelman's ideas, the interaction of neural clusters gives rise to a simple form of structural analogy.

Edelman's theory of "Neural Darwinism" divides the evolution of the brain into two phases. The first, which takes place during fetal development, is the phase of cluster formation. And the second, occurring throughout the remainder of life, is the phase of repermutation: certain arrangements of clusters are selected from the set of possible arrangements. This is not an outlandish hypothesis; Changeux (1985), among others, has made a similar suggestion. Edelman, however, has formulated the theory as a sequence of specific biochemical hypotheses, each of which is supported by experimental results.

Roughly speaking, a set of clusters which is habitually activated in a certain order is called a **map**. Mental process, according to Edelman's theory, consists of the **selection** of maps, and the actual **mapping** of input — each map receiving input from sensory sources and/or other maps, and mapping its output to motor control centers or other maps. Mathematically speaking, a map is not necessarily a function, since on different occasions it may conceivably give different outputs for the same input. A map is, rather, a dynamical system in which the output y^t at time t and the internal state S^t at time t are determined by $y^t=f(x^{t-1},S^{t-1})$, $S^t=g(x^{t-1},M^{t-1})$, where x^t is the input at time t. And it is a dynamical system with a special structure: each map may be approximately represented as a serial/parallel composition of simple maps which are composed of single clusters. One key axiom of Edelman's theory is the existence of numerous "degenerate" clusters, clusters which are different in internal structure but, in many situations, act the same (i.e. often produce the same output given the same input). This implies that each map is in fact a serial/parallel combination of simple component maps which are drawn from a fairly small set, or at least extremely similar to elements of a fairly small set.

There is much more to Neural Darwinism than what I have outlined here — for instance, I have not even mentioned Edelman's intriguing hypotheses as to the role of adhesion molecules in the development of mentality. But there are nevertheless a number of mysteries at the core of the theory. Most importantly, it is not known exactly how the behavior of a cluster varies with its strengths of interconnection and its internal state.

Despite this limitation, however, Neural Darwinism is in my opinion the only existing effective theory of low-to-intermediate-level brain structure and function. Philosophically, it concords well with our theory of mind: it conceives the brain as a network of "maps", or "functions". In previous chapters we spoke of a network of "programs," but the terms "program" and "map" are for all practical purposes interchangeable. The only difference is that a program is discrete whereas the brain is considered "continuous," but since any continuous system may be approximated arbitrarily closely by some discrete system, this is inessential.

So, consider a set of n processors P_i, each one possessing an internal state S_i^t at each time t. Assume, as above, that the output y_i^t at time t and the internal state S_i^t at time t are determined by $y_i^t = f_i(x_i^{t-1}, S_i^{t-1})$, $S_i^t = g_i(x_i^{t-1}, S^{t-1})$, where x^{it} is the input at time t. Define the "design" of each processor as the ₃et of all its possible states. Assume the processors are connected in such a way that the input of each processor is composed of subsets of the output of some set of k processors (where k is small compared to n, say O(logn)). This is a basic "network of processors".

Note that we have defined f and g to vary with i. Strictly speaking, this means that the different processors are different dynamical systems. In this case, what it really means, intuitively, is that f_i and g_i may vary with the pattern of flow of the dynamical system. In fact, from here on we shall assume $g_i = g$ for all i; we shall not consider the possibility of varying the g_i. However, we **shall** be concerned with minor variations in the f_i; in particular, with "strengthening" and "weakening" the connections between one processor and another.   For this purpose, we may as well assume that the space of outputs y_i^t admits is R^n or a discrete approximation of some subset thereof. Let $s_{i,j}$ denote the scalar strength of connection from P^i to P_j. For each P_i, let $_jf_i^t$ denote the portion of the graph of f_i which is connected to P_j at time t. Assume that if j and l are unequal, then $_jf_i^t$ and $_lf_i^t$ are disjoint for any t and r; and that $_jf_i^r = s_{i,j} _jf_i^t$ for all t and r. According to all this, then, the only possible variations of f_i over time are merely variations of strength of connectivity, or "conductance".

As observed above, our model of mind is expressed as a network of processors, and Edelman's theory expresses brain function as a result of the dynamics of a network of neuronal clusters, which are specialized processors. In the context of neuronal clusters, the "design" as defined above is naturally associated with the graph of interconnection of the neurons in the cluster; a particular state is then an assignation of charge levels to the neurons in the cluster, and a specification of the levels of various chemicals, most importantly those concerned with the modification of synaptic strength. According to Edelman's theory, the designs of the million or so processors in the brain's network are highly repetitive; they do not vary much from a much smaller set of fundamental designs. And it is clear that all the functions f_i regulating connection between neuronal clusters are essentially the same, except for variations in conductance.

THE NOISY HEBB RULE

D.O. Hebb, in his classic *Organization of Behavior* (1949), sought to explain mental process in terms of one very simple neural rule: when a synaptic connection between two neurons is used, its "conductance" is temporarily increased. Thus a connection which has proved somehow useful in the past will be reinforced. This provides an elegant answer to the question: where does the learning take place? There is now physiological evidence that Hebbian learning does indeed occur. Two types of changes in synaptic strength have been observed (Bliss, 1979): "post-tetanic potentiation", which lasts for at most a few minutes, and "enhancement", which can last for hours or days.

Hebb proceeded from this simple rule to the crucial concepts of the cell-assembly and the phase-sequence:

> Any frequently repeated, particular stimulation will lead to the slow development of a "cell-assembly", a diffuse structure comprising cells in the cortex and diencephalon... capable of acting briefly as a closed system, delivering facilitation to other such systems and usually having a specific motor facilitation. A series of such events constitutes a "phase sequence" — the thought process. Each assembly action may be aroused by a preceding assembly, by a sensory event, or — normally — by both.

This theory has been criticized on the physiological level; but this is really irrelevant. As Hebb himself said, "it is... on a class of theory that I recommend you to put your money, rather than any specific formulation that now exists" (1963, p.16). The more serious criticism is that Hebb's ideas do not really explain much about the most interesting aspects of mental process. Simple stimulus-response learning is a long way from analogy, associative memory, deduction, and the other aspects of thought which Hebb hypothesizes to be special types of "phase sequences".

Edelman's ideas mirror Hebb's on the level of **neural clusters** rather than neurons. In the notation given above, Edelman has proposed that if the connection from P_1 to P_2 is used often over a certain interval of time, then its "conductance" $s_{1,2}$ is temporarily increased. Physiologically, this is a direct consequence of Hebb's neuron-level principle; it is simply more specific. It provides a basis for the formation of maps: sets of clusters through which information very often flows according to a certain set of paths. Without this Hebbian assumption, lasting maps would occur only by chance; with it, their emergence from the chaos of neural flow is virtually guaranteed. At bottom, what the assumption amounts to is a neural version of the principle of induction. It says: if a pathway has been useful in the past, we shall assume it will be useful in the future, and hence make it more effective.

Unfortunately, there is no reason to believe that the cluster-level interpretation of Hebb's theory is sufficient for the explanation of higher mental processes. By constructing a simulation machine, Edelman has shown that a network of entities much like neural clusters, interacting according to the Hebbian rule, can learn to perceive certain visual phenomena with reasonable accuracy. But this work — like most perceptual biology — has not proceeded past the lower levels of the perceptual hierarchy.

In order to make a bridge between these neural considerations and the theory of mind, I would like to propose a substantially more general hypothesis: that if the connection between P_1 and P_3 is used often over a certain interval of time, and the network is structured so that P_2 can potentially output into P_3, then the conductance $s_{2,3}$ is likely to be temporarily increased.

As we shall see, this "noisy Hebb rule" leads immediately to a simple explanation of the emergence of analogy from a network of neural clusters. Although I know of no evidence either supporting or falsifying the noisy Hebb rule, it is certainly not biologically unreasonable. One way of fulfilling it would be a spatial imprecision in the execution of Hebbian neural induction. That is, if the inductive increase in conductance following repeated use of a connection were by some means spread liberally around the vicinity of the connection, this would account for the rule to within a high degree of approximation. This is yet another case in which imprecision may lead to positive results.

THE NOISY HEBB RULE AND STRUCTURAL ANALOGY

Consider the situation in which two maps, A and B, share a common set of clusters. This should not be thought an uncommon occurrence; on the contrary, it is probably very rare for a cluster to belong to one map only. Let B-A (not necessarily a map) denote the set of clusters in B but not A. The activation of map A will cause the activation of some of those clusters in map B-A which are adjacent to clusters in A. And the activation of these clusters may cause the activation of some of the clusters in B-A which are adjacent to them — and so on. Depending on what is going on in the rest of B, this process might peter out with little effect, or it might result in the activation of B. In the latter case, what has occurred is the most primitive form of structural analogy.

Structural analogy, as defined earlier, may be very roughly described as reasoning of the form: A and B share a common pattern, so if A is useful, B may also be useful. The noisy Hebb rule involves only the simplest kind of common pattern: the common subgraph. But it is worth remembering that analogy based on common subgraphs also came up in the context of Poetzsche's approach to analogical robot learning. Analogy by common subgraphs works. There is indeed a connection between neural analogy and conceptual analogy.

And — looking ahead to chapter 7 — it is also worth noting that, in this simple case, analogy and structurally associative memory are inextricably intertwined: A and B have a common pattern and are consequently stored near each other (in fact, interpenetrating each other); and it is this associative storage which permits neural analogy to lead to conceptual analogy.

7
Long-Term Memory

7.0 Structurally Associative Memory

It is clear that analogy cannot work effectively without recourse to an effective method of storing patterns. However, I suggest that an even stronger statement holds: the nature of analogy actually **dictates** a particular type of memory structure. The only way analogy can work effectively is if it is coupled with a memory that is specifically structured so as to support analogical reasoning.

This memory must, of course, be a "long-term memory": its contents must be sufficiently permanent to carry over from one situation to another. I will argue that the entire structure of the mind's long-term memory can be elicited through the study of analogy. On the other hand, the "short-term memory" of contemporary psychology is essentially a euphemism for "consciousness", and we shall deal with it in a later chapter.

In a completely different context, Jousselin (1987) has reached a similar conclusion regarding the relation between processing and memory. He has shown that, in a very general mathematical sense, the nature of the operations carried out by the processor of a computer actually **determine** the structure of the memory of that computer.

Strictly speaking, what is given here is not a model of how memories are physically stored in the brain or anywhere else, but rather a model of how memory **access** must work, of how the time required to access different memories in different situations must vary. However, following Jousselin, I hold that the structure of memory access **is** much if not all of the structure of memory. This point will be elaborated below.

ASSOCIATION AND PATTERN

The model which I will propose is **associative** in the sense that it stores related elements near each other (Kohonen, 1984; Palm, 1980). I have already suggested that mental process is founded on induction and analogy, which are based on **pattern recognition**. It follows from this hypothesis that, from the point of view of mental process, two entities should be considered to be **associated** if and only if they have patterns in common, or are bound together as the substrate of a common pattern.

As in Chapter 3, let IN(x,y;z) denote the intensity with which (x,y) is a pattern in z. Then the **network of emergence** associated with a set of functions is a weighted graph of which the nodes correspond to the functions, and in which each triple x, y an z is connected as follows:

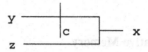

with weight c=IN(x,y;z). If IN(x,y;z)=0 then, of course, no zero-weight connection need actually be drawn. The essential aspect of this diagram is that each of x, y and z holds a unique position.

A **structurally associative memory**, associated with a set of functions, is also a weighted graph. The nodes correspond to the functions, and the nodes are connected in triples. In these respects it is similar to a network of emergence. But it need not possess the perfect structure of the network of emergence. Rather, if it does not possess this perfect structure, it is required to continually adjust itself so as to better approximate the structure of a network of emergence. It may contain the same entity at many different places. It may adjust itself by connecting nodes which were not previously connected, by adjusting the intensity of existing connections, or by adding new nodes (representing new or old entities).

The degree to which a graph is a structurally associative memory may be defined in a number of ways, the simplest of which are of the form: 1/[1-c*(the amount by which the graph deviates from the network-of-emergence structure)], where c is an appropriately chosen positive constant. But there is no need to go into the details.

From here on, I will occasionally refer to a structurally associative memory of this sort as a STRAM. Imperfection in the structure of a STRAM may stem from two sources: imperfect knowledge of the degrees to which a certain pair of functions is a pattern in other functions; or imperfect reflection of this knowledge in the structure of the network. The former is a pattern recognition problem and relates to the interconnection of cognition and memory, to be addressed below. For now let us concentrate on the latter difficulty: given a certain set of data, how can a structurally associative memory be intelligently reorganized?

In practice, a structurally associative memory cannot be given an unlimited number of nodes, and if it has a reasonably large number of nodes, then not every triple of nodes can be interconnected. The number of connecting wires would very soon grow unmanageable. This is the familiar combinatorial explosion. To be practical, one must consider a fixed set of n nodes each connected to a small number k of other nodes (say k=O(logn)), and one must arrange the given functions among these nodes in such a way as to approximate the structure desired. When a new function is created, it must take a node over from some other function; and likewise with a new connection. This requires an intricate balancing; it is a difficult optimization problem. What is required is a rapid iterative solution; an algorithm which is able to continually, incrementally improve the structure of the memory while the memory is in use. We shall return to this in Section 7.2.

7.1 Quillian Networks

It is rather difficult to study the structure of human long-term memory, since we cannot look into a person's brain or mind to determine the processes by which their memory organizes itself. The only aspect of memory which is open to study is memory access. In particular, a great deal of attention has been devoted to the time required for memory access.

One frequently studied phenomenon is "priming": an experimenter shows the subject one letter, then shows two other letters simultaneously, and measures how long it takes for the subject to determine if the two simultaneously presented letters are the same or different. The answer comes considerably faster when the one preliminary letter is the same as one of the two simultaneous letters (Posner and Snyder, 1975). This shows that when something is summoned from memory it is somehow "at the top" of the memory for a period afterwards, somehow more easily accessible.

According to the idea of structurally associative memory, if x is more easily accessible than y, those things which are similar to x should in general be more easily accessible than those things which are similar to y. This has been shown by many different experimenters, e.g. Rips et al (1973).

This is an essential result; however, it is clear that this simple feature would be predicted by all sorts of different memory models. Using similar techniques, psychologists have attempted to determine the structure of memory in further detail. For instance, Collins and Quillian (1969) performed several experiments to test Quillian's network theory of memory (Fig. 3), according to which concepts are stored as nodes in a digraph. For instance, chair, couch and table would be stored on nodes emanating from the furniture node; and coffee table and dinner table would be stored on nodes emanating from the table node. In their experiments, subjects were asked to verify statements of the form "an X is a Y" — say, "a couch is a table", or "a couch is furniture". Collins and Quillian predicted that the time required to verify the sentence would be a linear function of the number of links between the concepts in the memory digraph.

This hypothesis at first appeared to be correct; but further experiments showed that the model has difficulty dealing with negative responses. Therefore Rips et al proposed an alternate model of memory in which the similarity of two entities is defined as the amount by which their "semantic features" overlap. According to their experiments, this sort of similarity is a far better predictor of reaction time than Quillian's hierarchical distance.

Collins and Loftus (1975) responded with an improvement of the Quillian model, according which concepts are stored in the nodes of a network, and each link of the network is assigned a weight corresponding to the degree of association between the concepts that it connects. Memory access then involves two stages: 1) "spreading activation", in which an activated node spreads its activation to neighboring nodes, and 2) evaluation of the most active portion of the network. This accounts for the data because it incorporates the "feature overlap" of Rips et al into the network structure. Ratcliff (1989) has criticized the model for not adequately explaining the process of evaluation; but this seems to me to be beside the point.

The model of Collins and Loftus is somewhat similar to the structurally associative memory; the biggest difference is that in the Collins and Loftus model, "similarity" is imposed a priori from the outside. The model does not explain how the mind assigns these degrees of similarity. Psychologically, this is unsatisfactory. However, it must be noted that "Quillian networks" of the sort studied by Collins and Loftus have since become quite common in AI programs. The a priori nature of similarity is no problem here, since the writer or user of the program can specify the pertinent degrees of similarity. Quillian networks are a simple and effective way of representing knowledge.

A unique Quillian network may be derived from any network of emergence by a very simple process. To explain this we shall require one preliminary concept.

Definition 7.1: The **contextual distance** between x and y, relative to the set V, is the sum over all v in V of $d_*[St(x \cup v)-St(x),St(y \cup v)-St(v)]$. It will be denoted $d_{***}(x,y)$.

This measures the distance between x and y relative to the set V: not only direct structural similarities between x and y are counted, but also similarities in the ways x and y relate to elements of V.

Then, to form the Quillian network corresponding to a given network of emergence, one must simply create a new link between each two nodes, and weight it with the **contextual distance** between the entities stored at the nodes, relative to the other entities in the memory.

The structurally associative memory network refers to a deeper level than the Quillian network, but it is fully compatible with the Quillian network. It therefore seems reasonable to hypothesize that anything which the Quillian network explains, the structurally associative memory can also explain. However, there are certain phenomena which require a deeper analysis, and hence the full power of the structurally associative memory.

For example, it will be seen below that the details of the relationship between memory and analogy fall into this category. The Quillian network supports a very rough form of analogy based on a priori "similarity", but to explain the full subtlety of analogical reasoning, the structurally associative memory is required.

In general, it would seem that the Quillian network is not really suited to be a large-scale, adaptive, self-organizing memory. The structurally associative memory is based on pattern recognition and hence it can easily be modified on the basis of new pattern recognitions. And the STRAM stores more refined data: it stores information about the **type** of relation between two entities.

The remainder of this chapter will be devoted to showing that the STRAM is capable of functioning as a large-scale, adaptive, self-organizing memory; and showing how its structure relates to analogical reasoning.

7.2 Implications of Structurally Associative Memory

Let us now return to the problem of how a STRAM is to maintain its approximate network-of-emergence structure. One way to approach this optimization problem is via the multilevel methodology (Goertzel, 1989). This application of the multilevel methodology bears a strong similarity to Achi Brandt's (1985) multilevel algorithm for the Ising spin problem.

The first level would be the following procedure:

1. Assign nodes to any newly-introduced functions, and single out a number of pre-existing nodes, in such a way that the nodes assigned and selected are approximately evenly distributed across the network (so that no two are too close to each other). Call these functions x_i and their nodes $N(x_i)$.

2. Switch the node of each of these functions x_i with the node of one of the functions y with which it shares a pattern — that is, assign x_i node $N(y)$ and y node $N(x_i)$ — and see if, according to the new arrangement, the total amount of pattern which the network indicates in x_i and y is greater. If so, let $N(x_i)=N(y)$ and let $N(y)=N(x_i)$ — that is, make the switch permanent — and apply Step 2 to x_i again. If not, proceed to one of the other functions y with which x_i shares a pattern (say, proceeding through the x_i in order of decreasing intensity of shared pattern). Once all the functions with which x_i shares more than e (some small fixed number) worth of pattern have been exhausted, exit Step 2.

This algorithm moves functions through the network toward their "proper position." The problem is that, even if x_i is not in its optimal position, its position could well be better for it than the positions of its neighbors. Ideally, one might like to try each x_i out in every possible position; and although this is not possible, one may indeed improve upon the "neighbors-only" approach.

Following the multilevel methodology, one could seek to find the optimum node for x_i among those nodes at a distance between h_1 and h_2 from x_i in the network (where the distance between two nodes is measured by the number of links separating them). One could attempt this by the Monte Carlo method, randomly seeking to switch x_i with functions in this region, or one could attempt this by randomly beginning the neighbors-only search given above from points in this region.

And if one found a new home for x_i in this region, one could execute the neighbors-only search from the new home. And from the answer which this yielded, one could execute the second-level search. And one could repeat this entire process according on an arbitrary number of levels, according to the basic framework outlined in Chapter 2.

Of course, this is only one possibility; the multilevel philosophy could be applied in many different ways, and there are many other approaches to optimization. The important point is that, by some specially-tailored optimization method, the network must continually reorganize itself so as to better approximate the network of emergence structure, and so as to integrate new data in a manner which maintains this structure. It would seem to be completely impossible to determine, at this stage, the actual method by which the human brain reorganizes its memory network.

HOLISTIC MEMORY

It might seem that no organism could afford to continually subject its memory to such a risky, speculative optimization algorithm as that sketched above. It could be, of course, that there exists some optimization algorithm which is substantially more effective than those presently known. However, as emphasized in Chapter 2, most researchers doubt if there will ever exist a rapid, highly accurate algorithm for the solution of difficult optimization problems. In the context of associative memory, rapidity is of the essence, so it is probably true that rough approximate answers must suffice.

If one were designing a brain, one way of partially eliminating the risk involved in adjusting memory according to a highly approximate algorithm would be to provide it with a large number of structurally associative memories, each storing largely the same functions. In fact, it has often been observed that biological memory is holistic in the sense that it appears to "store almost everything almost everywhere". Any small section of the cortex appears to contain a large part of the data which the cortex stores. This an empirical observation, validated repeatedly in the laboratory (Hubel, 1988).

It has been suggested that holistic memory is necessary because of the error-prone nature of the brain's components. This is almost certainly true. However, the present considerations suggest another good reason: the nature of structurally associative memory seems to require that memory structure be continually subjected to radical, experimental transformations. In order for these transformations not to interfere too much with continual memory use, the mind must incorporate some sort of "workspace" in which unsuccessful trans-formations may be tried and discarded without global effect. In short: holistic memory may be necessary not only because of the error-prone nature of the brain's "hardware", but also because of the error-prone nature of high-level mental process.

PHYSICAL MEMORY STRUCTURES

In this context, let us return to the question of physical memory. A physical memory is, obviously, not a weighted graph. Nonetheless we would like to call certain physical memories structurally associative memories. Therefore it is necessary to assign to each physical memory M a set of "naturally correspondent" structurally associative memories. We know of no completely satisfactory way of doing this, but the following scheme is not unreasonable. It requires only that we assign to each pair of elements (x,y) stored by M a distance $D_M(x,y)$ which measures the difficulty of locating x in memory given that y has very recently been located. Let F be a mapping which takes the set S of elements stored by M into the nodes of a graph; let L(x,y) denote the number of links in the graph F(S) along the shortest path from(x) to F(y). Then the accuracy with which F represents M may be defined by the average, over all (x,y), of $|L(x,y)-D_M(x,y)|$. This definition requires that, in a rough sense, distance in the memory M correspond to distance in the graph F(S). Certainly there is more to be done in this direction, but the point is that it is indeed possible to model **any** sort of memory as a graph, and hence to analyze any sort of memory as structurally associative memory.

MEMORY AND ANALOGY

Finally, we must now explore the manner in which a structurally associative memory may be utilized by cognitive processes. In the notation of the definition of analogy given above, consider that f and y have already been chosen. The process of selection will be discussed briefly a bit later. Then, given x, an appropriate x' may be located by a simple process of "looking up" in STRAM.

In the case of structural analogy all that is required is to look for something which has a large amount of pattern in common with x. Specifically, a list must be made of the significant patterns in x, and then the other functions in which these functions are also patterns must be searched, with the objective of locating those which have a large number of these patterns in common. This may be a large search, and it will have to be approximate — e.g. a Monte Carlo search could be implemented, skipping over at random some of the neighbors. The point is that the making of the list of patterns in x, and of neighbors which may also possess these patterns, is merely a matter of looking at the actual graph of the network. Of course, this method will only be accurate to the extent that the STRAM approximates the network of emergence structure.

In the case of contextual analogy, a list must be made of all the patterns which emerge between x and v, and then a search of the neighbors of these patterns must be made, until a function x' is located such that many of the same patterns emerge between it and some other entity v'.

If f is not the identity mapping, then things are slightly more involved. One knows only that f(x') is close to x in the network; one knows nothing about x' itself. So, in general, a list must be made of all the patterns which emerge in x or between x and w, and then a search of the neighbors of these patterns must be made, until an entity z is located such that many of the same patterns emerge between it and some other entity w'. Then x' may be set equal to $f^{-1}(z)$. This involves the potentially difficult computation of f^{-1}, and it is generally much more difficult than structural or contextual analogy. However, as suggested earlier, even speculative modeling analogy may be useful, as in brainstorming.

The location of x' is Step 1 of the general process of analogy. The next step is the recognition of patterns in x'. This process may be decomposed into two stages: isolating the patterns already "known" by STRAM to be part of the structure of x', and finding new patterns not yet "known" by STRAM. Of course, if f is the identity mapping, then it is trivial to locate all patterns in x' that have been identified by STRAM; in fact, this was already done to some degree of approximation in the selection of x'. In this case the first stage is very easy to execute. But if f is not the identity, then in order to find out what STRAM knows about x', one must search through STRAM for x' (remember,it is f(x') which is near x, not necessarily x' itself). One may treat this search as a minimization, over the space of all nodes of STRAM, of the function $d_{\#}(x,x')$. It would not be wise to execute this minimization by local search (from each node proceeding to that neighboring node which minimizes the function), because the structure of STRAM is almost certainly imperfect; a focused Monte Carlo search, a simulated annealing search, or a multilevel search would be much more effective.

The second stage of Step 2, the location of new patterns in x', will be implicitly addressed later, when we discuss pattern recognition in general.

7.3 Image and Process

In Section 7.2 I explained the structurally associative memory by analogy to Quillian networks. But, as hinted there, the Quillian network has several undesirable properties not shared by the STRAM. Some of these are relatively technical, such the fact that the Quillian network has no connection with the details of analogical reasoning. But there are also more philosophical differences. In particular, I will argue that there are absolutely crucial phenomena which the Quillian network cannot even begin to explain.

What is at issue here is what Israel Rosenfeld (1988, p.3) has called

> a myth that has probably dominated human thought ever since human
> beings began to write about themselves: namely, that we can accurately
> remember people, places and things because images of them have been

imprinted and permanently stored in our brains; and that, though we may not be conscious of them, these images are the basis of recognition and hence of thought and action.

In Rosenfeld's opinion, a careful examination of classical neurological experiments shows that "the fundamental assumption that memories exist in our brains as fixed traces, carefully filed and stored, may be wrong" (p.5).

For instance, consider the well-known series of experiments carried out by Wilder Penfield, beginning in the 1930's. He stimulated various areas of the brain in conscious patients and noted that this appeared to elicit recollections of "forgotten memories." At first sight this would seem to speak against Rosenfeld's point — the natural interpretation is that Penfield was touching the areas of the brain in which those memories were stored. But actually things are not so clear. Recent experiments show that these forgotten memories are actually "fragmentary impressions, like pieces of a dream, containing elements that are not part of the patient's past experiences" (p. 7).

Also, these forgotten memories occur only when the brain stimulation is simultaneous activity with the limbic system. Since the limbic system is the seat of emotion, this is evidence in favor of Freud's observation that memory without emotion would be unrecognizable. As Gloor et al (1982) put it, describing their observations of epileptic patients:

> [W]hatever we experience with our senses... even after it has been elaborated as a percept in the temporal neocortex, must ultimately be transmitted to limbic structures in order to assume experiential immediacy. This may... imply that all consciously perceived events must assume kind sort of affective dimension, if only ever so slight.

Rosenfeld proposes that, rather than storing traces, memory stores **procedures**. According to him, what happened in Penfield's experiments was that certain processes were activated, which then **constructed** the so-called forgotten memories on the spur of the moment, based partly on emotional factors and partly on information somehow stored in nearby parts of the cortex.

Further support for this point of view is given by the work of Mahl et al (1964), who observed these forgotten memories depend significantly upon "the patient's mental content at the time of stimulation." Sometimes they may not be memories at all, but merely rearrangements of the ideas which occupied the patient's mind just prior to stimulation.

No one denies that **part** of memory consists of procedures. For instance, every time we form a spoken word from its syllables, we are applying certain phonological procedures. However, most contemporary psychologists would agree with Broca, who argued in 1861 that there is a crucial structural difference between the image-based memory responsible for the storage of words and their meanings, and the procedural "memory for the movements necessary for articulating words."

Against such arguments, Rosenfeld summons an impressive variety of evidence. In each case, a phenomenon which at first appears to depend on image-based memory is seen to require procedural memory. For instance, he refers to David Marr's demonstration that shapes can be recognized as shapes without any reference to previous knowledge, merely by executing certain procedures on the appropriate visual stimuli. This shows that shape recognition probably does not depend upon searching a memory store of shapes until a match is found — it may, rather, be a matter of summoning appropriate procedures from the memory. But if shape recognition does not require a store of shapes, then why should memory contain such a store at all?

Rosenfeld admits that "Marr did not totally abandon the idea of fixed memories, since ultimately the **naming** of a shape required, in his scheme, a memory search" (p. 113). To Rosenfeld, this is the major limitation of Marr's approach. However, it seems to me that this shows exactly where Rosenfeld goes too far. Clearly he is right that the brain does not hold, somewhere in its memory, little pictures of circles or ellipses or squares. Rather, it stores certain procedures or functions which characterize these shapes. But this fact does not imply all that he says it does.

For the purpose of illustration, let us consider a highly oversimplified example. Let y denote the function which, from P and r, generates the circle with radius r and center P; and let $z=(P,r)$. Then, roughly speaking, we may say that a certain collection of stimuli x is "representable as a circle" to the extent that (y,z) is a pattern in x. For each shape, there will be one or more such characterizing patterns. I do not mean to imply that the mind stores shapes by fitting them to their standard mathematical equations, but only that it characterizes shapes by certain "symmetries" or "computational shortcuts" which manifest themselves as patterns. Algebraic equations are one kind of specifying pattern, but not the only kind. For example, one of the patterns characterizing the shape "square" might be "invariance under reflection and ninety-degree rotation".

Let us suppose, then, that in the mind's "language" each shape is a certain collection of characterizing procedures. Then what is wrong with calling this **collection** a "label" or "trace" of the shape? It seems clear that, in general, a mind would do best to store such collections in proximity to each other. After all, they will very often be used to recognize the same shapes.

Rosenfeld thinks Marr is wrong to speak of a "memory search". But does he believe that a mind always immediately selects the most appropriate procedures? If a mind recognizes a shape by recognizing certain symmetries and other patterns in it, then what could possibly be wrong with the hypothesis that the mind has to search a little to determine the appropriate patterns?

A careful study of Rosenfeld's book reveals that the structurally associative memory accounts, schematically at least, not only for Marr's work but for **all** the phenomena which Rosenfeld adduces against the image-based model of memory. From the fact that most memory relies on procedures, one cannot conclude that these procedures are not organized and accessed according to a network structure. Returning to Quillian networks, I agree with Rosenfeld that "chair" is stored in the memory as a **collections of procedures** for determining what is a chair. But I still maintain that the Quillian network can be a useful approximation to the actual network of interrelations between the procedures associated with various entities.

INFORMATION AND RELATION

Extending this point of view, I concur with Erlich (1979, p. 200) that each item stored in memory should be "considered capable, by rights, of performing two different functions: the **informative function** and the **relational function**." That is: each item in memory is **acted on** by other items in memory, and also **acts on** other items in memory. The Quillian approach emphasizes the static, "acted-upon" aspect of memory; whereas the Rosenfeld approach stresses the dynamic, procedural, "acting-on" aspect, and considers actions on external stimuli as well as other memory items.

For instance, "chair", "house", "meal" and so forth are collections of procedures which act very little to transform other entities in memory — mainly they act on external stimuli. But logical and mathematical structures, as well as words such as "in", "on" and "besides", are primarily relational: they are collections of procedures which serve primarily to act on other entities stored in memory.

More precisely, what I mean here by "A acts on B" is simply: "A is a function which takes B as arguments." Those entities which are patterns between other entities in memory will thus "act on" many other entities. This definition is validated by the fact that such entities will very often be invoked by analogical searches proceeding from B to A; and by the fact that if A acts on B, recognition of B as a pattern in an entity will often be followed by recognition of A.

In sum: the STRAM is a memory model which 1) accounts for the procedural nature of memory, 2) recognizes the approximative value of static semantic networks, 3) explains the self-organizing, generative nature of memory, and 4) acknowledges the intricate structural interdependence of memory with cognition.

SPARSE DISTRIBUTED MEMORY

Another way to look at this dichotomy is to observe that the STRAM is superficially similar to Kanerva's (1988) "sparse distributed memory", in which entities are coded as binary sequences and stored, each in several places, near other sequences that are "similar". Kanerva measures similarity by the Hamming distance — the fewer places in which two sequences differ, the more similar they are. This is ideal for a memory storing images of physical objects, which may be conveniently characterized by a list of binary qualities. For instance, one could associate with a physical object A a binary sequence $a_1...a_n$ as follows: a_1 is 1 if and only if the object is red, a_2 is 1 if and only if the object is green, a_{77} is 1 if and only if the object is dirty, etc. Given any such assignation of sequences to objects, the similarity of two objects A and B could be plausibly measured by the number of places in which the sequences $a_1...a_n$ and $b_1...b_n$ differed.

But for a memory storing relations, procedures and so forth, it is much more direct to measure similarity **structurally**, as is done in the STRAM. It would certainly be **possible** to encode complete information about a complex procedure in a binary sequence. This possibility lies at the core of algorithmic information theory. But this is not a natural way to relate procedures. To make the Hamming distance mesh smoothly with analogical reasoning, one would have to enumerate all possible patterns $w_1,...,w_m$, and assign each entity A a binary sequence $a_1,...,a_n$ based on the formula: for some fixed C, and $0 \le r < k$, $a_{mk+r}=1$ if and only if w_m is a pattern in A with intensity greater than rC but less than $(r+1)C$.

Given this setup, Kanerva's sparse distributed memory would be extremely similar to the STRAM. But it would completely ignore the fact that the procedures being stored were **procedures** and not merely images of physical objects. The emphasis would be informational. The STRAM gives equal balance to the informational and relational functions of the entities stored in memory.

8
Deduction

8.0 Deduction and Analogy in Mathematics

In mathematical logic, deduction is analyzed as a thing in itself, as an entity entirely independent from other mental processes. This point of view has led to dozens of beautiful ideas: Godel's Incompleteness Theorem, the theory of logical types, model theory, and so on. But its limitations are too often overlooked. Over the last century, mathematical logic has made tremendous progress in the resolution of technical questions regarding specific deductive systems; and it has led to several significant insights into the general properties of deductive systems. But it has said next to nothing about the **practice** of deduction. There is a huge distance between mathematical logic and the practice of logic, and mathematical logic seems to have essentially lost interest in closing this gap.

Let us consider, first of all, deduction in mathematics. What exactly is it that mathematicians do? Yes, they prove theorems — that is, they deduce the consequences of certain axioms. But this is a highly incomplete description of their activity. One might just as well describe their work as **detecting analogies between abstract structures**. This process is just as universal to mathematical practice as the deduction of consequences of axioms. The two are inseparable.

No one proves a theorem by randomly selecting a sequence of steps. And very little theorem proving is done by logically deducing sequences of steps. Generally, theorems are proved by intuitively selecting steps based on analogy to proofs one has done in the past. Some of this analogy is highly specific — e.g. proving one existence theorem for partial differential equations by the same technique as another. And some of it is extremely generalized — what is known as "mathematical maturity"; the ability, gleaned through years of studious analogical reasoning, to know "how to approach" a proof. Both specific and general analogy are absolutely indispensable to mathematical research.

Uninteresting mathematical research often makes use of overly specific analogies — the theorems seem too similar to things that have already been done; frequently they merely generalize familiar results to new domains. Brilliant research, on the other hand, makes use of far subtler analogies regarding general strategies of proof. Only the most tremendously, idiosyncratically original piece of work does not display numerous analogies with past work at every juncture. Occasionally this does occur — e.g. with Galois's work on the unsolvability in radicals of the quintic. But it is very much the exception.

It might be argued that whereas analogy is important to mathematics, deduction from axioms is the defining quality of mathematics; that deduction is inherently more essential. But this does not stand up to the evidence. Even in Galois's work, there is obviously **some** evidence of analogical reasoning, say on the level of the individual steps of his proof. Although his overall proof strategy appears completely unrelated to what came before, the actual steps are not, taken individually, all that different from individual steps of past proofs. Analogical reasoning is ubiquitous, in the intricate details of even the most ingeniously original mathematical research.

And we must not forget Cauchy, one of the great mathematicians despite his often sloppy treatment of logical deduction. Cauchy originated a remarkable number of theorems, but many of his proofs were intuitive arguments, not deductions of the consequences of axioms. It is not that his proofs were explicitly more analogical than deductive — they followed consistent deductive lines of thought. But they did **not** proceed by rigorously deducing the consequences of some set of axioms; rather they appealed frequently to the intuition of the reader. And this intuition, or so I claim, is largely analogical in nature.

It is clear that both deduction and analogy are ubiquitous in mathematics, and both are present to highly varying degrees in the work of various mathematicians. It could be protested that Cauchy's proofs were not **really** mathematical — but then again, this judgment may be nothing more than a reflection of the dominance of mathematical logic during the last century. **Now** we say that they are not mathematical because they don't fit into the framework of mathematical logic, in which mathematics is defined as the step-by-step deduction of the consequences of axioms. But they **look** mathematical to anyone not schooled in the dogma of mathematical logic.

In sum: it is futile to try to separate the process of deduction of the consequences of axioms from the process of analogy with respect to abstract structures. This is true even in mathematics, which is the most blatantly deductive of all human endeavors. How much more true is it in everyday thought?

8.1 The Structure of Deduction

Let S be any set, and let $I=\{I_1, I_2, ..., I_n\}$ be a subset of S, called the set of **assumptions**. Let S^N denote the Cartesian product SxSxSx...xS, taken N times. And let $T=\{T_1,T_2,...,T_n\}$ be a set of **transformations**; that is, a set of functions each of which maps some subset of S^N into some subset of S. For instance, if S were a set of propositions, one might have $T_1(x,y)=$ x and y.

Let us now define the set D(I,T) of all elements of S which are **derivable** from the assumptions I via the transformations T. First of all, it is clear that I should be a subset of D(I,T). Let us call the elements of I the **depth-zero** elements of D(I,T). Next, what about elements of the form $x=T_i(A_1,...,A_m)$, for some i, where each $A_k=I_j$ for some j? Obviously, these elements are simple transformations of the assumptions; they should be elements of D(I,T) as well. Let us call these the **depth-one** elements of D(I,T). Similarly, we may define an element x of S to be a **depth-n** element of D(I,T) if $x=T_i(A_1,...,A_m)$, for some i, where each of the A_k is a depth-p element of D(I,T), for some p<n. Finally, D(I,T) may then be defined as the set of all x which are depth-n elements of D(I,T) for some n.

Deductive reasoning is nothing more or less than the construction of elements of D(I,T), given I and T. If the T are the rules of logic and the I are some set of propositions about the world, then D(I,T) is the set of all propositions which are logically equivalent to some subset of I. In this case deduction is a matter of finding the logical consequences of I, which are presumably a small subset of the total set S of all propositions.

8.2 Paraconsistency

Contemporary mathematical logic is not the only conceivable deductive system. In fact, I suggest that any deductive system which relies centrally upon Boolean algebra, without significant external constraints, is **not even qualified** for the purpose of general mental deduction. Boolean algebra is very useful for many purposes, such as mathematical deduction. I agree that it probably plays an important role in mental process. But it has at least one highly undesirable property: if any two of the propositions in I contradict each other, then D(I,T) is the entire set S of all propositions. From one contradiction, everything is derivable.

The proof of this is very simple. Assume both A and -A. Then, surely A implies A+B. But from A+B and -A, one may conclude B. This works for any B. For instance, assume A="It is true that my mother loves me". Then -A="It is not true that my mother loves me". Boolean logic implies that anyone who holds A and -A — anyone who has contradictory feelings about his mother's affection — also, implicitly, holds that 2+2=5. For from "It is true that my mother loves me" he may deduce "Either it is true that my mother loves me, or else 2+2=5." And from "Either it is true that my mother loves me, or else 2+2=5" and "It is not true that my mother loves me," he may deduce "2+2=5."

So: Boolean logic is fine for mathematics, but common sense tells us that human minds contain numerous contradictions. Does a human mind really use a deductive system that **implies everything**? It appears that somehow we keep our contradictions under control. For example, a person may contradict himself regarding abortion rights or the honesty of his wife or the ultimate meaning of life — and yet, when he thinks about theoretical physics or parking his car, he may reason deductively to one particular conclusion, finding any contradictory conclusion ridiculous.

It might be that, although we do use the "contradiction-sensitive" deduction system of standard mathematical logic, we carefully distinguish deductions in one sphere from deductions in another. That is, for example, it might be that we have **separate** deductive systems for dealing with physics, car parking, domestic relations, philosophy, etc. — so that we never, in practice, reason "A implies A+B", unless A and B are closely related. If this were the case, a contradiction in one realm would destroy only reasoning in that realm. So if we contradicted ourselves when thinking about the meaning of life, then this might give us the ability to deduce **any** statement whatsoever about other philosophical issues — but not about physics or everyday life.

In his Ph.D. dissertation, daCosta (1984) conceived the idea of a **paraconsistent** logic, one in which a single contradiction in I does **not** imply that D(I,T)=S. Others have extended this idea in various ways. Most recently, Avram (1990) has constructed a paraconsistent logic which incorporates the "relevance logic" discussed in the previous paragraph. Propositions are divided into classes and the inference from A to A+B is allowed only when A and B are in the same class.

I suggest that Boolean logic is indeed adequate for the purpose of common-sense deduction. My defense of this position comes in two parts. First, I believe that Avron is basically right in saying that contradictions are almost always localized. To be precise, I hypothesize that a mind does not tend to form the disjunction A+B unless $|\,|[(St(A \cup v)-St(v)]-[St(B \cup w)-St(w)]|\,|$ is small for some (v,w).

I do not think it is justified to partition propositions into disjoint sets and claim that each entity is relevant only to those entities in the same set as it. This yields an elegant formal system, but of course in any categorization there will be borderline cases, and it is unacceptable to simply ignore them away. My approach is to define relevance not by a partition into classes but rather using the theory of structure. What the formulation of the previous paragraph says is that two completely unrelated entities will only rarely be combined in one logical formula.

However, there is always the possibility that, by a fluke, two completely unrelated entities will be combined in some formula, say A+B. In this case a contradiction could spread from one context to another. I suspect that this is an actual danger to thought processes, although certainly a rare one. It is tempting to speculate that this is one possible route to insanity: a person could start out contradicting themselves only in one context, and gradually sink into insanity by contradicting themselves in more and more different contexts.

This brings us to the second part of the argument in favor of Boolean logic. What happens when contradictions **do** arise? If a contradiction arises in a highly specific context, does it remain there forever, thus invalidating all future reasoning in that context? I suspect that this is possible. But, as will be elaborated in later chapters, I suggest that this is rendered unlikely by the overall architecture of the mind. It is an error to suppose that the mind has only **one** center for logical deduction. For all we know, there may be tens of thousands of different deductive systems operating in different parts of the brain, sometimes perhaps more than one devoted to the same specialized context. And perhaps then, as Edelman (1987) has proposed in the context of perception and motor control, those systems which fail to perform a useful function will eventually be destroyed and replaced. If a deductive system has the habit of generating arbitrary propositions, it will not be of much use and will not last. This idea is related to the automata networks discussed in the final chapter.

One thing which is absolutely clear from all this is the following: if the mind **does** use Boolean logic, and it does harbor the occasional contradiction, then the fact that it does not generate arbitrary statements has nothing to do with deductive logic. This is one important sense in which deduction is dependent upon general structure of the mind, and hence implicitly on other forms of logic such as analogy and induction.

8.3 Deduction Cannot Stand Alone

When deduction is formulated in the abstract, in terms of assumptions and transformation, it is immediately apparent that deductive reasoning is incapable of standing on its own. In isolation, it is useless. For why would there be intrinsic value in determining which x lie in D(I,T)? Who cares? The usefulness of deduction presupposes several things, none of them trivial:

1. The elements of I must be accepted to possess some type of validity.
2. It must be assumed that, if the elements of I are important in this sense, then the elements of D(I,T) are also valid in this sense.
3. It must be the case that certain of the elements of D(I,T) are **important** in some sense.

The first requirement is the most straightforward. In mathematical logic, the criterion of validity is truth. But this concept is troublesome, and it is not necessary for deduction. Psychologically speaking, validity could just as well mean plausibility.

The second requirement is more substantial. After all, how is it to be **known** that the elements of D(I,T) will possess the desired properties? This is a big problem in mathematical logic. Using predicate calculus, one can demonstrate that if I is a set of true propositions, every statement derivable from I according to the rules of Boolean algebra is also true. But Boolean algebra is a very weak deductive system; it is certainly not adequate for mathematics. For nontrivial mathematics, one requires the predicate calculus. And no one knows how to prove that, if I is a set of true propositions, every statement derivable from I according to the rules of predicate calculus is true.

Godel proved that one can never demonstrate the consistency of any sufficiently powerful, consistent formal system within that formal system. This means, essentially, that if validity is defined as truth then the second requirement given above can never be verified by deduction.

To be more precise: if validity is defined as truth, let us say T is consistent if it is the case that whenever all the elements of I are true, all the elements of D(I,T) are true. Obviously, in this case consistency corresponds to the second requirement given above. Godel showed that one can never prove T is consistent using T. Then, given a deductive system (I,T), how can one deductively demonstrate that T is consistent? — i.e. that the second requirement given above is fulfilled? One cannot do so using T, so one must do so in some other deductive system, with a system of transformations T^1. But if one uses T^1 to make such a demonstration, how can one know if T^1 is consistent? If T^1 is inconsistent, then the demonstration means nothing, because an in an inconsistent system one can prove anything whatsoever. In order to prove T^1 is consistent, one must invoke some T^2. But in order to prove T^2 is consistent, one must invoke some T^3. Et cetera. The result is that, if validity is defined as truth, one can never use deduction to prove that the results of a given set of transformations are valid.

Yet we believe in mathematics — why? By induction, by analogy, by intuition. We believe in it because, at bottom, it **feels** right. It's never led us wrong before, says induction. It worked in all these other, similar, cases, so it should work here — says analogy. Even if validity is defined as truth, a recourse to induction and analogy is ultimately inevitable.

If validity is defined, say, as plausibility, then the situation is even worse. Clearly, any true statement is plausible, so that it's at least as hard to justify plausible reasoning as it is to justify "certain" reasoning. And, furthermore, the very concept of "plausibility" refers to induction and analogy. In sum, I contend that, in general and in specific cases, **deduction is only justifiable by recourse to induction and analogy**.

ANALOGY GUIDES DEDUCTION

Finally, let us consider the third requirement for the usefulness of deduction: certain of the elements of D(I,T) must be somehow **important**. Otherwise deduction would simply consist of the haphazard generation of elements of D(I,T). This is not the case. In mathematics or in everyday life, one wants to deduce things which are useful, beautiful, interesting, etc. This gives rise to the question: how does one know how to find the important elements of D(I,T)?

It seems clear that this is a matter of analogical reasoning. For instance, suppose one has a particular entity x in mind, and one wants to know whether x is an element of D(I,T). Or suppose one has a particular **property** P in mind, and one wants to find an element x of D(I,T) which has this property. How does one proceed? To an extent, by intuition — which is to say, to an extent, one does not consciously know how one proceeds. But insofar as one makes conscious decisions, one proceeds by considering what has worked in the past, when dealing with an entity x or a property P which is similar to the one under consideration.

For example, when studying mathematics, one is given as exercises proofs which go very much like the proofs one has seen in class or in the textbook. This way one knows how to go about doing the proofs; one can proceed by seeing what was done in similar cases. After one has mastered this sort of exercise, one goes on to proofs which are less strictly analogous to the proofs in the book — because one has grasped the subtler patterns among the various proofs; one has seen, in general, what needs to be done to prove a certain type of theorem.

Above I argued that deduction is only justifiable by analogy. Here the point is that deduction is impotent without analogy: that in order to use deduction to work toward any practical goal, one must be guided by analogy. Otherwise one would have no idea how to go about constructing a given proof.

This is, I suggest, exactly the problem with automatic theorem provers. There are computer programs that can prove simple theorems by searching through $D(I,T)$ according to a variety of strategies. But until these programs implement some form of sophisticated analogy — systematically using similar strategies to solve similar problems — they will never proceed beyond the most elementary level.

USEFUL DEDUCTIVE SYSTEMS

Another consequence of this point of view is that only certain deductive systems are of any use: only those systems about which it is **possible** to reason by analogy. To be precise, let x and y be two elements of $D(I,T)$, and let $G_{I,T}(x)$ and $G_{I,T}(y)$ denote the set of all proofs in (I,T) of x and y respectively.

> **Definition 8.1:** Let (I,T) be any deductive system, and take $a>0$. Let U equal the minimum over all v of the sum $a|v|+B$, where B is the average, over all pairs (x,y) so that x and y are both in $D(I,T)$, of the **correlation coefficient** between $d_\#[St(x\cup v)-St(x),St(y\cup v)-St(v)]$ and $d_I[G_{I,T}(x),G_{I,T}(y)]$. Then (I,T) is **useful** to degree U.

The relative distance $d_I[G_{I,T}(x),G_{I,T}(y)]$ is a measure of how hard it is to get a proof of x out of a proof of y, or a proof of y out of a proof of x. If v were assumed to be the empty set, then $|d_\#[St(x\cup v)-St(x),St(y\cup v)-St(v)] - d[G_{I,T}(x),G_{I,T}(y)]|$ would reduce to $|d_I(x,y) - d[G_{I,T}(x),G_{I,T}(y)]|$. The usefulness U would be a measure of how true it is that structurally similar theorems have similar proofs.

But in order for a system to be useful, it need not be the case that structurally similar theorems have similar proofs. It need only be the case that there is some system for determining, given any theorem x, which theorems y are reasonably likely to have similar proofs. This system for determining is v. In the metaphor introduced above in the section on contextual analogy, v is a codebook. A deductive system is useful if there is some codebook v so that, if one decodes x and y using v, the similarity of the resulting messages is reasonably likely to be close to the similarity of the proofs of x and y.

The constant a measures how much the complexity of the codebook v figures into the usefulness of the system. Clearly, it should count to some degree: if v is excessively complex then it will not be much use as a codebook. Also, if v is excessively complex then it is extremely unlikely that a user of the system will ever determine v.

Mathematically speaking, the usefulness of traditional deductive systems such as Boolean algebra and predicate calculus is unknown. This is not the sort of question that mathematical logic has traditionally asked. Judging by the practical success of both systems, it might seem that their usefulness is fairly high. But it should be remembered that certain **parts** of D(I,T) might have a much higher usefulness than others. Perhaps predicate calculus on a whole is not highly useful, but only those parts which correspond to mathematics as we know it.

It should also be remembered that, in reality, one must work with d_S rather than $d_\#$, and also with a subjective estimate of $|\ |$. Hence, in this sense, the subjective usefulness of a deductive system may vary according to who is doing the deducing. For instance, if a certain codebook v is very complicated to me, then a deductive system which uses it will seem relatively useless to me; whereas to someone who experiences the same codebook as simple, the system may be extremely useful.

DEDUCTION, MEMORY, INDUCTION

If the task of intelligence is essentially inductive, where does deduction fit in? One way to approach this question is to consider a deductive system as a form of memory. Deduction may then be understood as an extremely effective form of **data compaction**. Instead of storing tens of thousands of different constructions, one stores a simple deductive system that **generates** tens of thousands of possible constructions. To see if a given entity X is in this "memory" or not, one determines whether or not X may be derived from the axioms of the system. And, with a combination of deduction and analogy, one can determine whether the "memory" contains anything possessing certain specified properties.

Of course, a deductive system is not formed to serve strictly as a memory. One does not construct a deductive system whose theorems are precisely those pieces of information that one wants to store. Deductive systems are **generative**. They give rise to new constructions, by combining things in unforeseeable ways. Therefore, in order to use a deductive system, one must have **faith** in the axioms and the rules of transformation — faith that they will not generate nonsense, at least not too often.

How is this faith to be obtained? Either it must be "programmed in", or it must be arrived at inductively. AI theorists tend to implicitly assume that predicate calculus is inherent to intelligence, that it is hard-wired into every brain. This is certainly a tempting proposition. After all, it is difficult to see how an organism could **induce** a powerful deductive system in the short period of time allotted to it. It is not hard to show that, given a sufficiently large set of statements X, one may always construct a deductive system which yields these statements as theorems and which is a pattern in X. But it seems unlikely that such a complex, abstract pattern could be recognized very often. What the AI theorists implicitly suggest is that, over a long period of time, those organisms which **did** recognize the pattern of deduction had a greater survival rate; and thus we have evolved to deduce.

This point of view is not contradicted by the fact that, in our everyday reasoning, we do not adhere very closely to any known deductive system. For instance, in certain situations many people will judge "X and Y" to be more likely than "X". If told that "Joe smokes marijuana", a significant proportion of people would rate "Joe has long hair and works in a bank" as more likely than "Joe works in a bank". It is true that these people are not effectively applying Boolean logic in their thought about the everyday world. But this does not imply that their minds are not, on some deeper level, using logical deduction. I suspect that Boolean logic plays a role in "common sense" reasoning as in deeper intuition, but that this role is not dominant: deduction is mixed up with analogy, induction and other processes.

To summarize: recognizing that deductive systems are useful for data compaction and form generation is one thing; exalting deduction over all other forms of thought is quite another. There is no reason to assume that deduction is a "better", "more accurate" or "truer" mode of reasoning than induction or analogy; and there is no reason to believe, as many AI theorists do, that deduction is the core process of thought. Furthermore, it seems very unlikely that deduction can operate in a general context without recourse to analogy. However, because deduction is so effective **in the context of the other mental processes**, it may well be that deduction is essential to intelligence.

9
Perception

9.0 The Perceptual Hierarchy

In accordance with the philosophy outlined in Chapter 5, I define perception as **pattern recognition**. Pattern recognition is, of course, an extremely difficult optimization problem. In fact, the task of recognizing all the patterns in an arbitrary entity is so hard that no algorithm can solve it exactly — this is implied by Chaitin's (1987) algorithmic-information-theoretic proof of Godel's Theorem. As usual, though, exact solutions are not necessary in practice. One is, rather, concerned with finding a reasonably rapid and reliable method for getting fairly decent approximations.

I propose that minds recognize patterns according to a multilevel strategy. Toward this end, I hypothesize a hierarchy of perceptual levels, each level recognizing patterns in the output of the level below it, and governed by the level immediately above it. Schematically, the hierarchy may be understood to extend indefinitely in two directions (Fig. 2). It will often be convenient to, somewhat arbitrarily, pick a certain level and call it the zero level. Then, for n= ...-3,-2,-1,0, 1,2,3,..., the idea is that level n recognizes patterns in the output of level n-1, and also manipulates the pattern-recognition algorithm of level n-1.

PHENOMENOLOGY AND PERCEPTION

Physically speaking, any particular mind can deal only with a finite segment of this hierarchy. Phenomenologically speaking, a mind can never know exactly how far the hierarchy extends in either direction.

One may analyze consciousness as a process which moves from level to level of the perceptual hierarchy, but only within a certain restricted range. If the zero level is taken to represent the "average" level of consciousness, and consciousness resides primarily on levels from -L to U, then the levels below -L represent perceptions which are generally **below** conscious perception. And, on the other hand, the levels above U represent perceptions

116

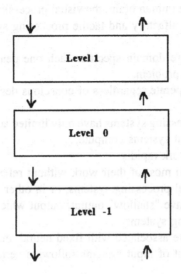

Figure 2.

that are in some sense **beyond** conscious perception: too abstract or general for consciousness to encompass.

Consciousness can never know how far the hierarchy extends, either up or down. Thus it can never encounter an ultimate physical reality: it can never know whether a perception comes from ultimate reality or just from the next level down.

Perception and motor control might be defined as the link between mind and reality. But this is a one-sided definition. Earlier we defined intelligence by dividing the universe into an organism and an environment. From this "God's-eye" point of view an organism's perceptual and motor systems are the link between that organism and its environment. But from the internal point of view, from the point of view of the conscious organism, there can be no true or ultimate reality, but only the results of perception.

Therefore, in a sense, the result of perception **is** reality; and the study of perception is the study of the construction of external reality. One of the aims of this chapter and the next is to give a model of perception and motor control that makes sense from **both** points of view — the objective and the subjective, the God's-eye and the mind's-eye, the biological and the phenomenological.

INPUT VERSUS CENTRAL PROCESSING

Fodor (1983) has proposed that, as a general rule, there are a number of significant structural differences between **input systems** and **central processing**

systems. He has listed nine properties which are supposed to be common to all the input systems of the human brain: the visual processing system, the auditory processing system, the olfactory and tactile processing systems, etc.:

1. Input systems are domain specific: each one deals only with a certain specific type of problem.
2. Input systems operate regardless of conscious desires; their operation is mandatory.
3. The central processing systems have only limited access to the representations which input systems compute.
4. Input systems work rapidly.
5. Input systems do most of their work without reference to what is going on in the central processing systems, or in other input systems.
6. Input systems have "shallow" output, output which is easily grasped by central processing systems.
7. Input systems are associated with fixed neural architecture.
8. The development of input systems follows a certain characteristic pace and sequence.

I think these properties are a very good characterization of the lower levels of the perceptual hierarchy. In other words, it appears that the lower levels of the perceptual hierarchy are strictly **modularized.** Roughly speaking, say, levels -12 to -6 might be as depicted in Figure 3, with the modular structure playing as great a role as the hierarchical structure.

If, say, consciousness extended from levels -3 to 3, then it might be that the modules of levels -12 to -6 melded together **below** the level of consciousness. In this case the results of, say, visual and auditory perception would **not** present themselves to consciousness in an entirely independent way. What you saw might depend upon what you heard.

HIERARCHY IN HUMAN VISUAL PERCEPTION

A decade and a half ago, Hubel and Wiesel (1988) demonstrated that the brain possesses specific neural clusters which behave as processors for judging the orientation of line segments. Since then many other equally specific visual processors have been found. It appears that Area 17 of the brain, the primary visual cortex, which deals with relatively low-level vision processing, is composed of various **types** of neuronal clusters, each type corresponding to a certain kind of processing, e.g. line orientation processing.

And, as well as perhaps being organized in other ways, these clusters do appear to be organized in levels. At the lowest level, in the retina, gradients are enhanced and spots are extracted — simple mechanical processes. Next come simple moving edge detectors. The next level, the second level up from the retina, extracts more sophisticated information from the first level up — and so

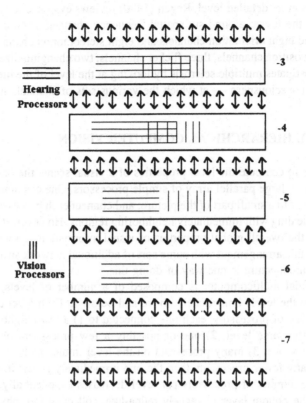

Figure 3.

on. Admittedly, little is known about the processes two or more levels above the retina. It is clear (Uhr, 1987), however, that there is a very prominent hierarchical structure, perhaps supplemented by more complex forms of parallel information processing. For instance, most neuroscientists would agree that there are indeed "line processing" neural clusters, and "shape processing" neural clusters, and that while the former pass their results to the latter, the latter sometimes direct the former (Rose and Dobson, 1985).

And there is also recent evidence that certain features of the retinal image are processed in "sets of channels" which proceed several levels up the perceptual hierarchy without intersecting each other — e.g. a set of channels for color, a set of channels for stereoposition, etc. This is modular perception at a level lower than that considered by Fodor. For instance, Mishkin et al (1983) have concluded from a large amount of physiological data that two major pathways pass through the visual cortex and then diverge in the subsequent visual areas: one pathway for color, shape and object recognition; the other for motion and spatial interrelations. The first winds up in the inferior temporal areas; the second leads to the inferior parietal areas.

And, on a more detailed level, Regan (1990) reviews evidence for three color channels in the fovea, around six spatial frequency channels from each retinal point, around eight orientation channels and eight stereomotion channels, two or three stereoposition channels, three flicker channels, two changing-size channels, etc. He investigates multiple sclerosis by looking at the level of the hierarchy — well below consciousness — at which the various sets of channels intersect.

PARALLEL HIERARCHICAL COMPUTER VISION

If one needs to compute the local properties of a visual scene, the best strategy is to hook up a large parallel array of simple processors. One can simply assign each processor to a small part of the picture; and connect each processor to those processors dealing with immediately neighboring regions. However, if one needs to compute the overall global properties of visual information, it seems best to supplement this arrangement with some sort of additional network structure. The **pyramidal** architecture is one way of doing this.

A pyramidal multicomputer is composed of a number of levels, each one connected to the levels immediately above and below it. Each level consists of a parallel array of processors, each one connected to 1) a few neighboring processors on the same level, 2) one or possibly a few processors on the level immediately above, 3) many processors on the level immediately below. Each level has many fewer processors than the one immediately below it. Often, for instance, the number of processors per level decreases exponentially.

Usually the bottom layer is vaguely retina-like, collecting raw physical data. Then, for instance, images of different resolution can be obtained by averaging up the pyramid: assigning each processor on level n a distinct set of processors on level n-1, and instructing it to average the values contained in these processors.

Or, say, the second level could be used to recognize edges; the third level to recognize shapes; the fourth level to group elementary shapes into complex forms; and the fifth level to compare these complex forms with memory.

Stout (1986) has proved that there are certain problems — such as rotating a scene by pi radians — for which the pyramidal architecture will perform little better than its base level would all by itself. He considers each processor on level n to connect to 4 other processors on level n, 4 processors on level n-1, and one processor on level n+1. The problem is that, in this arrangement, if two processors on the bottom level need to communicate, they may have to do so by either 1) passing a message step by step across the bottom level, or 2) passing a message all the way up to the highest level and back down.

However, Stout also shows that this pyramidal architecture is optimal for so-called "perimeter-bound" problems — problems with nontrivial communication requirements, but for which each square of s^2 processors on the base level needs to exchange only $O(s)$ bits of information with processors outside that square. An example of a perimeter-bound problem is labeling all the connected components of an image, or finding the minimum distance between one component and another.

In sum, it seems that strict pyramidal architectures are very good at solving problems which require processing that is global, but not too global. When a task requires an extreme amount of global communications, a parallel architecture with greater interconnection is called for — e.g. a "hypercube" architecture.

Thinking more generally, Levitan et al (1987) have constructed a three-level "pyramidal" parallel computer for vision processing. The bottom level deals with sensory data and with low-level processing such as segmentation into components. The intermediate level takes care of grouping, shape detection, and so forth; and the top level processes this information "symbolically", constructing an overall interpretation of the scene. The base level is a 512x512 square array of processors each doing exactly the same thing to different parts of the image; and the middle level is composed of a 64x64 square array of relatively powerful processors, each doing exactly the same thing to different parts of the base-level array. Finally, the top level contains 64 very powerful processors, each one operating independently according to programs written in LISP (the standard AI programming language). The intermediate level may also be augmented by additional connections, e.g. a hypercube architecture.

This three-level perceptual hierarchy appears be an extremely effective approach to computer vision. It is not a strict pyramidal architecture of the sort considered by Stout, but it retains the basic pyramidal structure despite the presence of other processes and interconnections.

IS PERCEPTION JUST A BAG OF TRICKS?

In sum, it is fairly clear that human perception works according to a "perceptual hierarchy" of some sort. And it is also plain that the perceptual hierarchy is a highly effective way of doing computer vision. However, there is no general understanding of the operation of this hierarchy. Many theorists, such at Uttal (1988), suspect that such a general understanding may be impossible — that perception is nothing more than a largely unstructured assortment of very clever tricks. In 1965, Hurvich et al made the following remark, and it is still apt: "the reader familiar with the visual literature knows that this is an area of many laws and little order" (p.101).

I suggest that there is indeed an overall structure to the process. This does not rule out the possibility that a huge variety of idiosyncratic tricks are involved; it just implies that these tricks are not 100% of the story. The structure which I will propose is abstract and extremely general; and I am aware that this can be a limitation. As Uttal has observed,

> Perceptual psychophysics has long been characterized by experiments specific to a microscopically oriented theory and by theories that either deal with a narrowly defined data set at one extreme or, to the contrary, a global breadth that is so great that data are virtually irrelevant to their construction. Theories of this kind are more points of view than analyses. (p. 290)

Uttal would certainly put the theory given here in the "more point of view than analysis" category. However, it seems to me that, if the gap between psychophysical theory and data is ever to be bridged, the first step is a better point of view. And similarly, if the gap between biological vision and computer vision is ever to be closed, we will need more than just superior technology — we will need new, insightful general ideas. Therefore I feel that, at this stage, it is absolutely necessary to study the abstract **logic** of perception — even if, in doing so, one is guided as much by mathematical and conceptual considerations as by psychophysical or other data.

9.1 Probability Theory

The branch of mathematics known as probability theory provides one way of making inferences regarding uncertain propositions. But it is not a priori clear that it is the only reasonable way to go about making such inferences. This is important for psychology because it would be nice to assume, as a working hypothesis, that the mind uses the rules of probability theory to process its perceptions. But if the rules of probability theory were just an arbitrary selection from among a disparate set of possible schemes for uncertain inference, then there would be little reason to place faith in this hypothesis.

Historically, most attempts to derive general laws of probability have been "frequentist" in nature. According to this approach, in order to say what the statement "the probability of X occurring in situation E is 1/3" means, one must invoke a whole "ensemble" of situations. One must ask: if I selected an situation from among an ensemble of n situations "identical" to E, what proportion of the time would X be true? If, as n tended toward infinity, this proportion tended toward 1/3, then it would be valid to say that the probability of X occurring in situation E is 1/3.

In some cases this approach is impressively direct. For instance, consider the proposition: "The face showing on the fair six-sided die I am about to toss will be either a two or a three". Common sense indicates that this proposition has probability 1/3. And if one looked at a large number of similar situations — i.e. a large number of tosses of the same die or "identical" dice — then one would indeed find that, in the long run, a two or a three came up 1/3 of the time.

But often it is necessary to assign probabilities to **unique** events. In such cases, the frequency interpretation has no meaning. This occurs particularly often in geology and ecology: one wishes to know the relative probabilities of various outcomes in a situation which is unlikely ever to recur. When the problem has to do with a bounded region of space, say a forest, it is possible to justify this sort of probabilistic reasoning using complicated manipulations of integral calculus. But what is really required, in order to justify the general application of probability theory, is some sort of proof that the rules of probability theory are **uniquely** well-suited for probable inference.

Richard Cox (1961) has provided such a proof. First of all, he assumes that any possible rule for assigning a "probability" to a proposition must obey the following two rules:

> The probability of an inference on given evidence determines the probability of its contradictory on the same evidence. (p. 3)

> The probability on given evidence that both of two inferences are true is determined by their separate probabilities, one on the given evidence, the other on this evidence with the additional assumption that the first inference is true. (p. 4)

The probability of a proposition on certain evidence is the probability that logically **should** be assigned to that proposition by someone who is aware **only** of this evidence and no other evidence. In Boolean notation, the first of Cox's rules says simply that if one knows the probability of X on certain evidence, then one can deduce the probability of -X on that same evidence without using knowledge about anything else. The second rule says that if one knows the probability of X given certain evidence E, and the probability that Y is true given EX, then one can deduce the probability that Y is true without using knowledge about anything else.

These requirements are hard to dispute; in fact, they don't seem to say very much. But their simplicity is misleading. In mathematical notation, the first requirement says that $P(XY|E)= F[(X|E),(Y|XE)]$, and the second requirement says that $P(-X|E)=f[P(X|E)]$, where F and f are unspecified functions. What is remarkable is that these functions need not remain unspecified. Cox has shown that the laws of Boolean algebra dictate specific forms for these functions.

For instance, they imply that $G[P(XY|E)] = CG[P(X|E)]G[P(Y|XE)]$, where C is some constant and G is some function. This is **almost** a proof that for any measure of probability P, $P(XY|E)=P(X|E)P(Y|XE)$. For if one sets $G(x)=x$, this rule is immediate. And, as Cox points out, if $P(X|E)$ measures probability, then so does $G[P(X|E)]$ — at least, according to the two axioms given above. The constant C may be understood by setting X=Y and recalling that XX=X according to the axioms of Boolean algebra. It follows by simple algebra that C = $G[P(X|XE)]$ — i.e., C is the probability of X on the evidence X, the numerical value of certainty. Typically, in probability theory, C=1. But this is a convention, not a logical requirement.

As for negation, Cox has shown that if $P(X)=f[P(-X)]$, Boolean algebra leads to the formula $X^r+[f(X)]^r=1$. Given this, we could leave r unspecified and use $P(X)^r$ as the symbol of probability; but, following Cox, let us take r=1.

Cox's analysis tells us in exactly what sense the laws of probability theory are arbitrary. All the laws of probability theory can be derived from the rules $P(X|E)=1-P(-X|E)$, $P(XY|E)=P(X|E)P(Y|XE)$. And these rules are essentially the only ways of dealing with negation and conjunction that Boolean algebra allows. So, if we accept Boolean algebra and Cox's two axioms, we accept probability theory.

Finally, for a more concrete perspective on these issues, let us turn to the work of Krebs, Kacelnik and Taylor (1978). These biologists studied the behavior of birds (great tits) placed in an aviary containing two machines, each consisting of a perch and a food dispenser. One of the machines dispenses food p% of the times that its perch is landed on, and the other one dispenses food q% of the times that its perch is landed on. They observed that the birds generally visit the two machines according to the optimal strategy dictated by Bayes' rule and Laplace's Principle of Indifference — a strategy which is not particularly obvious. This is a strong rebuttal to those who raise philosophical objections against the psychological use of probability theory. After all, if a bird's brain can use Bayesian statistics, why not a human brain?

BAYES' RULE

Assume that one knows that **one** of the propositions $Y_1, Y_2, ..., Y_n$ is true, and that **only** one of these propositions can possibly be true. In mathematical language, this means that the collection $\{Y_1, ..., Y_n\}$ is **exhaustive** and **mutually exclusive**. Then, Bayes' rule says that

$$P(Y_n \mid X) = \frac{P(Y_n)P(X \mid Y_n)}{P(Y_1)P(X \mid Y_1) + ... + P(Y_n)P(X \mid Y_n)} .$$

In itself this rule is unproblematic; it is a simple consequence of the two rules of probable inference derived in the previous section. But it lends itself to controversial applications.

For instance, suppose Y_1 is the event that a certain star system harbors intelligent life which is fundamentally dissimilar from us, Y_2 is the event that it harbors intelligent life which is fundamentally similar to us, and Y_3 is the event that it harbors no intelligent life at all. Assume these events have somehow been precisely defined. Suppose that X is a certain sequence of radio waves which we have received from that star system, and that one wants to compute $P(Y_2 \mid X)$: the probability, based on the message X, that the system has intelligent life which is fundamentally similar to us. Then Bayes' rule applies: $\{Y_1, Y_2, Y_3\}$ is exhaustive and mutually exclusive. Suppose that we have a good estimate of $P(X \mid Y_1)$, $P(X \mid Y_2)$, and $P(X \mid Y_3)$: the probability that an intelligence dissimilar to us would send out message X, the probability that an intelligence similar to us would send out message X, and the probability that an unintelligent star system would somehow emit message X. But how do we know $P(Y_1)$, $P(Y_2)$ and $P(Y_3)$?

We cannot deduce **these** probabilities directly from the nature of messages received from star systems. So where does $P(Y_i \mid X)$ come from? This problem, at least in theory, makes the business of identifying extraterrestrial life extremely tricky. One might argue that it makes it impossible, because the only things we know about stars are derived from electromagnetic "messages" of one kind or another — light waves, radio waves, etc. But it seems reasonable to assume that spectroscopic information, thermodynamic knowledge and so forth are separate from the kind of message-interpretation we are talking about. In this case there might be some kind of a priori physicochemical estimate of the probability of intelligent life, similar intelligent life, and so forth. Carl Sagan, among others, has attempted to estimate such probabilities. The point is that we need some kind of **prior** estimate for the $P(Y_i)$, or Bayes' rule is useless here.

This example is not atypical. In general, suppose that X is an effect, and $\{Y_i\}$ is the set of possible causes. Then to estimate $P(Y_1|X)$ is to estimate the probability that Y_1, and none of the other Y_i, is the true cause of X. But in order to estimate this using Bayes' rule, it is not enough to know how likely X is to follow from Y_i, for each i. One needs to know the probabilities $P(Y_i)$ — one needs to know how likely each possible cause is, in general.

One might suppose these problems to be a shortcoming of Bayes' rule, of probability theory. But this is where Cox's demonstration proves invaluable. Any set of rules for uncertain reasoning which satisfy his two simple, self-evident axioms — must necessarily lead to Bayes' rule, or something essentially equivalent with a few G's and r's floating around. Any reasonable set of rules for uncertain reasoning must be essentially identical to probability theory, and must therefore have no other method of deducing causes from effects than Bayes' rule.

The perceptive reader might, at this point, accuse me of inconsistency. After all, it was observed above that quantum events may be interpreted to obey a different sort of logic. And in Chapter 8 I raised the possibility that the mind employs a weaker "paraconsistent" logic rather than Boolean logic. How then can I simply assume that Boolean algebra is applicable?

However, the inconsistency is only apparent. Quantum logic and paraconsistent logic are both weaker than Boolean logic, and they therefore cannot not lead to any formulas which are not also formulas of Boolean logic: they cannot improve on Bayes' rule.

So how **do** we assign prior probabilities, in practice? It is not enough to say that it comes down to instinct, to biological programming. It is possible to say something about how this programming works.

THE PRINCIPLE OF INDIFFERENCE

Laplace's "Principle of Indifference" states that if a question is known to have exactly n possible answers, and these answers are mutually exclusive, then in the absence of any other knowledge one should assume each of these answers to have probability $1/n$ of being correct.

For instance, suppose you were told that on the planet Uxmylarqg, the predominant intelligent life form is either blue, green, or orange. Then, according to the Principle of Indifference, if this were the only thing you knew about Uxmylargq, you would assign a probability of 1/3 to the statement that it is blue, a probability of 1/3 to the statement that it is green, and a probability of 1/3 to the statement that it is orange. In general, according to the Principle of Indifference, if one had **no** specific knowledge about the n causes $\{Y_1,...,Y_n\}$ which appear in the above formulation of Bayes' rule, one would assign a probability $P(Y_i)=1/n$ to each of them.

Cox himself appears to oppose the Principle of Indifference, arguing that "the knowledge of a probability, though it is knowledge of a particular and limited kind, is still knowledge, and it would be surprising if it could be derived from... complete ignorance, asserting nothing". And in general, that is exactly what the Principle of Indifference does: supplies knowledge from ignorance. In certain specific cases, it may be proved to be mathematically correct. But, as a general rule of uncertain inference, it is nothing more or less than a way of getting something out of nothing. Unlike Cox, however, I do not find this surprising or undesirable, but rather exactly what the situation calls for.

9.2 The Maximum Entropy Principle

If the Principle of Indifference tells us what probabilities to assign given **no** background knowledge, what is the corresponding principle for the case when one **does** have some background knowledge? Seeking to answer this question, E.T. Jaynes studied the writings of J. Willard Gibbs and drew therefrom a rule called the maximum entropy principle. Like the Principle of Indifference, the maximum entropy principle is provably correct in certain special cases, but in the general case, justifying it or applying it requires ad hoc, something-out-of-nothing assumptions.

The starting point of the maximum entropy principle is the entropy function

$$H(p_1,...,p_n) = - [p_1 \log p_1 + p_2 \log p_2 + ... + p_n \log p_n],$$

where $\{Y_i\}$ is an exhaustive, mutually exclusive collection of events and $p_i=P(Y_i)$. This function first emerged in the work of Boltzmann, Gibbs and other founders of thermodynamics, but its true significance was not comprehended until Claude Shannon published *The Theory of Communication* (1949). It is a measure of the **uncertainty** involved in the distribution $\{p_i\}$.

The entropy is always positive. If, say, $(p_1,...,p_n)=(0,0,1,..,0,0,0)$, then the entropy $H(p_1,...,p_n)$ is zero[1] — because this sort of distribution has the minimum possible uncertainty. It is **known** which of the Y_i is the case, with absolute certainty. On the other hand, if $(p_1,...,p_n)=(1/n,1/n,...,1/n)$, then $H(p_1,...,p_n)=\log n$, which is the maximum possible value. This represents the maximum possible uncertainty: each possibility is equally likely.

---

[1] Although log0 is infinite, 0log0 may be assigned the value 0 because the limit as x goes to zero of xlogx is zero.

The maximum entropy principle states that, for any exhaustive, mutually exclusive set of events $(Y_1,...,Y_n)$, the most likely probability distribution $(p_1,...,p_n)$ **with respect to a given set of constraints on the** Y_i is that distribution which, among all those that satisfy the constraints, has maximum entropy. The "constraints" represent particular knowledge about the situation in question; they are what distinguishes one problem from another.

For instance, what if one has absolutely no knowledge about the various possibilities Y_i? Then, where $p_i=P(Y_i)$, can we determine the "most likely" distribution $(p_1,...,p_n)$ by finding the distribution that maximizes $H(p_1,...,p_n)$? It is easy to see that, given no additional constraints, the maximum of $H(p_1,...,p_n)$ occurs for the distribution $(p_1,...p_n)= (1/n,1/n,...,1/n)$. In other words, when there is no knowledge whatsoever about the Y_i, the maximum entropy principle reduces to the Principle of Indifference.

MAXIMUM ENTROPY WITH LINEAR CONSTRAINTS

In thermodynamics the Y_i represent, roughly speaking, the different possible regions of space in which a molecule can be; p_i is the probability that a randomly chosen molecule is in region Y_i. Each vector of probabilities $(p_1,...,p_n)$ is a certain distribution of molecules amongst regions. The question is, what is the **most likely** way for the molecules to be distributed? One assumes that one knows the energy of the distribution, which is of the form $E(p_1,...,p_n)=c_1p_1+...+c_np_n$, where the $\{c_i\}$ are constants obtained from basic physical theory. That is, one assumes that one knows an equation $E(p_1,...,p_n)=K$. Under this assumption, the answer to the question is: the most likely $(p_1,...,p_n)$ is the one which, among all those possibilities that satisfy the equation $E(p_1,...,p_n)=K$, **maximizes the entropy** $H(p_1,...,p_n)$. There are several other methods of obtaining the most likely distribution, but this is by far the easiest.

What is remarkable is that this is not just an elegant mathematical feature of classical thermodynamics. In order to do the maximum entropy principle justice, we should now consider its application to quantum density matrices, or radio astronomy, or numerical linear algebra. But this would take us too far afield. Instead, let us consider Jaynes's "Brandeis dice problem", a puzzle both simple and profound.

Consider a six-sided die, each side of which may have any number of spots between 1 and 6. The problem is (Jaynes, 1978):

> Suppose [this] die has been tossed N times, and we are told only that the average number of spots up was not 3.5, as we might expect from an 'honest' die but 4.5. Given this information, **and nothing else**, what probability should we assign to i spots on the next toss? (p. 49)

Let Y_i denote the event that the next toss yields i spots; let $p_i=P(Y_i)$. The information we have may be expressed as an equation of the form

$A(p_1,...,p_n)=4.5$, where $A(p_1,...,p_n)=(p_1+...+p_n)/n$ is the average of the p_i. This equation says: whatever the most likely distribution of probabilities is, it must yield an average of 4.5, which is what we know the average to be.

The maximum entropy principle says: given that the average number of spots up is 4.5, the **most likely distribution** $(p_1,...,p_n)$ is the one that, among all those satisfying the constraint $A(p_1,...,p_n)=4.5$, maximizes the entropy $H(p_1,...,p_n)$. This optimization problem is easily solved using Lagrange multipliers, and it has the approximate solution $(p_1,...,p_n) = (.05435, .07877, .11416, .16545, .23977, .34749)$. If one had $A(p_1,...,p_n)=3.5$, the maximum entropy principle would yield the solution $(p_1,...,p_n)=(1/6, 1/6, 1/6, 1/6, 1/6, 1/6)$; but, as one would expect, knowing that the average is 4.5 makes the higher numbers more likely and the lower numbers less likely.

For the Brandeis dice problem, as in the case of classical thermodynamics, it is possible to prove mathematically that the maximum entropy solution is far more likely than any other solution. And in both these instances the maximization of entropy appears to be the most efficacious method of locating the optimal solution. The two situations are extremely similar: both involve essentially random processes (dice tossing, molecular motion), and both involve linear constraints (energy, average). Here the maximum entropy principle is at its best.

MAXIMUM ENTROPY AS A GENERAL RULE OF INFERENCE

The maximum entropy principle is most appealing when one is dealing with linear constraints. There is a simple, straightforward proof of its correctness. But when talking about the general task of intelligence, we are not necessarily restricted to linear constraints. Evans (1978) has attempted to surmount this obstacle by showing that, given any constraint $F(p_1,...,p_n)=K$, the overwhelmingly most likely values $p_i=P(Y_i)$ may be found by maximizing

$$H(p_1,...,p_n) - H(k_1,...,k_n) = p_1\log(p_1/k_1) + ... + p_n\log(p_n/k_n)$$

where $k=(k_1,k_2,...,k_n)$ is some "background distribution". The trouble with this approach is that the only known way of determining k is through a complicated sequence of calculations involving various ensembles of events.

Shore and Johnson (1980) have provided an alternate approach, which has been refined considerably by Skilling (1989). Extending Cox's proof that probability theory is the only reasonable method for uncertain reasoning, Shore and Johnson have proved that if there is any reasonably general method for assigning prior probabilities in Bayes' Theorem, it has to depend in a certain way upon the entropy. Here we will not require all the mathematical details; the general idea will suffice.

Where D is a subset of $\{Y_i\}$, and C is a set of constraints, let $f[D|C]$ denote the probability distribution assigned to the domain D on the basis of the constraints C. Let m={$m_1,m_2,...m_n$} denote some set of "background information" probabilities. For instance, if one actually has no background information, one might want to implement the Principle of Indifference and assume $m_i=1/n$, for all i.

Assume f[D|C] is intended to give the most likely probability distribution for D, given the constraints C. Then one can derive the maximum entropy principle from the following axioms:

Axiom I: Subset Independence

If constraint C_1 applies in domain D_1 and constraint C_2 applies in domain D_2, then f[D_1|C_1]$\cup$f[D_2|C_2] = f[$D_1\cup D_2$|$C_1\cup C_2$]. (Basically, this means that if the constraints involved do not interrelate D_1 and D_2, neither should the answer). This implies that f[D|C] can be obtained by maximizing over a sum of the form $S(p,m)=m_1Q(p_1)+...+m_nQ(p_n)$, where Q is some function.

Axiom II: Coordinate Invariance

This is a technical requirement regarding the way that f[$(p_1,...,p_n)$|C] relates to f[$(p_1/q_1,....,p_n/q_n)$|C]: it states that if one expresses the regions in a different coordinate system, the probabilities do not change. It implies that $S(p,m)=m_1Q(p_1/m_1)+...+m_nQ(p_n/m_n)$.

Axiom III: System Independence

Philosophically, this is the crucial requirement. "If a proportion q of a population has a certain property, then the proportion of any sub-population having that property should properly be assigned as q.... For example, if 1/3 of kangaroos have blue eyes... then [in the absence of knowledge to the contrary] the proportion of left-handed kangaroos having blue eyes should be 1/3."

It can be shown that these axioms imply that f[Y|C] is proportional to the maximum of the entropy $H(p_1,...,p_n)$ subject to the constraints C, **whatever** the constraints C may be (linear or not). And since it must be proportional to the entropy, one may as well take it to be equal to the entropy.

These axioms are reasonable, though nowhere near as compelling as Cox's stunningly simple axioms for probable inference. They are not simply mathematical requirements; they have a great deal of philosophical substance. What they do **not** tell you, however, is by what amount the most likely solution f[Y|C] is superior to all other solutions. This requires more work.

More precisely, one way of summarizing what these axioms show is as follows. Let m=$(m_1,...,m_n)$ be some vector of "background" probabilities. Then f[D|C] must be assigned by maximizing the function

$$S(p,m)=[p_1-m_1-p_1\log(p_1/m_1)]+...+[p_n-m_n-p_n\log(p_n/m_n)].$$

Evans has shown that, for any constraint C, there is some choice of m for which the maximum entropy principle gives an distribution which is not only correct but dramatically more likely than any other distribution. It is implicit, though not actually stated, in his work that **given the correct vector** $(m_1,...,m_n)$, the prior probabilities $\{p_i\}$ in Bayes' formula must be given by

$$p_i = exp[aS/Z],$$

where $S = S(p,m)$ as given above, $Z = exp(aS)/[n(p_1p_2...p_n)^{1/2}]$, and a is a parameter to be discussed below. Skilling has pointed out that, in every case for which the results have been calculated **for any** $(m_1,...,m_n)$, with linear or nonlinear constraints, this same formula has been the result. He has given a particularly convincing example involving the Poisson distribution.

In sum: the maximum entropy principle appears to be a very reasonable general method for estimating the best prior probabilities; and it often seems to be the case that the best prior probabilities are considerably better than any other choice. Actually, none of the details of the maximum entropy method are essential for our general theory of mentality. What is important is that, in the maximum entropy principle, we have a widely valid, practically applicable method for estimating the prior probabilities required by Bayes' Theorem, given a certain degree of background knowledge. The existence of such a method implies the possibility of a unified treatment of Bayesian reasoning.

DEDUCTION, INDUCTION

In order to use Bayes' rule to determine the $P(Y_i|X)$, one must know the $P(X|Y_i)$, and one must know the $P(Y_i)$. Determining the $P(X|Y_i)$ is, I will propose, a fundamentally **deductive** problem; it is essentially a matter of determining a property of the known quantity Y_i. But the $P(Y_i)$ are a different matter. The maximum entropy principle is remarkable but not magical: it cannot manufacture knowledge about the $P(Y_i)$ where there isn't any. All it can do is work with **given** constraints C and **given** background knowledge m, and work these into a coherent overall guess at the $P(Y_i)$. In general, the background information about these probabilities must be determined by **induction**. In this manner, Bayes' rule employs both inductive and deductive reasoning.

THE REGULARIZATION PARAMETER

It is essential to note that the maximum entropy method is not entirely specified. Assuming the formulas given above are accurate, there is still the problem of determining the parameter a. It appears that there is no way to assign it a universal value once and for all — its value must be set in a context-specific way. So if the maximum entropy principle is used for perception, the value of a must be set differently for different perceptual acts. And, furthermore, it seems to me that even if the maximum entropy principle is not a central as I am assuming, the problem of the parameter a is still relevant: any other general theory of prior probability estimation would have to give rise to a similar dilemma.

Gull (1989) has demonstrated that the parameter a may be interpreted as a "regularizing parameter". If a is large, prior probabilities are computed in such a way that distributions which are far from the background model m are deemed relatively unlikely. But if a is very small, the background model is virtually ignored.

So, for instance, if there is no real background knowledge and the background model m is obtained by the Principle of Indifference, the size of a determines the tendency of the maximum entropy method to assign a high probability to distributions in which all the probabilities are about the same. Setting a high would be "over-fitting". But, on the other hand, if m is derived from real background knowledge and the signal of which the Y_i are possible explanations is very "noisy," then a low a will cause the maximum entropy principle to yield an optimal distribution with a great deal of random oscillation. This is "under-fitting". In general, one has to keep the parameter a small to get any use out of the background information m, but one has to make it large to prevent the maximum entropy principle from paying too much attention to chance fluctuations of the data.

BAYESIAN PARAMETER ESTIMATION

As an alternative to setting the parameter a by intuition or ad hoc mathematical techniques, Gull has given a method of using Bayesian statistics to estimate the most likely value of a for particular p and m. Often, as in radioastronomical interferometry, this tactic or simpler versions of it appear to work well. But, as Gull has demonstrated, vision processing presents greater difficulties. He tried to use the maximum entropy principle to turn blurry pictures of a woman into accurate photograph-like images, but he found that the Bayesian derivation of a yielded fairly unimpressive results.

He devised an ingenious solution. He used the maximum entropy principle to take the results of a maximum entropy computation using the value of a arrived at by the Bayesian method — and get a new background distribution $m'=(m_1',...,m_n')$. Then he applied the maximum entropy principle using this new background knowledge, m'. This yielded beautiful results — and if it hadn't, he could have applied the same method again. This is yet another example of the power of hierarchical structures to solve perceptual problems.

Of course, one could do this over and over again — but one has to stop somewhere. At some level, one simply has to set the value of a based on intuition, based on what value a usually has for the **type of problem** one is considering. This is plainly a matter of induction.

In general, when designing programs or machines to execute the maximum entropy principle, we can set a by trial and error or common sense. But this, of course, means that we are using deduction, analogy and induction to set a. I suggest that similar processes are used when the mind determines a internally, unconsciously. This hypothesis has some interesting consequences, as we shall see.

As cautioned above, if the maximum entropy method were proved completely incorrect, it would have no effect on the overall model of mind presented here — so long as it were replaced by a reasonably simple formula, or collection of formulas, for helping to compute the priors in Bayes' formula; and so long as this formula or collection of formulas was reasonably amenable to inductive adjustment. However, I do not foresee the maximum entropy principle being "disproved" in any significant sense. There may be indeed be psychological systems which have nothing to do with it. But the general idea of filling in the gaps in incomplete data with the "most likely" values seems so obvious as to be inevitable. And the idea of using the maximum entropy values — the values which "assume the least", the most unbiased values — seems almost as natural. Furthermore, not only is it conceptually attractive and intuitively attractive — it has been shown repeatedly to work, under various theoretical assumptions and in various practical situations.

9.3 The Logic of Perception

Now, let us return to the perceptual hierarchy as briefly discussed in Section 9.0. I propose that this hierarchy is composed of a network of processors, each one of which operates **primarily** as follows:

1. Take in a set of entities consisting of stimuli, patterns in stimuli, patterns in   patterns in stimuli, etc.
2. Use Bayes' rule and the maximum entropy principle (or some other tool for determining priors) — perhaps aided by induction, deduction and analogy — to obtain a small set of most likely "interpretations" of what its input represents.
3. Seek to recognize the **most meaningfully complex** approximate patterns in these interpretations. Where $|x|$ is the minimum complexity assigned to x by any processor that inputs to processor P, processor P should use $|\ |'$ as   its measure of complexity.
4. Output these newly recognized patterns, along with perhaps portions of its input.

Step 3 is basically a form of Occam's razor: it states that the mind looks for the simplest interpretation of the data presented to it.

On lower levels, this pattern recognition will have to be severely limited. Processors will have to be restricted to recognizing certain **types** of patterns — e.g. lines, or simple shapes — rather than executing the optimizations involved in pattern recognition over a general space of functions. This is similar to the situation considered in Chapter 3, when we discussed "substitution machines." A substitution machine was a very special kind of pattern, but it turned out that much more general types of patterns could be formed from **hierarchies** of substitution machines. Here we have a hierarchy of restricted pattern recognizers, which as a whole is not nearly so restricted, because it deals routinely with patterns in patterns, patterns in patterns in patterns, and so on.

And what about the "aid" provided to Bayes' rule in Step 2? This also will have to be severely restricted on the lower levels, where speed is of the essence and access to long-term memory is limited. For instance, calculating the $P(X|Y_i)$ is a matter of deduction; and on lower levels this deduction may be carried out by rigid "hardware" routines, by fixed programs specific to certain **types** of X and Y_i. But as the level becomes higher, so does the chance that a processor will refer to more general, more intricate deductive systems to compute its $P(X|Y_i)$. And, of course, one cannot use a general, flexible deductive system without recourse to sophisticated analogical reasoning and therefore to a structurally associative memory.

Also, as the level becomes higher and higher, the $P(Y_i)$ are more and more likely to be calculated by sophisticated inductive processing rather than, say, simple entropy maximization. Technically speaking, induction may be used to provide a good background knowledge vector $\{m_1,...,m_n\}$ and meaningful constraints C. On the lower levels, the set of possible interpretations Y_i is provided by the hardware. But on the higher levels, the Y_i may be entirely determined by induction: recall that the output of the general induction algorithm is a set of **possible worlds**. Once the level is high enough, no or essentially no entropy maximization may be necessary; the prior may be supplied entirely or almost entirely by induction. The regularization parameter a may be set very low. On the other hand, intermediate levels may get **some** of the Y_i from induction and some from hardware, and entropy maximization may be invoked to a significant degree.

Also, the regularization parameter a may be adapted by induction to various degrees on various levels. On very low levels, it is probably fixed. Around the level of consciousness, it is probably very small, as already mentioned. But on the intermediate levels, it may be **adaptively modified**, perhaps according to some specialized implementation of the adaptation-of-parameters scheme to be given in the following chapter.

In sum: on the lower levels of the perceptual hierarchy, experience does **not** affect processing. The structurally associative memory is **not** invoked, and neither are any general pattern recognition algorithms. Lower level processors apply Bayes' rule, using hardware to set up the $\{Y_i\}$ and to deduce the $P(X|Y_i)$, and maximum entropy hardware to get the $P(Y_i)$. One result of this isolation is that prior knowledge has no effect on low-level pattern recognition — e.g. familiar shapes are not necessarily more easily perceived (Kohler, 1947).

On higher levels, however, the structurally associative memory must be invoked, to aid with the analogical reasoning required for estimating the $P(X|Y_i)$ either by induction or according to a flexible deductive system. Also, as will be discussed below, induction is required to set up the $\{Y_i\}$ — which are not, as on lower levels, "wired in." And sophisticated parameter adaptation is required to intelligently the regularization parameter a and, possibly, other parameters of the process of prior estimation. The structure of the perceptual hierarchy is still important, but it is interconnected with the structure of the central processing systems related to induction, deduction, analogy and parameter adaptation.

WHOLE AND PART

So far I have only discussed the progression of information **upward** through the perceptual hierarchy. Upward progression builds more complex, comprehensive forms out of simpler, more specific ones. But downward progression is equally essential.

It was the genius of the Gestalt psychologists to recognize that **the understanding of the whole guides the perception of the part**. This may be reconciled with the present framework by assuming that, in many cases, a processor on level n and a processor on level n-1 will refer to respectively more and less "local" aspects of the same phenomenon. For instance, a processor on level -8 might refer to lines, and a processor on level -7 to shapes composed of lines. In this framework, the Gestalt insight means: the results obtained by processors on level n of the perceptual hierarchy are used to tell processors on level n-1 what to look for. Specifically, I suggest that they are used to give the processors on level n-1 some idea of what the set $\{Y_i\}$ should be, and what the $P(X \mid Y_i)$ are.

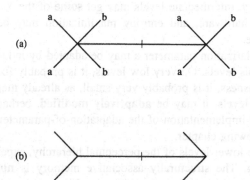

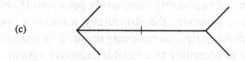

Figure 4.

A figure that at first looks like a meaningless array of fragments,
but looks entirely different when recognized.

Figure 5.

In *Gestalt Psychology*, Wolfgang Kohler (1947, p.99) gave several classic examples of this kind of top-down information transmission. For instance, if someone is shown Figure 4a and asked to draw it from memory, they will correctly draw the point P on the center of the segment on which it lies. But if someone is shown Figure 4b and asked to draw it from memory, they will place P to the **right** of the center. And, on the other hand, if they are shown Figure 4c and asked to draw it from memory, they will usually place it to the **left** of the center. Hundreds of experiments point to the conclusion that this sort of thing is not a quirk of memory but rather a property of **perception** — we actually **see** dots in different places based on their surroundings.

This is only the most rudimentary example. It has been conclusively demonstrated (Rock, 1983) that a stationary object appears to move if it is surrounded by a moving object, that a vertical line appears tilted if it is seen within a room or rectangle that is tilted, that the perceived speed of a moving object is a function of the size of the aperture through which it is perceived, et cetera. And Figure 5 (Rock, 1983) is an example of a picture which at first looks like a meaningless arrangement of fragments, but actually **looks** entirely different once recognized.

All these examples illustrate that the operation of a processor at level n can be affected by the conclusions of a processor at level n+1. Each one of these particular cases is undoubtedly highly complex. For the purpose of illustration, however, let us take a drastically oversimplified example. Say the processor which perceives points and lines is on level -8. Then perhaps the processor which put points and lines together into shapes is on level -7. According to this setup, Kohler's simple example illustrates that the operation of level -8 is affected by the results of a level -7 computation. Roughly speaking, the processor on level -7 takes in a bunch of points and lines and guesses the "most likely shape" formed out of them. It then gives the processor on level -8 a certain probability distribution $\{m_i\}$, which indicates in this case that the point is more likely to be to the right of the center of the line.

COGNITION OR SPONTANEOUS INTERACTION?

Above I said that on lower levels, a great deal of perceptual processing is executed by "hardware", by biological programs that may have little to do with deduction, induction, analogy or probability theory. But it is very difficult to estimate exactly **how much** this "great deal!" is — and this difficulty has nothing to do with the specifics of the present model. There is little consensus in biology or psychology as to how much of the processing involved in perception is "thoughtlike" as opposed to "hardware-like". In fact, there is little consensus as to what "thoughtlike" means.

In the past, there have essentially been two camps. The Gestalt psychologists believed that, in the words of Irwin Rock,

> the determinant of a perception is not the stimulus but spontaneous interactions between the representations of several stimuli or interactions between the stimulus and more central representations. Such interaction could take any form consistent with the known principles of neurophysiology. The essence of this theory is that... complex interactive events that ensue following stimulation... can allow for known effects such as those of context, constancy, contrast, perceptual changes without stimulus changes, illusions, and the like. (p.32)

Rock opposes this "spontaneous interaction theory" to the "cognitive theory", in which "reference is made... to thoughtlike processes such as description, rule following, inference or problem solving."

The theory given here is plainly cognitive in nature. However, it leaves a great deal of room for "spontaneous interaction." First of all, as mentioned above, the theory assigns a significant role to "hardware", which in the case of the human brain is likely to be independently operating self-organizing neural circuitry. How great or how small the role of this independently operating circuitry is, we cannot yet say.

In any event, the entire debate may be a matter of semantics. I have made no restrictions on the nature of the physical systems underlying minds, except that they must behave similarly to the way they would if they followed the algorithms given. It is certainly not unlikely that the brain "spontaneously" self-organizes in such a way as to execute processes of cognition. As observed in Chapter 1, **some** structure must be involved; an unstructured neural network will virtually never demonstrate intelligent behavior. The self-organizing neurodynamics in which the Gestaltists placed so much faith may indeed play a dominant role.

So, this **is** a cognitive theory, but it does not rule out the existence of noncognitive processes underlying or supplementing cognition.

For instance, consider Figure 5. The framework I have given provides a rather cognitive analysis of this phenomenon. Suppose that, say, the part of the vision processing module that resides on level -3 contains a "shape interrelation" or "form organization" processor. Assume that this processor works by **recognizing**

patterns in the input provided to it by level -4 processors, such as "shape detection processors". Then, once it has recognized the pattern "horse and rider", which greatly simplifies the picture, things change significantly. First of all, if the memory stores the picture it will most likely store it as a specific instantiation of the pattern "horse and rider", very differently from the way it would store it if no such prominent pattern had been recognized. And, more to the point, the level -3 processor will adjust the $\{Y_i\}$ used by a level -4 shape recognition processor in a very specific way: it will tell it to look for shapes that look like legs, tails, feet, et cetera. And, perhaps more significantly, it will adjust the $P(Y_i)$, too — it will tell the shape recognition processor that a shape is more likely if it looks like some part of a horse.

It is possible that these changes will propagate further down. For instance, suppose that the level -4 shape recognition processor receives output from a level -5 curve recognition processor. What if the new shapes on which the shape recognition processor has been instructed to concentrate all have some common factor, say a gentle sloping organic nature rather than an angular nature or a spiraling nature? Then the shape recognition processor might well instruct the curve recognition processor to look for the appropriate curves — i.e. it might supply the curve recognition processor with new Y_i, or with new $P(Y_i)$.

Again, this analysis is highly oversimplified, but it indicates the general direction that a detailed analysis might take. It is cognitive in that it implies that reasoning is indeed occurring below the conscious level. But does how the shape recognition, or the form organization recognition, or the curve recognition take place? I have little doubt that these pattern recognition problems are solved by specific self-organizing networks of neural clusters. In this sense, "spontaneous interaction" undoubtedly plays an essential role. Neural networks seem to be very good at self-organizing themselves so as to obtain the solutions to pattern-recognition problems. But I think that certain very general cognitive structures are also necessary, in order to systematically direct these solutions toward the goal of intelligent behavior.

MULTILEVEL OPTIMIZATION IN THE PERCEPTUAL HIERARCHY

I have suggested that information can progress downward through the perceptual hierarchy, but I have not yet said exactly how this information transmission is organized. The most natural strategy for this purpose is multilevel optimization.

This is especially plain when, as in vision processing, lower and lower levels refer to more and more local aspects of the same phenomenon. In cases such as this, operations on lower levels roughly correspond to searches in smaller subsets of the space of all patterns in the phenomenon in question, so that the regulation of the perceptual hierarchy appears very much like the regulation of a search, as discussed in Chapter 2.

In general, what the multilevel philosophy dictates is that, after a processor on level n makes its best guess as to the k most likely probability distributions $p^i=(p_1^i,...,p_n^i)$, it sends down messages to L>k processors on level n-1. To each of these processors it "assigns" one of the p^i — the most likely distribution gets more processors than the second most likely, and so on. The proportion of processors to be assigned each distribution could be set approximately equal to $S(p^i,m)/[S(p^1,m)+...+S(p^k,m)]$, in the notation of the previous chapter.

To the processors it has assigned p^i, it sends a new background distribution m^i, based on the assumption that p^i is actually the case. Also, it may send the processor new possibilities Y_i, based on this assumption. These are not trivial tasks: determining a new m^i and determining new possibilities Y_i both require deductive reasoning, and hence indirectly analogy and associative memory.

The parameter k need not be constant from level to level, but in the case of visual perception, for instance, it seems plausible that it is approximately constant. Obviously, this requires that the number of processors increases exponentially as the level decreases. But if the individual processors on lower levels deal with progressively simpler tasks, this is not unreasonable.

The perceptual hierarchy may thus be understood to operate by interconnecting multilevel optimization, Bayes' rule and the maximum entropy principle — and on the higher levels integrating induction and analogy-driven deduction as well.

SIMPLICITY AND PERCEPTION

Finally, let us consider the Gestaltists' basic law of visual perception: **Any stimulus pattern tends to be seen in such a way that the resulting structure is as simple as the given conditions permit.** This rule was formulated to explain the results of numerous well-known experiments involving, for instance, drawings with multiple interpretations. As mentioned above, it has been shown that the interpretation which one places on a drawing can affect the way one actually sees the drawing.

The key shortcoming of this Gestaltist principle is, in my opinion, the vagueness of the word "simplicity." Some Gestaltists have implied that there is a biologically innate measure of simplicity. However, experiments indicate that perception of visual stimuli is definitely influenced by culture (Segal et al, 1966). This provides a particularly strong argument for the need for a precise definition of simplicity: it shows that simplicity is not a universal intuition, but is to some extent learned.

Shortly after the discovery of information theory, Hochberg and McAlister (1953) attempted to use it to make Gestalt theory precise. They proposed that "other things being equal, the probabilities of occurrence of alternative perceptual responses to a given stimulus (i.e. their 'goodness') are inversely proportional to the amount of information required to define such alternatives differentially; i.e., **the less the amount of information needed to define a given organization as compared to the other alternatives, the more likely that figure will be so perceived.**"

They defined "goodness" as "the response frequency or relative span of time ... devoted to each of the possible perceptual responses which may be elicited by the same stimulus." And they defined information as "the number of different items we must be given, in order to specify or reproduce a given pattern or 'figure', along some one or more dimensions which may be abstracted from that pattern, such as the number of different angles, number of different line segments of unequal length, etc." Wisely, they did not blindly equate intuitive "information" with information in the communication-theoretic sense. However, their definition is not really much more precise than the standard Gestalt doctrine.

What if we replace "amount of information needed to define" in Hochberg's hypothesis with "complexity of defining relative to the patterns already in the mind," in the sense defined in Chapter 4? This seems to me to capture what Hochberg and McAlister had in mind. The "number of different items" in a set is a crude estimate of the effort it takes the mind to deal with the set, which is (according to the present model of mind) closely related to the algorithmic complexity of the set relative to the contents of the mind. To get a better estimate one must consider not only the raw quantity of items but also the possibility that a number of items which are all minor variations on one basic form might be "simpler" to the mind than a smaller number of more various items. And this line of thought leads directly to the analysis of pattern and complexity proposed in Chapter 4.

Next, what if we associate these "alternative perceptual responses" with complementary patterns in the set of stimuli presented, in the sense given in Chapter 4? Then we have a pattern-theoretic formulation of the Gestalt theory of perception: **Among a number of complementary patterns in a given stimulus, a perceiving mind will adopt the one with the least complexity relative to its knowledge base**. Note that this refers not only to visual stimuli, but to perception in general. It is easy to see that this principle, obtained as a modification of standard Gestalt theory, is a consequence of the model of perception given above. Given a set of stimuli, Bayes' rule picks the most likely underlying form. But it needs some sort of prior assumption, and on the higher levels of the perceptual hierarchy this is supplied by a network of processes involving analogy, and therefore long-term memory. Thus, to a certain extent, what we deem most likely is based on what we **know**.

To a large extent, therefore, we see what we know. This does not imply that the patterns we perceive aren't "there" — but only that, among the immense variety of patterns in the universe, we automatically tend to see those which are more closely related to what we've seen or thought before.

This has an interesting consequence for our analysis of induction. Above, we postulated that the universe possesses a "tendency to take habits," arguing that otherwise induction could not possibly work. But induction is only the process of recognizing patterns in **what one perceives**, and assuming they will continue. Therefore, if we assume that

1. as the Gestaltist rule suggests, when given a "choice" we tend to perceive what is most closely related to our knowledge base;
2. the set of "external" patterns simple enough to be contained in our minds are presented in a fairly "unbiased" distribution (e.g. a distribution fairly close to uniform, or fairly close the distribution given in which probability of occurrence is proportional to intensity, etc.);

then it follows that the universe as we perceive it **must** possess the tendency to take habits. Of course, this line of thought is circular, because our argument for the general Gestalt rule involved the nature of our model of mind, and our model of mind is based on the usefulness of pattern-recognitive induction, which is conditional on the tendency to take habits. But all this does serve to indicate that perception is not merely a technical issue; it is intricately bound up with the nature of mind, intelligence, and the external world.

10
Motor Learning

10.0 Generating Motions

Twenty years ago, Marr (1969) and Albus (1971) suggested that the circuitry of the cerebellum resembles the learning machine known as the "perceptron." A perceptron learns how to assign an appropriate output to each input by obeying the suggestions of its "teacher". The teacher provides encouragement when the perceptron is successful, and discouragement otherwise. Marr and Albus proposed that the climbing fibers in the cerebellum play the role of the teacher, and the mossy fibers play the role of the input to which the perceptron is supposed to assign output.

Perceptrons are no longer in vogue. However, the general view of the cerebellum as a learning machine has received a significant amount of experimental support. For instance, Ito (1984) has studied the way the brain learns the vestibulo-ocular reflex — the reflex which keeps the gaze of the eye at a fixed point, regardless of head movement. This reflex relies on a highly detailed program, but it is also situation-dependent in certain respects; and it is now clear that the cerebellum can change the gain of the vestibulo-ocular reflex in an adaptive way.

The cerebellum, in itself, is not capable of coordinating complex movements. However, Fabre and Buser (1980) have suggested that similar learning takes place in the motor cortex — the part of the cortex that is directly connected to the cerebellum. In order to learn a complex movement, one must do more than just change a few numerical values in a previous motion (e.g. the gain of a reflex arc, the speed of a muscle movement). Sakamoto, Porter and Asanuma (1987) have obtained experimental evidence that the sensory cortex of a cat can "teach" its motor cortex how to retrieve food from a moving beaker.

Asanuma (1989) has proposed that "aggregates of neurons constitute the basic modules of motor function", an hypothesis which is in agreement with Edelman's theory of Neural Darwinism. He goes on to observe that "each module has multiple loop circuits with many other modules located in various areas of the brain" — a situation illustrated roughly by Figure 10. In this view, the motor

141

cortex is a network of "schemes" or "programs", each one interacting with many others; and the most interesting question is: how is this network structured?

10.1 Parameter Adaptation

Consider an algorithm $y=A(f,x)$ which takes in a guess x at the solution to a certain problem f and outputs a (hopefully better) guess y at the solution. Assume that it is easy to compute and compare the quality $Q(x)$ of guess x and the quality $Q(y)$ of guess y. Assume also that A contains some parameter p (which may be a numerical value, a vector of numerical values, etc.), so that we may write $y=A(f,x,p)$. Then, for a given set S of problems f whose solutions all lie in some set R, there may be some value p which **maximizes** the average over all f in S of the average over all x in R of $Q(A(f,x,p)) - Q(x)$. Such a value of p will be called **optimal** for S.

The determination of the optimal value of p for a given S can be a formidable optimization problem, even in the case where S has only one element. In practice, since one rarely possesses a priori information as to the performance of an algorithm under different parameter values, one is required to assess the performance of an algorithm with respect to different parameter values in a real-time fashion, as the algorithm operates. For instance, a common technique in numerical analysis is to try $p=a$ for (say) fifty passes of A, then $p=b$ for fifty passes of A, and then adopt the value that seems to be more effective on a semi-permanent basis. Our goal here is a more general approach.

Assume that A has been applied to various members of S from various guesses x, with various values of p. Let U denote the $nx2$ matrix whose i'th row is (f_i,x_i), and let P denote the $nx1$ vector whose i'th entry is (p_i), where f_i, x_i and p_i are the values of f, x and p to which the i'th pass of A was applied. Let I denote the $nx1$ vector whose i'th entry is $Q(A(f_i,x_i,p_i))-Q(x_i)$. The crux of adaptation is finding a connection between parameter values and performance; in terms of these matrices this implies that what one seeks is a function $C(X,Y)$ such that $|C(U,P)-I|$ is small, for some norm $|\ |$.

So: once one has by some means determined C which thus relates U and I, then what? The overall object of the adaptation (and of A itself) is to maximize the size of I (specifically, the most relevant measure of size would seem to be the l_1 norm, according to which the norm of a vector is the sum of the absolute values of its entries). Thus one seeks to maximize the function $C(X,Y)$ with respect to Y.

PARAMETER ADAPTATION AS A BANDIT PROBLEM

The problem here is that one must balance three tasks: experimenting with p so as to locate an accurate C, experimenting with P so as to locate a maximum of C with respect to Y, and at each stage implementing the what seems on the basis of current knowledge most appropriate p, so as to get the best answer out of A. This sort of predicament, in which one must balance experimental variation with use of the best results found through past experimentation, is known as a "bandit problem" (Gittins, 1989). The reason for the name is the following question: given a "two-armed bandit", a slot machine with two handles such that pulling each handle gives a possibly different payoff, according to what strategy should one distribute pulls among the two handles? If after a hundred pulls, the first handle seems to pay off twice as well, how much more should one pull the second handle just in case this observation is a fluke?

To be more precise, the bandit problem associated with adaptation of parameters is as follows. In practice, one would seek to optimize C(X,Y) with respect to Y by varying Y about the current optimal value according to some probability distribution. The problem is: **what** probability distribution? One could, of course, seek to determine **this** adaptively, but this leads to a regress: how does one solve the bandit problem associated with this adaptation?

10.2 The Motor Control Hierarchy

I propose a motor control hierarchy which is closely analogous to the perceptual hierarchy, but works in the opposite direction. In the motor control hierarchy, the lower levels deal directly with muscle movements, with bodily functions; whereas the higher levels deal with patterns in bodily movements, with schemes for arranging bodily movements. This much is similar to the perceptual hierarchy. But in the motor control hierarchy, the primary function of a processor on level n is to instruct processors on level n-1 as to what they should do next. The most crucial information transmission is top-down. Bottom-up information transmission is highly simplistic: it is of the form "I can do what you told me to do with estimated effectiveness E".

Let us be more precise. When we say a processor on the n'th level tells a processor on the n-1'th level what to do, we mean it gives it a certain **goal** and tells it to fulfill it. That is, we mean: it poses it a certain **optimization problem**. It tells it: do something which produces a result as near to this goal as possible. The processor on the n-1'th level must then implement some **scheme** for solving this problem, for approximating the desired goal. And its scheme will, in general, involve giving instructions to certain n-2'nd level processors. The important point is that each level need know nothing about the operation of processors 2 or 3 levels down from it. Each processor supplies its subordinates with ends, and the subordinates must conceive their own means.

As with the perceptual hierarchy, consciousness plays a role only on certain relatively high levels. So, from the point of view of consciousness, the motor control hierarchy has no definite end. But, from the point of view of external reality, there is an indisputable bottom level: physical actions. The lowest level of the motor control hierarchy therefore has no subordinates except for physical, nonintelligent systems. It must therefore prescribe means, not merely ends.

Now, where do these "schemes" for optimization come from? Some are certainly preprogrammed — e.g. a human infant appears to have an inborn "sucking reflex". But — as observed above — even a cursory examination of motor development indicates that a great deal of learning is involved.

Let us assume that each processor is not entirely free to compute any function within its capacity; that it has some sort of general "algorithm scheme", which may be made more precise by the specification of certain "parameter values". Then there is first of all the problem of parameter adaptation: given an optimization problem and a method of solution which contains a number of parameter values, which parameter values are best? In order to approximately solve this problem according to the scheme given above, all that is required is an estimate of how "effective" each parameter value tends to be. In the motor control hierarchy, a processor on level n must obtain this estimate from the processors on level n-1 which it has instructed. The subordinate processors must tell their controlling processor how well they have achieved their goal. The effectiveness with which they have achieved their goal is a rough indication of how effective the parameter values involved are for that particular problem.

So, on every level but the lowest, each processor in the hierarchy tells certain subordinate lower-level processors what to do. If they can do it well, they do it and are not modified. But if then cannot do their assigned tasks well, they are experimentally modified until they can do a satisfactory job. The only loose end here is the nature of this experimental modification. Parameter adaptation is only part of the story.

MOTOR CONTROL AND ASSOCIATIVE MEMORY

Knowing how effective each vector of parameter values is for each particular problem is useful, but not adequate for general motor control. After all, what happens when some **new** action is required, some action for which optimal parameter values have not already been estimated? It would be highly inefficient to begin the parameter optimization algorithm from some random set of values. Rather, some sort of educated guess is in order. This means something very similar to analogical reasoning is required. Presented with a new task, a motor control processor must ask: what parameter values have worked for **similar** tasks?

So, each motor control processor must first of all have access to the structurally associative memory, from which it can obtain information as to which tasks are similar to which tasks. And it must also have access to a memory bank storing estimates of optimal parameter values for given tasks. In this way it can select appropriate schemes for regulating action.

Based on the biological facts reviewed above, it is clear that this aspect of motor control is native to the motor cortex rather than the cerebellum. To learn a complex action, the brain must invoke the greater plasticity of the cortex.

LEARNING TO THROW

Introspectively speaking, all this is little more than common sense. To figure out how to throw a certain object, we start out with the motions familiar to us from throwing similar objects. Then, partly consciously but mainly unconsciously, we modify the "parameters" of the motions: we change the speed of our hand or the angle at which the object is tilted. Based on trial-and-error experimentation with various parameters, guided by intuition, we arrive at an optimal, or at least adequate, set of motions.

This process may be simple or sophisticated. For instance, when first throwing a frisbee with a hole in the middle, one throws it as if it were an ordinary frisbee; but then one learns the subtle differences. In this case the major problem is fine-tuning the parameters. But when learning to throw a shot-put, or a football, the only useful item to be obtained from memory is the general scheme of "throwing" — all the rest must be determined by conscious thought or, primarily, experiment.

And when learning to juggle, or when learning to throw for the first time, the mind must synthesize whole new patterns of timing and coordination: there is not even any "scheme" which can be applied. Fragments of known programs must be pieced together and augmented to form a new program, which then must be fine-tuned.

More and more difficult tasks require higher and higher levels of the motor control hierarchy — both for learning and for execution. Even the very low levels of the motor control hierarchy are often connected to the perceptual hierarchy; but the higher levels involve a great deal of interaction with yet other parts of the mind.

10.3 A Neural-Darwinist Perceptual-Motor Hierarchy

In Chapter 6 we used Edelman's theory of Neural Darwinism to explore the nature of neural analogy. However, we did not suggest how the "lower-to-intermediate-level" details discussed there might fit into a theory of higher-level brain function. It is possible to give a partial Neural-Darwinist analysis of the perceptual and motor hierarchies. This entails wandering rather far from the biological data; however, given the current state of neuroscience, there is little choice.

Assume that the inputs of certain neural clusters are connected to **sensory input,** and that the outputs of certain clusters are connected to **motor controls.** The purpose of the brain is to give "appropriate" instructions to the motor controls, and the determination of appropriateness at any given time is in large part dependent upon the effects of past instructions to the motor controls — i.e. on using sensory input to **recognize patterns** between motor control instructions and desirability of ensuing situation.

In order to make sense of this picture, we must specify exactly how appropriateness is to be determined. Toward this end I will delineate a hierarchy of maps. Maps which are connected to both sensory inputs and motor controls (as well as, naturally, other clusters) we shall call **level 1** maps. These maps are potentially able to "sense" the effect of motor control instructions, and formulate future motor control instructions accordingly.

One question immediately arises: How are appropriate level 1 maps arrived at and then maintained? In the simple Hebb rule discussed in Chapter 6, we have a mechanism by which any map, once repeatedly used, will be reinforced and hence maintained; but this says nothing about the problem of arriving at an appropriate map in the first place. Rather than proposing a specific formula, let us dodge the issue by asserting that the appropriateness of level 1 maps should be determined on the basis of the degree to which the levels of certain chemical substances in their vicinity are maintained within biologically specified "appropriate" bounds. This cowardly recourse to biological detail can serve as the "ground floor" of an interesting general definition of appropriateness.

Define a map which is not a level-1 map to be appropriate to the extent that the maps or motor controls to which it outputs are appropriate. The idea is that a map is appropriate to the extent that the entities over which it has (partial) control are appropriate. The appropriateness of a level 1 map is partially determined by the extent to which it directs motor controls to make appropriate actions. And in the long run — barring statistical fluctuations — this is roughly **equivalent** to the extent to which it represents an emergent pattern between 1) results of motor control and 2) appropriateness as measured by sensory data and otherwise. This is the crucial observation. In general, the appropriateness of a map is determined by the extent to which it directs other maps to effect appropriate actions, either directly on motor controls or on other maps. And, barring statistical fluctuations, it is plain that this is roughly equivalent to the extent to which it represents an emergent pattern between 1) results of outputs to other maps and 2) inputs it obtains from various sources.

It is important to remember that we are not hypothesizing the brain to contain distinct "pattern recognition processors" or "analogical reasoning processors" or "memory cells": our model of mind is schematic and logical, not necessarily physical; it is a model of patterns and processes. We have hypothesized a neural mechanism which tends to **act** much like a pattern recognition processor, and that is all that can reasonably be expected.

Now, let us go beyond the level 1 maps. Define a **degree 2** map as a map which outputs to level 1 maps (as well as possibly inputting from level 1 maps and other maps and outputting to other maps). Define a **degree 3** map as one which outputs to degree 2 maps (as well as possibly level 1 maps, etc.). One may define maps of degree 4, 5, 6,.. in a similar way. The **level** of a map is then defined as the highest degree to which it possesses. If a level k map accepted inputs only from maps of level k-1 or lower, the network of maps would have a strictly hierarchical structure. There would be a "top" level n, and our definition of appropriateness would define appropriateness on all levels less than n in terms of top-level appropriateness, but say nothing about the appropriateness of a map on level n. But in fact, the maps of the brain are arranged in a far less orderly fashion. Although there is a bottom level — the level of perception and action — there is no distinct top level.

The nonhierarchical interconnection of the maps of the brain implies that the evaluation of appropriateness is a very tricky matter. If A and B both input and output to each other, then the appropriateness of A is determined in part as an increasing function of the appropriateness of B, and vice versa. The hierarchy of maps does bottom out at level 1, but it also re-enters itself multiply. In a very rough way, this explains a lot about human behavior: our internal definition of "appropriateness" is determined not only by low-level biological factors but also by a subtle, probably unstable dynamical system of circularly reinforcing and inhibiting patterns.

We have not yet specified what exactly happens to inappropriate maps. Clearly, an inappropriate map should be dissolved, so that it will no longer direct behavior, and so that a new and hopefully better map can take its place. The easiest way to effect this would be to **inhibit** the connections between clusters of the map — to **decrease** their conductances (roughly speaking, proportionally to the lack of appropriateness). Naturally, if a connection belonged to more than one map, this decrease would be mitigated by the increase afforded by membership in other maps, but this effect need not rob inhibition of its effectiveness.

Biologically, how might such a system of inhibition work? It is known that if a once-frequently-used connection between clusters is unused for a time, its conductance will gradually revert to the level of other infrequently-used neurons. Naturally, the presence of inhibitory connections between individual neurons plays a role in this. However, it is not presently known whether this effect is sufficient for the suppression of inappropriate maps.

At this point, just as we are beginning to move toward the higher levels of mental process, we must abandon our discussion of the brain. We have already left our starting point, Neural Darwinism, too far behind. On the positive side, we have constructed a hierarchy of neural maps which is, intuitively, a combination of the perceptual and motor control hierarchies: it recognizes patterns and it controls actions, using a simple form of analogy, in an interconnected way. However, we have accounted for only a few of the simpler aspects of the master network to be described in Chapter 12 — we have spoken only of pattern recognition and a simple form of structural analogy. We have said nothing of induction, deduction, Bayesian inference, or modeling or contextual analogy, or even more general forms of structural analogy. It is difficult to see how these subtler aspects of mentality could be integrated into the Neural Darwinist framework without altering it beyond recognition. It seems to me that they may require somewhat more structure than the self-organizing network of maps which Neural Darwinism proposes.

11
Consciousness and Computation

11.0 Toward A Quantum Theory of Consciousness

For sixty years physicists have struggled with the paradox of quantum measurement. However, despite a number of theoretical advances, rather little progress has been made toward resolution of the basic dilemma. The problem is one of physics versus phenomenology. According to quantum physics, no physical entity is ever in a definite state; the most one can ever say about a given entity is that it has certain probabilities of being in certain states. And yet, both in daily life and in the laboratory, things do sometimes appear to have definite states.

For instance, the equations of quantum physics predict that, in many situations, an electron has a 50% "chance" of having a positive spin, and a 50% "chance" of having a negative spin. Yet when the physicist probes the electron in his laboratory, it appears to have either a positive spin or a negative spin. According to the equations of quantum physics — the Heisenberg equation and the Schrodinger equation — such a reduction to a definite state is impossible. O f course, one may have various degrees of probabilistic knowledge. In certain situations, one might know an electron to have a 90% "chance" of having positive spin, and a 10% "chance" of having negative spin. But there can never be 100% definite knowledge. Heisenberg's indeterminacy principle says that one can never have complete knowledge of the state of any particle: the greater the accuracy with which one knows its position, the less the accuracy with which one can know its momentum; and vice versa. In order to predict what the particle will do in the future, one needs to know both the position and the momentum; but according to quantum physics, this is possible only probabilistically.

This sort of indeterminacy is a proven scientific fact, inasmuch as quantum theory is the only known theory that correctly explains the behavior of microscopic particles, and it predicts only probabilities. Classical mechanics and electromagnetism gave definite answers about the behavior of microscopic particles, but these answers were experimentally wrong. Furthermore, it seems likely that, if quantum theory is someday superseded, the theory which follows it will build on the probabilistic nature of quantum theory, rather than regressing to classical ideas. In fact, it has been proved mathematically (Bell, 1964, 1987) that any physical theory satisfying certain simple requirements must necessarily have properties similar to those of quantum theory: it must deal only in probabilities.

BEYOND THE PROJECTION POSTULATE

In his classic treatise on quantum theory, John von Neumann (1936) introduced the "projection postulate", an addition to the basic principles of quantum physics which states that, when an entity is measured, it reduces to a definite state. This approach appears to be adequate for most practical problems of quantum mechanics; and, although, many physicists find it unacceptable, there is no equally elegant alternative. The only trouble is that no one has ever given a satisfactory definition of "measurement".

Originally it was thought that a microscopic event could be considered to be measured when it "registered" an effect on some macroscopic entity. The justification for this was the belief that, as entities become larger and larger, the probabilistic nature of quantum physics becomes less and less relevant to their behavior. For instance, according to quantum physics a baseball dropped from a window has an infinity of possible paths, but one of them, or one small class of them, is overwhelmingly more likely than the others.

But this naive identification of measurement with macroscopic effect cannot stand up to criticism. Spiller and Clark (1986) have constructed a Super-conducting Quantum Interference Device (SQUID) which is about the size of a thumbnail and yet displays the same sort of uncertainty as an electron. One can never know both the intensity and the flux of its magnetic field with perfect accuracy; there is a finite limit beyond which further accuracy is impossible. Its state is fundamentally a probabilistic superposition.

And it appears that the brain may display a similar form of quantum indeterminacy (Changeaux, 1985; Penrose, 1990). Recall that a neuron fires when its charge exceeds a certain threshold amount. It follows that, on occasion, highly unpredictable quantum phenomena may push the charge of a neuron over the threshold. And this neuron may then set other neurons off, and so on — in this manner a tiny quantum indeterminacy may give rise to a huge neurophysiological uncertainty. If the extra charge has a fifty-fifty chance of being there, then the entire pattern of neuronal firing that ensues from its presence probably has about a fifty-fifty chance of being there. A pattern of neuronal firing might, for instance, represent a state of mind. And when you consider the fact that there are over a hundred billion neurons in the brain, the possibilities for interlocking quantum uncertainties are astounding. The exact numbers are difficult to estimate, but it appears that this may be a significant phenomenon.

One intriguing alternative to the projection postulate is Everett's (1957) "many-worlds hypothesis", which assigns to each uncertain situation an array of universes, one corresponding to each possible outcome. For instance, according to the many-worlds hypothesis, every time a physicist observes an electron to have positive spin, there is an alternate universe which is exactly identical to this one, except that in the alternate universe the physicist observes the electron to have negative spin. This is an interesting possibility, but it is empirically indistinguishable from the projection postulate, since these alternate universes can never be observed.

THE QUANTUM THEORY OF CONSCIOUSNESS

Another alternative, first proposed by Wigner (1962), is that "measurement" may be defined as "registration into consciousness." To see the motivation for this radical idea, let us turn to the infamous paradox of Schrodinger's cat (1948). Here the peculiarity of quantum theory is elevated to the level of absurdity. Put a cat in a soundproofed cage with a radioactive atom, a Geiger counter and a vial of poison gas. Suppose that the atom has a half-life of one hour. Then it has a fifty-fifty chance of decaying within the hour. According to the dynamical equations of quantum physics, this is **all one can know** about the atom: that it has a fifty-fifty chance of decaying. There is no possible way of gaining more definite information.

Assume that, if the atom decays, the Geiger counter will tick; and if the Geiger counter ticks, the poison vial will be broken. This set-up is bizarre but not implausible; a clever engineer could arrange it or something similar. What is the state of the cat after the hour is up? According to quantum theory without the projection postulate, it is neither definitely alive nor definitely dead — but half and half. Because the atom **never** either definitely decays or definitely doesn't decay: quantum physics deals only in probabilities. And if the atom never either definitely decays or definitely doesn't decay, then the cat never definitely dies or definitely doesn't die.

One might argue that the cat is not in a state of superposition between life and death, but rather has a fifty percent chance of being alive and a fifty percent chance of being dead. But according to quantum theory without the projection postulate, the cat will never collapse into a definite state of being either alive or dead. What sense does it make to suggest that the cat has a fifty percent chance of entering into a state which it will never enter into? The function of the projection postulate is to change the statement that the cat is half dead and half alive into a statement about the probabilities of certain definite outcomes.

Of course, the fact is that if we look in the box after the hour is up, we either see a dead cat or a living cat. Phenomenologically, by the time the observation is made, one of the two possibilities is selected — **definitely** selected. But **when**, exactly, does this selection occur? Since measurement cannot be defined as macroscopic registration, this is a very serious problem.

And the problem is resolved very neatly by the hypothesis that **probabilistic occurrences are replaced by definite occurrences when they enter consciousness.**

For instance, this implies that Schrodinger's cat is not half dead and half alive, but rather has a fifty percent chance of being dead and a fifty percent chance of being alive. The cat becomes definitely dead or definitely alive **when a conscious being sees it.** As Goswami put it,

> it is our consciousness whose observations of the cat resolves its dead-or-alive dichotomy. Coherent superpositions, the multifaceted quantum waves, exist in the transcendent order until consciousness brings them to the world of appearance with the act of observation. And, in the process, consciousness chooses one facet out of two, or many, that are permitted by the mathematics of quantum mechanics, the Schrodinger equation; it is a limited choice, to be sure, subject to the overall probability constraint of quantum mathematics (i.e. consciousness is lawful).... [C]onsciousness... **is not about doing something to objects via observing, but consists of choosing among the alternative possibilities that the wave function presents and recognizing the result of choice.** (1990, p. 142)

That is, the mind does not create the world in the sense of reaching out and physically modifying events. But it creates the world by selecting from among the wide yet limited variety of options presented to it by the probabilistic equations of physics.

11.1 Implications of the Quantum Theory of Consciousness

The measurement paradox is not the only philosophically troublesome aspects of quantum physics. Bell's Theorem (1987), with its implication of instantaneous communication between distant events, is equally unsettling. The simplest example of this is the Einstein-Podolsky-Rosen (EPR) thought experiment. Two electrons, initially coupled, are shot off in different directions. It is assumed that each one flies for millions of miles without hitting anything. Each one, according to quantum physics, has a fifty-fifty chance of spinning to the right or to the left — there is no way to make a more accurate prediction. However, the rules of quantum physics **do** imply that the two are spinning in opposite directions: if one is spinning to the right, then the other one is spinning to the left; and vice versa.

Now suppose someone measures **one** of the electrons, and that it all of a sudden assumes a definite value. Then the other electron will **immediately** also assume a definite value — because it is known that the two are spinning in opposite directions. If one is measured to be spinning to the right, then the other is instantaneously known to be spinning to the left. When Einstein conceived this example, he thought he had disproved quantum mechanics — because nothing so absurd could possibly be true. After all, he asked **how does the one electron tell the other one which way to spin?** Special relativity forbids information to travel faster than the speed of light; so it would seem that if the particles were sufficiently distant, the value of the spin of one particle could take eons to reach the other particle.

But, absurd as this may be, it is an experimentally proven fact (Aspect and Grangier, 1985). Scenarios very similar to the original EPR thought experiment have been tested in the lab. It turns out that, mathematically speaking, this peculiar "nonlocality" does not contradict special relativity, because no **information** is being transmitted, only a **correlation**. But this is very little consolation: it is a violation against the spirit, if not the letter, of special relativity.

Reality does not consist of pairs of electrons, coupled and then shot out into space a million miles in opposite directions. Consider the following thought experiment. Split apart two coupled physical systems, say A and B. Suppose that, from the state of A, one could infer the state of B, and vice versa. Leave A alone but let B interact with C for a while, and then separate B from C. Finally, measure A. A is collapsed into some definite state. If B had not interacted with C, one could say that the state of B would also, immediately, collapse into some definite state. But the state of B now depends also upon the state of C, which according to quantum physics has no definite value but is rather an array of possibilities. So the measurement of A does not collapse B to a definite state. But it does, however, decrease the uncertainty involved in the state of B. It increases the "closeness" of B to a definite state.

Technically speaking, assume that $p=(p_1,p_2,...,p_n)$ denotes the probabilities of the various possible states in which B might be. Then one may show that, in the situation described above, the measurement of A necessarily changes p into a new set of probabilities $p'=(p_1',...,p_n')$ so that $H(p_1,...,p_n) < H(p_1',...,p_n')$, where H is the entropy function

$$H(p_1,...,p_n) = -[p_1 \log p_1 + ... + p_n \log p_n].$$

A similar statement may be made when the possible states of B form a continuum rather than a discrete set. Recall that the entropy of a probability distribution is a measure of its uncertainty, or its distance from the most certain distribution.

This thought experiment may be generalized. What if the state of B **cannot** be completely determined from the state of A? If the state of A yields any information at all about the state of B, then it is plain that the same result holds. If A and B were ever coupled, no matter how loosely, no matter what they have done since, measurement of A reduces the uncertainty of the probability distribution characterizing the states of B. Bell's Theorem implies that this sort of propagation of certainty is a necessary aspect of any physical theory that is mathematically similar to quantum theory.

In terms of the quantum theory of consciousness, what does this mean? A little consciousness can go a long way! If two sets of possibilities have been coupled in the past, and are then separated, then whenever consciousness makes one of them definite, the other one becomes definite automatically, instantaneously, without any physical causation involved.

QUANTUM CONSCIOUSNESS AND BIOLOGICAL CONSCIOUSNESS

By introducing consciousness, one obtains a philosophically elegant resolution of the paradox of quantum measurement. But in a way we are abusing the word "consciousness". What qualities does this abstract entropy-decreasing consciousness share with the common-sense understanding of consciousness? We have reconciled the physics of measurement with the phenomenology of measurement only by separating the physics of consciousness from the phenomenology of consciousness.

Mandler has proposed that

> ... [C]onscious constructions represent the most general interpretation that is appropriate to the current scene in keeping with both the intentions of the individual and the demands of the environment. ...Thus, we are aware of looking at a landscape when viewing the land from a mountaintop, but we become aware of a particular road when asked how we might get down or of an approaching storm when some dark clouds "demand" inclusion in the current construction. In a problem-solving task, we are conscious of those current mental products that are closest to the task at hand, i.e. the likely solution to the problem. (1985, p. 81)

Whether or not this particular formulation is exactly correct, it seems plain that some similar characterization must hold true. Consciousness seems to have a role in planning and decision-making, but it is rarely involved in the minute details of everyday life: walking, turning the pages of a book, choosing words in conversation, doing arithmetic with small numbers, etc. In the language of the previous chapters, this means that — as already stated — consciousness has contact with only a certain restricted range of the perceptual hierarchy.

The decision-making aspect of consciousness is intuitively harmonious with quantum theory: in making a decision, one is reducing an array of possibilities to one definite state. There is a sense in which making a decision corresponds to selecting one of many possible universes. But the quantum theory of consciousness gives us no indication of why certain decisions are submitted to consciousness, but others are not.

One of the main problems here is that it is not clear what function the quantum theory of consciousness is supposed to serve. In Wigner (1962) or Goswami (1990), consciousness is essentially **defined** as the reduction to a definite state, or more generally as the decrease of the entropy of an array of possible states. This interpretation gives a transcendentalist resolution of the mind-body problem, made explicit by Goswami when he suggests that, as a heuristic tool, we consider the mind to be a coupling of two computers, a classical computer and a quantum computer. The quantum computer behaves in a way which transcends ordinary biophysics, and it is this transcendence which is responsible for consciousness.

But there is another, more radical, way of interpreting the quantum theory of consciousness. One may begin with the assertion that consciousness is a **process** which is part of the dynamics of certain physical systems, e.g. human brains. This means that consciousness has some direct physical effect: that, for instance, when a pattern of neural firings enters consciousness, consciousness changes it in a certain characteristic way. The biochemical nature of this process is of course largely unknown. However, Edelman (1989) has made some very interesting hypotheses. In his notation, consciousness may be described as the continual interaction between C(W) and C[C(W). C(I)], where

C(I) is the neural basis for categorization of I, the interoceptive input — autonomic, hypothalamic, endocrine. It is evolutionarily earlier, driven by inner events, mediated by limbic and brain-stem circuits coupled to biochemical circuits, and it shows slow phasic activity. C[W] is the neural basis for perceptual categorization of W, the exteroceptive input — peripheral, voluntary motor, proprioceptive and polymodal sensory signals — and is mediated by the thalmus and cortical areas. It is driven largely by outer events, is fast, and handles many more signals in parallel. C(W).C(I) represents the neural basis of interaction and comparison of two categorical systems that occurs, for example, at the hippocampus, septum, and cingulate gyri. C[C(W).C(I)] is the neural basis of conceptual recategorization of this comparison, which takes place in the cingulate gyri, temporal lobes, and parietal and frontal cortex. (The boldface C indicates conceptual categorization.)

Less technically, what Edelman proposes is that consciousness is the interaction between two processes: 1) the recognition of patterns in perceptions, and 2) the interaction between the recognition of patterns of perception and the recognition of patterns in internal, emotional, chemical stimuli.

Given this biological characterization of consciousness, one may then hypothesize that the entropy reduction of arrays of possible states is **correlated with** those changes the states of conscious systems which correspond to conscious acts. This point of view — which I will call the **strong interaction** postulate — places less responsibility on quantum theory than the interpretation of Wigner and Goswami: it does not require quantum theory to explain psychological facts. Rather, it portrays consciousness as the point of connection between psycho-biological dynamics and physical dynamics; the bridge between the mind and the world.

The quantum theory of consciousness, as presented by Wigner or Goswami, implies a transcendentalist resolution of the mind-body problem. But though it is useful for intuitively understanding quantum theory, it is not at all adequate for understanding consciousness. The strong interaction postulate is not merely a reinterpretation of quantum theory: it states that consciousness, in some sense, plays an active role in forming the physical world.

In terms of the many-worlds interpretation, strong interaction implies that the brain-states of conscious entities put a **special bias** on the possible universes of the future. Everything in the universe figures into the array of probabilities of possible future universes — but conscious systems are involved in an additional feedback process with this array.

The idea of strong interaction may be worked out in much more detail, but that would lead us too far astray. It may be that future developments in physics will render this entire discussion nonsensical. However, as Penrose (1989) has pointed out, it is also possible that the relation between mind and body will be essential to the next revolution in physics.

SELF-AWARENESS

Finally, I would like to point out that the quantum view of consciousness yields an interesting interpretation of that intangible feeling of self-awareness that accompanies consciousness of external objects or definite ideas. Consider the following scenario. P and Q are closely coupled algorithms, each one continually modifying the other. Simultaneously, consciousness greatly reduces the uncertainty of both the distribution of possible states of P and the distribution of possible states of Q. The reduction of the uncertainty P then reduces the uncertainty of Q yet further; and vice versa. The result is that the combined entity P∪Q has, in effect, **looked at itself** and reduced its own entropy.

It is not justifiable to say that P∪Q did not really look at itself, that what really happened was that P and Q looked at each other. Because according to quantum physics, if we **observed** P ∪ Q to see what was really happening, this would change the probability distributions. P and Q are quantum coupled, and this means they are effectively one entity. Clearly, this situation is not rare: feedback between different prominent structures is probably not the exception but the rule.

According to this analysis, the feeling of self-awareness is not logically inherent to consciousness; it is rather an extremely common by-product of consciousness. This accounts for the fact that we are **not** continually absorbed with the sensation of self-awareness: it flits in and out of consciousness. Self-awareness is not quite the same as consciousness, but the two are inextricably interlinked.

INTELLIGENCE AND CONSCIOUSNESS

Clearly, the quantum theory of consciousness is in a very early stage of development. However, none of the details are really essential here. The primary point of our excursion through quantum theory was to arrive at one simple hypothesis: that whereas Turing machines cannot possess consciousness, quantum computers can.

This hypothesis has profound implications for the relation between consciousness and intelligence. To see this, we must consider a certain crucial but vastly under appreciated shortcoming of the theory of Turing machines. Mathematically, it is easy to deal with Turing machines of arbitrarily large processing capacity. But in physical reality, it is impossible to build an arbitrarily powerful Turing machine.

If the parts of a machine are very small or very closely packed, then they are susceptible to quantum effects, and the machine is a quantum computer, not strictly a Turing machine: its behavior depends crucially on the peculiar properties of indeterminacy and nonlocality. But if the parts of a machine are not very small, and not very closely packed, then they must spread over a large expanse of space. However, according to the theory of special relativity, information cannot travel any faster than the speed of light. Therefore, there is a limit to the speed of a machine made of large and/or sparse parts.

From these considerations it follows that, for any given time period T, there is a certain limit to the amount of computation that a physical Turing machine can do in time T. Even without estimating the specific numbers, it is clear that this limit is considerably smaller than the total amount of computation which a quantum computer can do in time T. Deutsch has shown that an abstract quantum computer cannot compute any functions which an abstract Turing machine cannot also compute. However, within any specified period of time, there is some physical quantum computer which can compute functions that no physical Turing machine can.

Now, intelligence depends not only on absolute computing power but also on speed. Therefore it follows from our assumptions that there is a certain degree of intelligence which quantum computers can attain but Turing machines cannot. Coupling this with the hypothesis that quantum computers but not Turing machines possess consciousness, one obtains the following intriguing conclusion: **there may be a certain level of intelligence which can be attained only by conscious entities.**

11.2 Consciousness and Emotion

One often hears comments to the effect that "even if a computer could somehow think, it could never *feel*." And Dreyfus (1978), among others, has argued that this imposes strict limitations on the potential power of computer thought. After all, what is intuition but a sense of what "feels right"?

The weakest point of such arguments is that they do not refer to any particular definition of emotion. Without a definition of emotion broad enough to apply, at least potentially, to entities substantially different from human beings, how can one make a fair judgement as to the emotional capacity of computers?

One might argue that no such general definition is possible; that the only way to understand human emotions is through human biology, which is inherently applicable only to entities substantially similar to human beings. This argument is bolstered by the numerous vagaries and self-contradictions which plague psychoanalysis and other classical theories of emotion, and also by the many impressive achievements of molecular psychology. However, it is nonetheless not implausible that there is a general **structure of emotion**.

In his 1887 classic *Laws of Feeling*, Paulhan made an intriguing suggestion as to what this structure might be. And more recently, Mandler (1985) has outlined a theory very similar to Paulhan's, and gathered together a great deal of data in favor of it. These theories are preliminary and incomplete, and they are not essential to the main ideas of this book. However, they do indicate how one might develop a theory of emotion compatible with the ideas of the previous chapters.

MacCurdy, a psychoanalyst, expressed Paulhan's core idea excellently in his 1925 *Psychology of Emotion*: it is precisely

> when instinctive reactions are stimulated that do not gain expression, that affect is most intense. It is the prevention of the expression of instinct either in behavior or conscious thought that leads to intense affect. In other words, the energy of the organism, activating an instinct process, must be blocked by repression before poignant feeling is excited.

In his own words, Paulhan's general law of feeling is simply that

> desires ... only give rise to affective phenomena when the tendency awakened undergoes inhibition.

Throughout *Laws of Feeling*, Paulhan implicitly assumes that "tendencies" are the stuff of mind. Since he never actually defines the word "tendency", I see no problem with reading "tendency" as "behavioral pattern".

In the language of the preceding chapter, a "desire" is an instruction passed down the motor control hierarchy. Very low-level instructions probably do not deserve the label "desire", but there is no rigid cut-off point: the higher the level of an instruction, the more it is a "desire". Paulhan's hypothesis is that emotions occur only when such an instruction is not obeyed. This disobeyal may be due to mental incapacity or to the uncooperativeness of external reality. Emotion would never occur in an all-powerful, all-knowing, perfectly-running machine, because all of its internal instructions would invariably be fulfilled. Livesey, in the first volume of his 1986 *Learning and Emotion*, has sketched out similar ideas, although his analysis is less specific and hence less controversial.

HAPPINESS

Paulhan apparently did not try very hard to apply his theory to particular emotions. He considered this to be an elementary exercise. Unfortunately, I cannot agree with him on this point: I have found this "exercise" to be formidably difficult. However, Paulhan did make two clear definitions, so let us consider these: **happiness is the feeling of increasing order; unhappiness is the feeling of decreasing order.**

Paulhan did not define order; in the present context, it seems most straightforward to define the order of a set of patterns X as the sum over all x in X of the average, over all neighbors (y,z) of x in the mind's STRAM, of $IN[x;(y,z)]$. This implies that the "feeling of increasing order" is the "feeling of increasingly simple representation of the contents of one's subjective world."

To put it rather pedantically, this means that happiness is the feeling of recognizing patterns more effectively than in the immediate past; and, on the other hand, unhappiness is the feeling of recognizing patterns less effectively than in the immediate past. Or, more intuitively: happiness is the feeling of increasing unity.

The only puzzling thing about this is that, according to Paulhan's definition, all emotion derives from inhibition; and therefore the "feeling of increasing simplicity" must mean the inhibition of those patterns which are rendered unnecessary or impossible by the advent of increasing simplicity. Is happiness, then, the feeling of **stifling** all the fruitless attempts to order the world which are rendered irrelevant by success? And is unhappiness, the feeling of **stifling** the habits instilled by a previously successful simplifying order of the world, in favor of further laborious attempts?

This may seem a little bit bizarre. I would argue that, at any rate, this is **one** important meaning of the word "happiness." For instance, it explains, in a very rough way, why young children (who are continually presented with highly novel stimuli) obtain such pleasure from exploring and understanding. And, conversely, it also explains the human tendency toward closed-mindedness: the intrusion of novel patterns into a mental world of familiar ideas and routines will usually, at first anyhow, cause a decrease in the simplicity of one's representation of the world.

BEAUTY

Next, let us consider the experience of aesthetic appreciation, of "beauty." One may define the beauty of X to Y as the amount of happiness gained by Y from the patterns which Y perceives in X, and this is not unsatisfactory, but it would be nice to have a definition which provided insight into the internal structure of the beautiful object. This we shall draw not from Paulhan, but from a loose interpretation of the work of Georg Simmel.

In his essay on "The Face", Simmel (1959) proposed that "the closer the interrelation of the parts of a complex, and the livelier their interaction (which transforms their separateness into mutual dependence)," the greater the aesthetic significance of that complex. It seems to me that this "unity out of and above diversity," this "interaction" and "interrelation of the parts" is very well summed up by the concept of structural complexity. After all, an entity is not a priori divided into "parts"; the mind divides it into parts as part of the process of perception and comprehension — the "parts" are patterns. And the "degree of interrelation" of the various patterns is, I suggest, simply the amount of pattern tying together the various patterns — in other words, the structural complexity. Thus, it seems reasonable that the beauty of x to y is the happiness associated with that portion of St(x) which is perceived by y. Simmel's conception of beauty as emergent order coincides perfectly with Paulhan's idea of happiness as increasing order.

FREE WILL

Free will and consciousness are often considered identical. Conscious decisions are considered freely willed. However, this point of view is unjustified. The first argument against free will is that, physiologically and psychologically, it is clear that conscious decisions are far from unpredictable. They are influenced very strongly by unconscious memories and biases, i.e. by parts of the brain which have no direct role in consciousness. This argument might be contradicted as follows: perhaps other influences **bias** consciousness, but they do not determine its behavior completely. They influence the likelihood of consciousness making one decision or another, but this only permits us to predict the outcome of consciousness in a rough probabilistic sense.

But, if this is the case, then how does consciousness actually make a choice? Empirically, there is no way of distinguishing between the hypothesis that a choice is made by free will, and the hypothesis that it is made **at random subject to the probability distribution induced by outside influences.**

So the existence of free will is essentially a moot point. I suspect that, in the future, it will be more fruitful to analyze free will as an **emotion.** To see how this might be done, consider Nietzsche's analysis of "freedom of the will" as

> the expression for the complex state of delight of the person exercising volition, who commands and at the same time identifies himself with the executor of the order — who, as such, enjoys also the triumph over obstacles, but thinks within himself that it was really his will itself that overcame them. In this way the person exercising volition adds the feelings of delight of his successful executive instruments, the useful 'underwills' or undersouls — indeed, our body is but a social structure composed of many souls — to his feelings of delight as commander. **L'effet c'est moi**: what happens here is what happens in every well-constructed and happy commonwealth; namely, the governing class identifies itself with the successes of the commonwealth. (1968, p. 216)

The feeling of free will, according to Nietszche, involves 1) the feeling that there is indeed an entity called a "self", and 2) the assignation to this "self" of "responsibility" for one's acts. It is easy to see how such a feeling would fall under the category of happiness, because it certainly does serve to impose a simple "order" on the confusing interplay of patterns underlying mental action.

But what is this pattern called the "self", which the mind recognizes in its own operation? Given a definition of "self", free will could be defined as the emotion resulting from the "belief" or "recognition of the pattern" that, in the absence of the self, effective pattern recognition (i.e. happiness) would not be possible. But even then the question why this belief would emerge would not be answered. Clearly there is a great deal of subtlety involved here, and we do not yet possess the tools with which to probe it.

EMOTION, COMPUTATION, AND CONSCIOUSNESS

Regarding the emotional capacity of computers, Paulhan's theory yields an ambiguous verdict. Emotion is analyzed to involve a certain characteristic **structure**. One may say that this characteristic structure only becomes true **emotion** when it enters consciousness, in which case it might well be that a quantum computer but not a Turing machine can experience emotion. Or, on the other hand, one may say that this structure is **always** emotion, whether or not it is consciously experienced. Essentially this is a matter of semantics.

Mandler (1975) has made a similar point, observing that emotions have a "hot" aspect and a "cold" aspect. The cold aspect is the abstract structure of nonfulfillment of expectation. The hot aspect has to do with the presence of certain chemical factors which cause the vivid, visceral experience of emotion. One might say also that the cold aspect has to do with mind, the hot aspect with body. It may be that consciousness is a prerequisite for "hotness". The hot aspect of emotion is the bodily effect of the abstract mental nonfulfillment of expectation. The means by which this effecting takes place — by which structure affects chemical levels — is essentially unknown.

And, if consciousness is a prerequisite for emotion, is it perhaps also true that emotion is a necessary part of consciousness? It is well known that, when a person summons something from long-term memory into consciousness, the limbic system is activated. The exact reason for this is a mystery, but it is also well known that the limbic system is the center of emotion. This reflects a psychological concept that goes back at least to Freud, who suggested that it may be **impossible** to remember something unless that something possesses some emotional content.

This "Freudian" hypothesis coincides well with the present model of mind. We have hypothesized that consciousness contains the most "prominent" patterns in the mind, where a "prominent" pattern is both intense as a pattern, and the object of a great deal of activity on high levels of the motor control hierarchy. Is it not reasonable that a great deal of activity will center around those instructions which are **not** obeyed the first time around? Merely by virtue of their failure, they will receive more attention — they have to be tried again, or alternatives have to be found.

In conclusion: all that can be said with certainty is that consciousness and emotion are closely related. The nature of this relation is not yet clear. It appears that emotion may be understood to consist of two aspects: "hot" and "cold", or perhaps "conscious" and "structural". Perhaps the structural aspect of emotion may exist independently of the conscious, hot aspect; but in practice the two seem to usually occur together.

12
The Master Network

12.0 The Structure of Intelligence

The ideas of the previous chapters fit together into a coherent, symbiotic unit: the master network. The master network is neither a network of physical entities nor a simple, clever algorithm. It is rather a vast, self-organizing network of self-organizing programs, continually updating and restructuring each other. In previous chapters we have discussed particular components of this network; but the whole is much more than the sum of the parts. None of the components can be fully understood in isolation.

A self-organizing network of programs does not lend itself well to description in a linear medium such as prose. Figure 6 is an attempt to give a schematic diagram of the synergetic structure of the whole. But, unfortunately, there seems to be no way to summarize the all-important details in a picture. In Appendix 1, lacking a more elegant approach, I have given a systematic inventory of the structures and processes involved in the master network: optimization, parameter adaptation, induction, analogy, deduction, the structurally associative memory, the perceptual hierarchy, the motor hierarchy, consciousness, and emotion.

These component structures and processes cannot be arranged in a linear or treelike structure; they are fundamentally interdependent, fundamentally a network. At first glance it might appear that the master network is impossible, since it contains so many circular dependencies: process A depends on process B, which depends on process C, which depends on process A. But, as indicated in the previous chapters, each process can be executed independently — just not with maximal effectiveness. Each process must do some proportion of its work according to crude, isolated methods — but this proportion may be reduced to a small amount.

Figure 6 and Appendix 2 provide the background necessary for my central hypothesis: that the master network is both necessary and sufficient for intelligence.

As in Chapter 4, let us define **general intelligence** as the average of L-intelligence, S-intelligence, and R.S.-intelligence, without specifying exactly what

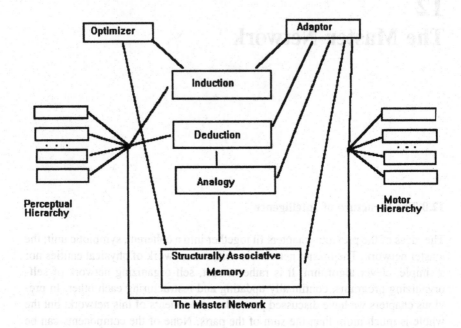

Figure 6.

sort of average is involved. Then, using the ideas of Chapters 4 and 5, one may easily prove the following:

Theorem 12.1: For any computable set of patterns C, and any degree D of general intelligence, there is some master network which has general intelligence D relative to C.

However, it is also clear from Chapter 5 that most of the master network is not essential for this result. In particular, we have:

Theorem 12.2: Theorem 12.1 holds even if the perceptual and motor control hierarchies only have one level each, and even if the global optimizer works by the Monte Carlo method.

In fact, even this assumes too much. The essential core of the master network consists the induction processor, the global optimizer and the parameter adaptor. One may show

Theorem 12.3: Theorem 12.1 holds even if all perception, induction and parameter adaptation are executed by Monte Carlo optimization, and the analogy and deduction processors do not exist.

FEASIBLE INTELLIGENCE

The problem is that Theorem 12.1 and its offshoots do not say **how large** a master network needs to be in order to attain a given degree of intelligence. This is absolutely crucial. As discussed in Chapter 11, it is not physically possible to build a Turing machine containing arbitrarily many components and also working reasonably fast. But it is also not possible to build a **quantum** computer containing arbitrarily many components and also working reasonably fast. Quantum computers can be made smaller and more compact than classical Turing machines, but Planck's constant would appear to give a minimum limit to the size of any useful quantum computer component. With this in mind, I make the following hypothesis:

> **Hypothesis 12.1**: Intelligent computers satisfying the restrictions imposed by Theorem 12.3, or even Theorem 12.2, are **physically impossible** if C is, say, the set of all N'th order Boolean functions (N is a very large number, say a billion or a trillion).

This is not a psychological hypothesis, but it has far-reaching psychological consequences, especially when coupled with the hypotheses made at the end of Chapter 4, which may be roughly paraphrased as

> **Hypothesis 12.2**: Every generally intelligent system, relative to the C mentioned in the Hypothesis 12.2, contains a master network as a significant part of its structure.

Taken together, these two hypotheses imply that **every intelligent system** contains **every component** of the master network.

In conclusion, I think it is worth getting even more specific:

> **Hypothesis 12.3**: Intelligent computers (relative to the C mentioned in Hypothesis 12.2) in which a high proportion of the work of each component of the master network is done independently of the other components — are physically impossible.

All this does not imply that every intelligent system — or **any** intelligent system — contains physically distinct modules corresponding to "induction processor", "structurally associative memory," and so on. The theorems imply that the master network is a **sufficient** structure for intelligence. And the hypotheses imply that the master network a **necessary** part of the structure of intelligence. But we must not forget the definition of structure. All that is being claimed is that the master network is a significant **pattern** in every intelligent system.

According to the definition given in Chapter 4, this means that the master network is a part of every mind. And, referring back to the definition of pattern, this means nothing more or less than the following: **representing (looking at)** an intelligent system in terms of the master network always yields a significant amount of simplification; and one obtains more simplification by using the entire master network than by using only part.

PHILOSOPHY OR SCIENCE?

To demonstrate or refute these hypotheses will require not only new mathematics but also new science. It is clear that, according to the criterion of falsification, the hypotheses are indeed scientific. For instance, Hypothesis 12.2 could be tested as follows:

1. Prove that system X is intelligent by testing its ability to optimize a variety of complex functions in a variety of structurally sensitive environments.
2. Write the physical equations governing X, mathematically determine the set of all patterns in X, and determine whether the master network is a significant part of this set.

We cannot do this experiment now. We must wait until someone constructs an apparently intelligent machine, or until neuroscientists are able to derive the overall structure of the brain from the microscopic equations. But, similarly, no one is going to make a direct test of the Big Bang theory of cosmology or the theory of evolution by natural selection, at least not any time soon. Sometimes, in science, we must rely on indirect evidence.

The theory of natural selection is much simpler than the theory of the master network, so indirect evidence is relatively easy to find. The Big Bang theory is a slightly better analogy: it is not at all simple or direct. But the theories of differential geometry, functional analysis, differential equations and so forth permit us to deduce a wide variety of indirect consequences of the original hypothesis. In principle, it should be possible to do something similar for the theory of the master network. However, the master network involves a very different sort of mathematics — theoretical computer science, algorithmic information theory, the theory of multiextremal optimization, etc. These are very young fields and it will undoubtedly be difficult to use them to derive nontrivial consequences of the theory of the master network.

12.1 Design for a Thinking Machine

A theory of mind and a theory of brain are two very different things. I have sketched an abstract Platonic structure, the master network, and claimed that the structure of every intelligent entity must contain a component approximating this structure. But it would be folly to deny that different entities may approximate this structure in very different ways.

A general study of the emergence of minds from physical systems would require a general theory of networks of programs. But of course no such theory presently exists (see Appendix 2 for a summary of certain preliminary results in the field). Thus we cannot give a comprehensive answer to the question: what sorts of machines, if constructed, would be able to think? In talking about thinking machines, we will have to be contented with very specialized considerations, improvising on the themes of computer science and neuroscience.

Most of the workings of the brain are still rather obscure. We have an excellent understanding of the workings of individual brain cells (Hille, 1984); and we have long known which regions of the brain concentrate on which functions. What is lacking, however, is a plausible theory of the intermediate scale. The study of the visual cortex, reviewed above, has brought us a great deal closer to this goal. But even here there is no plausible theory relating thoughts, feelings and "mind's-eye" pictures to the microscopic details of the brain.

In Chapters 6 and 10, lacking a truly effective theory of intermediate-level brain structure, we have made use of what I consider to be the next best thing: Edelman's "Neural Darwinism," a slightly speculative but impressively detailed model of low-to-intermediate-scale brain structure. I suspect that Neural Darwinism is incapable of explaining the higher levels of cognition and memory; but, be that as it may, the theory is nonetheless essential. As suggested in Chapters 6 and 10, it indicates how one might go about establishing a nontrivial connection between brain and mind. And furthermore, it leads to several interesting ideas as to how, given sufficient technology, one might go about constructing an intelligent machine. In closing, let us sketch one of these ideas.

OMPs, AMPs, and nAMPs

In what follows I will speculate as to what global neural structure **might** conceivably look like. This should not be considered a theory of the brain but a **design** for a brain, or rather a sketch of such a design — an indication of how one might draw blueprints for a thinking machine, based loosely on both the idea of the master network and the theory of Neural Darwinism. The "zero level" of this design consists of relatively sophisticated "optimization/memory processors" or OMPS, each of which stores one function or a fairly small set of related functions, and each of which has the capacity to solve optimization problems over the space of discrete functions — e.g. to search for patterns in an input — using the functions which it stores as initial guesses or "models". For instance, the multi-leveled "Neural Darwinist" network of maps described at the end of Chapter 10 could serve as an OMP. It is biologically plausible that the brain is composed of a network of such networks, interconnected in a highly structured manner.

Next, define an "analogy-memory processor," an AMP, as a processor which searches for patterns in its input by selecting the most appropriate — **by induction/analogy/deduction** — from among an assigned pool of OMPs and setting them to work on it. Each AMP is associated with a certain specific subset of OMPs; and each AMP must contain within it procedures for general deductive, inductive and analogical reasoning, or reasonable approximations thereof. Also, each AMP must be given the power to reorganize its assigned pool of OMPs, so as to form a structurally associative memory. There should be a large amount of duplication among the OMP pools of various AMPs.

And similarly, define a "second-level analogy-memory processor," a 2AMP, as a processor which assigns to a given input the AMP which it determines — by induction/analogy/deduction — will be most effective at recognizing patterns in it. Define a 3AMP, 4AMP, etc., analogously. Assume that each nAMP (n>1) refers to and has the power to reorganize into rough structural associativity a certain pool of (n-1)AMPS.

Assume also that each nAMP, n=2,..., can cause the (n-1)AMPs which it uses frequently to be "replicated" somehow, so that it can use them as often as necessary. And assume that each AMP can do the same with OMPs. Physically speaking, perhaps the required (n-1)AMPs or OMPs could be put in the place of other (n-1)AMPs or OMPs which are almost never used.

A high-level nAMP, then, is a sort of fractal network of networks of networks of networks... of networks. It is, essentially, an additional control structure imposed upon the Neural Darwinist network of maps. I suspect that the Neural Darwinist network of maps, though basically an accurate model, is inadequately structured — and that, in order to be truly effective, it needs to be "steered" by external processes.

I will venture the hypothesis that, if one built a nAMP with, say, 15 levels and roughly the size and connectivity of the human brain — and equipped it with programs embodying a small subset of those special techniques that are already standard in AI — it would be able to learn in roughly the same way as a human infant. All the most important aspects of the master network are implicitly or explicitly present in the nAMP: induction, pattern recognition, analogy, deduction structurally associative memory, and the perception and motor control hierarchies.

In conclusion: the nAMP, whatever its shortcomings, is an example of a design for an intelligent machine which is neither AI-style nor neural-network-style. It is neither an ordinary program nor an unstructured assemblage of programs; nor a self-organizing network of neurons or neural clusters without coherent global structure. It is a program, and a network of physical entities — but more importantly it is a network of networks of networks ... of networks of programs; a network of networks of networks... of networks of neural clusters. In this context it seems appropriate to repeat Hebb's words, quoted above: "it is... on a class of theory that I recommend you to put your money, rather than any specific formulation that now exists." The details of the nAMP are not essential. The point is that, somehow, the dynamics of neurons and synapses must intersect with the abstract logic of pattern. And the place to look for this intersection is in the behavior of extremely complex networks of interacting programs.

Appendix 1
Components of the Master Network

Structure: Perceptual Hierarchy

Internal Structure: Composed of a hierarchy of levels, each level containing a number of processors which may interact with each other and with processors on lower or higher levels.

Internal Processes: Each processor obtains input from processors on lower levels, and sends output to processors operating on higher levels. Each processor operates by guessing the most likely, simplest "reality" underlying its input, using Bayes' rule and probably, on lower levels, the maximum entropy principle.

The range of possibilities is given by hard-wiring and/or induction and/or deduction and/or analogy; the a priori background distribution is given by hard-wiring and/or induction and/or deduction and/or analogy; and the properties of potential realities are given by hard-wiring and/or induction and/or deduction and/or analogy. As one goes higher and higher up the hierarchy, induction, analogy and deduction are relied upon more heavily, and the estimation sticks closer and closer to the background distribution. And as induction, analogy and deduction are relied upon more heavily, the processing becomes slower and slower.

Information is passed from the top down when a processor tells one of the processors that gives it input what sort of things it should look for. This overall regulation operates according to the multilevel optimization methodology.

Dependencies: Induction processor, deduction processor, analogy processor.

Functions: Supplies the induction processor and the parameter adaptor with the pattern recognition they require.

Structure: Motor Control Hierarchy

Internal Structures: Composed of a hierarchy of levels, each level containing a number of processors which may interact with each other and with processors on lower or higher levels.

Internal Processes: Each processor gives processors on lower levels **goals**, and each processor refers to the parameter adaptor for information on how to achieve these goals. The success of each processor is continually relayed to the parameter adaptor.

Dependencies: Parameter adaptor.

Functions: Directly controls the action of the system; the effect of mind on body and therefore world.

Structure: Structurally Associative (Long-term) Memory

Internal Structures: A network of processors, each one containing a certain pattern, which is continually reorganizing itself to approximate the structure of a network of emergence (i.e. of a network in which X and Y are stored near all functions which are patterns emergent between X and Y). Any particular pattern may be stored in a number of different places. Along with each pattern is stored the parameters by which the global optimizer can best recognize patterns in it.

Internal Processes: Reorganization must follow some special-case optimization algorithm. In order for structurally associative organization to be possible, it must be known what functions are patterns in what functions.

Dependencies: Perceptual hierarchy (for pattern recognition).

Functions: Analogy could not exist without it.

Structure: Analogy Processor

Internal Structures: Must contain processors capable of applying the general analogy algorithm to many functions at once.

Internal Processes: Searches for patterns according to general analogy algorithm, which requires numerous searches through structurally associative memory and also, in the case of modeling analogy, special-case global optimization in order to invert certain functions. May determine which types of analogy to use according to analogy.

Dependencies: Structurally associative memory, global optimizer.

Functions: Guides the perceptual hierarchy in its pattern recognition; guides the process of deduction.

Structure: Induction Processor

Internal Structures/Processes: Must be able to continually take in large sets of patterns and operate on them according to rapid, specialized approximation algorithms so as to construct a consistent model of the world. Parameters of these algorithms may be modified by parameter adaptor.

Dependencies: Perceptual hierarchy (for the patterns it takes as input), parameter adaptor.

Functions: Aids the perceptual hierarchy in its recognition of patterns.

Structure: Deduction Processor

Internal Structures/Processes: Must be able to rapidly carry out chains of deductions according to hard-wired or otherwise specified rules. Which chains of deductions are executed is determined by an optimization routine whose initial guesses are determined by analogy. Which sets of rules are used may also be determined, to some extent, by parameter adaptation.

Dependencies: Analogy processor, global optimizer, parameter adaptor.

Functions: Guides the perceptual hierarchy.

Structure: Parameter Adaptor

Internal Structures/Processes: Executes a specific set of optimization problems, some involving pattern recognition, induction and analogy.

Dependencies: Induction processor, analogy processor, perceptual hierarchy global optimizer.

Functions: Guides the motor control hierarchy and, to a lesser extent, the deduction, induction and analogy processors. Supplies the structurally associative memory with information.

Structure: Global Optimizer

Internal Structures/Processes: Minimizes and maximizes functions according to some widely applicable strategy. Adapts the particulars of its strategy to the nature of the function in question.

Dependencies: Parameter adaptor.

Functions: Aids the parameter adaptor, the analogy processor and the deduction processor.

Process: Consciousness

Related Structures: Resides, apparently, fairly high up on the perceptual and motor control hierarchies; ventures into all regions of the mind but never too far from there (e.g. never too deeply into the structurally associative memory).

Functions: According to the quantum theory of consciousness, consciousness has no deterministic effect on mental function; it is rather the means by which the mind participates in the creation of the world.

Phenomenon: Emotion

Related Structures: It is hypothesized that emotion occurs when a processor in the motor control hierarchy which notably fails to reach its goal is also a part of consciousness.

Functions: Emotion, like consciousness, appears to serve no deterministic role in mental function. It is, however, a necessary consequence of significant mental change in any conscious system.

Appendix 2
Automata Networks

The master network is a large, intricately interconnected network of programs. In this context, it is interesting to ask: what, in general, is known about the behavior of large interconnected networks of programs? The most important work in this area is Stuart Kauffmann's (1988) theory of random automata networks, which was initiated in the late 1960's. Kauffmann's method is very simple: construct networks of N random Boolean automata (i.e., programs), connect them to each other, and let them run for thousands of iterations. His results, however, are striking. Let K denote the number of other automata to which each automaton is connected.

One of Kauffman's first questions was: what is the long-term dynamical behavior of the networks? Since the networks are finite, for any given initial condition each one must eventually converge to a stable state or lock into a repetitive "limit cycle" (say, from state 1 to state 2 to state 3, and then back to state 1). The question is, how many different limit cycles are there, and how many distinct states are involved in each cycle? Where k=1, the networks operate in a largely independent, well-understood manner. Where k=N, the case of complete connectivity, the problem is also analytically soluble. For intermediate k, there is as yet no mathematical answer to Kauffmann's question — but in every case, the numerical results are extremely clear. The total number of attractors (steady states or limit cycles) is roughly **proportional** to the number of automata in the network. But the average period of a cycle is exponential in the number of automata. Thus an arbitrary automata network, supplied an arbitrary initial condition, will almost certainly display "pseudo-chaotic" behavior — it will eventually lock into a cycle of states that is so long as not to be humanly recognizable as a cycle.

This tells us little about the behavior of highly structured automata networks like the master network. But Kauffmann's more recent work (1988) tells us a bit more. He has set up a network of automata according to a certain scheme called the "NK model". Each automaton seeks to optimize its state according to certain criteria, and the criteria used by each automaton depend in a certain way upon the states of certain other automata. His model is very specific, but philosophically, it represents a very common situation: a network of programs each optimizing some function of an environment which is continually changed by the action of each program. His network is much simpler than the master network, but there are certain qualitative similarities: it is much closer to the master network than is a random automata network.

Kauffman's main result regarding the NK model is that the interdependence of criteria makes a tremendous qualitative difference. If the criteria for each optimizing automaton were independent of the other automata, then as the optimization problems became more and more complex, the approximate optima found would be further and further from the true optimum. And this is true in the interdependent case, if the number of other automata to which each automaton is connected is increased proportionally to the complexity the problem. But if the complexity of the problem is increased while the connectivity is kept much smaller, the network tends to settle into a state in which each automaton can solve its problem relatively well.

I am being vague about the exact nature of Kauffmann's NK model because it is not relevant here. The model is tied to evolutionary biology rather than psychology or neuroscience. But similar results have been obtained from models of the immune system (Kauffmann et al, 1985); and it is only a matter of time until someone attempts a similar model of the simpler aspects of neurodynamics. What interests us here is Kauffman's general conclusion:

> [I]t is a reasonable bet that low connectivity... is a sufficient and perhaps necessary feature in complex systems which must be perfected in the face of conflicting constraints... which are themselves complex adapting entities with many parts and processes which must mesh well to meet their external worlds.... [L]ow connectivity may be a critical feature of **coadaptation** of entities....

The mind and brain are clearly systems of the sort Kauffmann describes.

The nAMP meets the criterion of low connectivity, because its structure is based on hierarchy, and inherently low-connectivity inter-neural-cluster connections. And, in general, the master network meets the criterion of low connectivity: in the STRAM each memory item is directly connected to only a small proportion of others; in the perceptual and motor hierarchies each processor is connected to only a few processors on the same or immediately adjacent levels; etc.

Admittedly, the observation that the master network has low connectivity is not particularly exciting or profound. If it did not have low connectivity, it could not feasibly be constructed. But it is enchanting to think that it might somehow be possible to use the general theory of automata networks to deduce more interesting properties of the network of programs that is the brain, or the network of programs that is the mind. This would be the exact opposite of the psychological approach to mind. Instead of explaining particular behaviors with highly specific ad hoc theories, one would be analyzing the overall structure and dynamics of intelligence from a perspective inclusive of all complex self-organizing systems: minds, brains, ecosystems, immune systems, bodies,....

Appendix 3
A Quick Review of Boolean Logic

Leibniz was probably the first person to make a serious attempt to analyze thought mathematically. But Leibniz's pioneering efforts in this direction never inspired much enthusiasm. The project never really got off the ground until George Boole published *Laws of Thought*. Boole, like Leibniz before him, had the idea of formulating a mathematical theory which does for ideas what ordinary algebra does for numbers. And, unaware that Leibniz had worked on the problem, he began by duplicating Leibniz's efforts.

One might think that an algebra of thought would have to be something dramatically new. But in fact what Leibniz and Boole independently conceived was a synthesis of numerical algebra and ordinary language. Anthropologically, one might observe that, having committed themselves to expressing thoughts in terms of sequences of ink marks, they turned immediately to the two best-developed systems of sequences of ink marks. They arrived at the concept of a "proposition."

PROPOSITIONS

A proposition is a simply a statement which is either true or false, and not both. For instance, it seems fairly clear that "George Boole wrote a book called "Laws of Thought" and "There is an Arab ruler who can play the bagpipes through his ear" are propositions. The first one is true and, as far as I know, the second is false. On the other hand, it also seems fairly clear that "Ione Skye is ten times prettier than Kim Basinger" and "Why are you reading this claptrap?" and "XXXXPPGttkeykeykey" are **not** propositions. The first is not really well-defined, and the second and third are not statements at all.

Strictly speaking, propositions are not sentences. A proposition is an abstraction. A sentence can **represent** a proposition. But two different sentences can represent the same proposition. For instance, "The U.S. is capitalist and Russia is socialist" represents the same proposition as "Russia is socialist and the U.S.

is capitalist." The two sentences are not word-for-word identical, but they are **equivalent** in the sense that if either one is true, then the other is true; and if either one is false, then the other is false.

One way to deal with this situation is to introduce the strange notion of **possible worlds**. That is: consider the set of **all** universes that might possibly exist. Then a proposition may be considered as a sort of cosmic labeling device which assigns to each possible universe either the label "true," the label "false," or the label "meaningless" — depending on whether, given the conditions of that universe, the proposition is true, false or meaningless. And it is clear that two statements which assign the same label to every universe correspond to the same proposition.

For example, to a universe in which the Bolshevik revolution failed and Russia became a democratic-capitalist constitutional monarchy like England, the proposition "The U.S. is capitalist and the Russia is socialist" would assign the label "false." In that universe, the proposition is false. To a universe in which a comet pulverized the earth in 10,000 B.C., the proposition "The U.S. is capitalist and Russia is socialist" would assign the label "meaningless" — in that universe, there is no such thing as the U.S. To our universe, of course, this proposition would assign the label "true". And it would also assign the label "true" to an infinity of alternate possible universes — for example, the universe which is exactly the same as ours except that the last word in this sentence is not "pomegranates."

There are certain propositions, such as "2+2=4," which we would like to say are true in **any** possible world. Philosophers refer to propositions of this sort as **analytic** propositions. More poetically, Saint Augustine called them "eternal verities." Those propositions which are true in some possible worlds but false in others are called **contingent** propositions. This distinction is interesting from a metaphysical point of view, and it is particularly relevant to the theory of mind if one takes a Nietzschean point of view. According to Nietzsche, true propositions are true only in that they are so extremely useful we cannot imagine giving them up. In this interpretation an analytic proposition is one which is useful to an intelligent entity in **any** environment whatsoever.

The possible worlds approach obviously rests upon shaky ground: after all, how do we decide which worlds are **possible**? We only live in one world, all the rest are just conjecture. However, it is indisputable that each of us makes his way through the world by continually speculating as to how the future might turn out, and also how the past might have been. In each of our minds, there is an array of possible worlds. It turns out that the notion of possible worlds also arises in the analysis of consciousness.

BOOLEAN ALGEBRA

The fundamental operations of numerical algebra are addition and multiplication. Correspondingly, Boole suggested, the fundamental operations of mental algebra must be "or" and "and" (disjunction and conjunction). In order to write these mental operations, Boole borrowed the notation of numerical algebra. For instance, if we set

X   =   "George Boole wrote a book called *Laws of Thought*"

and

Y   =   "There is an Arab nation whose ruler can play the bagpipes through his ear,"

then

X+Y = "Either George Boole wrote a book called *Laws of Thought*, or there is an Arab nation whose ruler can play the bagpipes through his ear."

and

XY =   "George Boole wrote a book called *Laws of Thought*, and there is an Arab nation whose ruler can play the bagpipes through his ear."

That is, in Boole's notation, "X and Y" is written XY, and "X or Y" is written X+Y.

Now, addition and multiplication are only two of the four operations of numerical algebra. What about subtraction and division? It turns out that there is no real counterpart to division in the realm of propositions. But subtraction is a different matter. Subtraction, Boole observed, is analogous to negation. In his scheme, "minus" in the realm of numbers corresponded to "not" in the realm of thought. So, for example, where X is as defined above,

-X   =   "George Boole did not write a book called *Laws of Thought*"

and

-Y   =   "There is not an Arab nation whose ruler can play the bagpipes through his ear."

In numerical algebra, we have the rule X+0=X, for any X whatsoever. In the Boolean scheme, this rule can be translated into the algebra of thought by using the symbol "0" to denote the "empty proposition," the proposition which says nothing whatsoever. In symbols: 0=" ". The statement X+0 then means "either X, or nothing whatsoever." And since "either X, or nothing whatsoever" is true whenever X is true, and false whenever X is false, it is equivalent to X. By similar reasoning, it follows that 0xX=0.

Boolean algebra has its own set of rules, similar but not equivalent to the rules of numerical algebra. For instance, in Boolean algebra $-X + -Y = - XY$. This is easy to see — all it means is that "either x is false or y is false" is the same as "not both x and y are true." But the same rule obviously does not hold for numerical algebra. The complete list is as follows, where 0 is the "zero element" (the proposition which says nothing) and 1 is the "unit element" (the proposition which contains all other propositions):

Commutative Laws:
   $X+Y=Y+X$, $XY=YX$

Distributive Laws:
   $X+(YZ)=(X+Y)(X+Z)$, $X(Y+Z)=XY+XZ$

Identity Laws:
   $X+0=0$, $1X=X$

Complement Laws:
   $A+(-A)=1$, $A(-A)=0$

These rules form an interesting and important mathematical structure. However, it seems rather unlikely that they are the "laws of thought", for three reasons.

For one thing, they govern only deduction, whereas (as will be emphasized in the pages to follow) induction and analogy are equally important to mental process. I think it is a mistake to assume, as is often done among computer scientists (Indurkhya, 1988), that induction and analogy may be understood as special cases of deduction.

Also, it is not at all clear that the mind actually deduces according to Boolean algebra. As pointed out in Chapter 8, there are serious contradictions between Boolean algebra and common sense logic. Contemporary logicians are seeking to remedy these with new axioms systems called "paraconsistent" and "relevance" logics, but the case is far from closed.

And, finally, it is not obvious that the **brain** gets along well with Boolean algebra. For instance, the distributive rule $X(Y+Z) = XY + XZ$ seems very straightforward: all it says is that "X and either Y or Z" is the same as "either X and Y or X and Z". However, quantum theory indicates that when X, Y and Z represent propositions about physical situations, this is not always true. This simple observation, first made by Birkhoff and von Neumann (1932) has given rise to an entire new field: quantum logic (Mittelstaedt, 1978).

LOGICAL PARADOXES

The first recorded logical paradox is that of Epiminides the Cretan, who proclaimed that "All Cretans are liars." If we believe him, then we should disbelieve him. But if we disbelieve him, then that is evidence that we should believe him.

Of course, this is a very rough paradox. After all, it could be that only Epiminides is a liar. What is generally referred to as Epiminides' Paradox is the refined version: "This sentence is false." Here there is no escape. If it is false, it is true; if it is true, it is false.

Berry's paradox is equally intriguing. What is the smallest number that cannot be described in English in one hundred characters or fewer? Whatever it is, is it not described by the phrase "the smallest number that cannot be described in English in one hundred characters or less"? This phrase is in English, and it uses fewer than one hundred characters. Therefore there is no number that cannot be described in English in one hundred characters or less. And yet this is not possible: there is an infinity of numbers, but only a finite number of English sentences of length less than one hundred.

And consider Russell's paradox. The barber in a certain town shaves all the residents except those who shave themselves. Who shaves the barber? In mathematical language: let R denote the set of all sets which do not contain themselves. Does R contain itself?

For centuries such conundrums were considered childish irrelevancies. But suddenly, around the turn of the century, they came to assume a tremendous importance for philosophers and mathematicians.

Mathematical logicians had succeeded in unifying all of mathematics into a small set of rules for manipulating a small set of symbols — into a simple "formal system". Actually there was not just one formal system, there were many varieties. None of them was quite as simple as Boolean algebra, but most of them were similar to it in many respects. Through the efforts of Peano, Frege, Bertrand Russell, Alfred North Whitehead and others, everything from geometry to calculus to number theory was expressed in terms of these elementary ideas. It appeared that mathematics had finally been made completely exact.

It is important to understand the full implications of this (apparent) achievement. First of all, it implied that every single mathematical statement could be expressed in this one formal language — every statement about triangles, quadratic equations, calculus, nine-dimensional spheres, abstract topologies, whatever. And secondly, it indicated that every single true mathematical statement — but no false mathematical statements — could be arrived at by an application of the rules of this system. Therefore, doing mathematics was reduced to dealing with the symbols and the rules of this system. Or so it was thought at the time.

But before long this tremendous leap, the result of decades of ingenious research, was plagued with two serious difficulties — both of which centered around simple conundrums like the Paradox of Epiminides. The second, and most damaging, of these difficulties was Godel's Theorem. The first was the Theory of Types.

The formalizations of mathematics that they had arrived at permitted certain forms of these paradoxes (Russell's paradox in particular) as valid mathematical statements. The problem was the following elementary fact: if a system of mathematical rules permits one of these paradoxes as valid, then for every X which is valid in it, -X is also valid.

To see this, assume for instance that Epiminides' Paradox is an admissible statement in a formal system S which incorporates Boolean algebra. Let G = "This sentence is false". Then G implies -G, and -G implies G. So if G is true in S, then so is -G. But given this fact, one can prove that any statement whatsoever is true. For take an arbitrary statement B. Then, since G is true, "G + B" is true. Hence "-G(G+B)" is true. But "-G(G+B)" implies B.

What good is a system of mathematics which cannot prove any statement true without also proving it false? Not much good, everyone realized — you have to get rid of the paradoxes. Russell and Whitehead came up with one way of doing so: the theory of types. This is not essentially a mathematical idea: it has more to do with the general theory of reference. The theory of types can be applied to any language, formal or informal. It is nothing more or less than a way of organizing a set of statements.

THE THEORY OF LOGICAL TYPES

In order to organize a set of statements according to the theory of types, one must first distinguish a set of "basic elements." These basic elements are supposed to be what the statements are fundamentally about. For instance, they might be numbers, or physical objects. These basic elements are assigned logical type 0.

Next, one must isolate a set of statements which are statements **about** the basic elements. These statements are assigned logical type 1. For instance, if the basic elements are physical objects, then statements like "the cat is on the mat" and "the log is in the bog" are of logical type 1.

Next, one isolates a set of statements which are statements about either basic elements or type 1 statements, or both. These are assigned logical type 2. For instance, "You were lying when you said the cat was on the mat" is of logical type 2 — it is a statement about a statement about physical objects.   Similarly, a statement of logical type 3 is a statement about entities of logical type 0,1 or 2. A statement of logical type 4 is a statement about entities of logical type 0, 1, 2 or 3. And so on. What's the point of all this? Well, where does a statement like "This statement is false" fit in? It is a statement about itself. There is no way to reduce it to a statement about basic elements, or a statement about statements about basic elements, or a statement about statements about statements about basic elements.... The point is that an statement of logical type n cannot refer to another statement of logical type n. For instance, it cannot refer to itself.

If one requires that all mathematical statements have a logical type, then the paradoxes disappear. They are no longer well-formed mathematical statements. There is a problem with this, however: it also rules out innocuous self-referential statements like "This sentence is true." It is not paradoxical to say "this sentence is true", and there is no real reason to forbid such utterances.

It may seem that there is no great harm in getting rid of statements like "this sentence is true." After all, what good did saying "this sentence is true" ever do anyone? But there is no need to pursue this point, because the recent work of Paul Aczel has rendered it moot. He has given a formalization of mathematics which permits nonparadoxical self-reference without permitting paradoxical self-reference.

In fact, it turns out that not only is there no need to rule out "this sentence is true" and other innocuous self-references — but there are some circumstances where "vicious" self-references like "this sentence is false" may come in handy. Certainly, we should forbid them to enter our mathematical deductions. But the work of G. Spencer-Brown (1970), Gregory Bateson (1980) and others has shown that, treated carefully, they can be useful.

The theory of types is indirectly relevant to the perceptual/motor hierarchy as described in Chapter 9, in which higher and higher levels may be understood to correspond to higher and higher logical types.

References

Agrawala, ed. (1977). *Machine Recognition of Patterns,* IEEE Press, NY

Amari, Shun-ichi (1983). "Field Theory of Self-Organizing Neural Nets," *IEEE Transactions on Systems, Man and Cybernetics* **13**, pp. 741–748

Aspect and Grangier (1985). "Tests of Bell's Inequality with Pairs of Low-Energy Correlated Photons," in *Symposium on the Foundations of Modern Physics: 50 Years of the EPR Gedankenexperiment,* ed. Lahti and Mittelstaedt, World Scientific Publishers, Singapore

Atlan, Henri (1988). "Measures of Biologically Meaningful Complexity," in *Measures of Complexity,* ed. Peliti et al., Springer-Verlag, NY

Bateson, Gregory (1980). *Mind and Nature: A Necessary Unity,* Bantam, NY

Bell, J.S. (1964). "On the EPR Paradox," *Physics* **I**, pp. 195–200

Bell, J.S. (1987). *Speakable and Unspeakable in Quantum Mechanics,* Cambridge University Press

Birkhoff and von Neumann (1936). *Annals of Mathematics* **37**, p. 823

Borzeszowski and Treder (1988). *The Meaning of Quantum Gravity,* Kluwer Academic, NY

Carnap (1959). *The Continuum of Inductive Methods*

Casti, John (1978). *Complexity, Connectivity and Catastrophe,* North-Holland, NY

Chaitin, Gregory (1974). "Information-Theoretic Computational Complexity," *IEEE Transactions on Information Theory* **IT-20**, pp. 10–15

Chaitin, Gregory (1978). "Toward a Mathematical Definition of Life," in *The Maximum Entropy Principle,* ed. Levine and Tribus, MIT Press, Cambridge, MA

Chaitin, Gregory (1987). *Algorithmic Information Theory,* Cambridge Press, NY

Changeaux, Jean-Pierre (1985). *Neuronal Man,* Oxford Press, NY

Cox (1962). *The Algebra of Probable Inference*

da Costa (1984). "On the Theory of Inconsistent Formal Systems," *Notre Dame Journal of Formal Logic,* pp. 497–510

Deutsch (1985)

deWitt, Bryce (1973). *The Many-Worlds Interpretation of Quantum Mechanics*, Princeton, NJ

Dreyfus (1979). *What Computers Can't Do*, Harper and Row, NY

Einstein, Albert (1931). *Relativity: The Special and General Theory*, Crown, NY

Einstein, Podolsky, and Rosen (1935). "Can the Quantum Mechanical Description of Reality Be Considered Complete?" *Physics Reviews* **47**, pp. 777–780

Etzione (1968). *The Active Society*, The Free Press, NY

Evans, R.B. (1979). "A New Approach for Deciding Upon Constraints in the Maximum Entropy Formalism," in *The Maximum Entropy Formalism*, ed. Levine and Tribus, MIT Press, Cambridge, MA

Franklin, Jon (1987). *Molecules of the Mind*, Dell, NY

Fukanaga, Keinosuke (1972). *Introduction to Statistical Pattern Recognition*, Academic Press, NY

Gittins, John C. (1989). *Multi-armed Bandit Allocation Indices*, Wiley, NY

Goertzel, Ben (1989). "A Multilevel Approach to Global Optimization," Ph.D. thesis, Temple University, Philadelphia, PA (To appear in *Journal of Optimization Theory and Applications*)

Goertzel, Ben (1990). "Information, Complexity and Meaning," talk delivered at Irvine AMA Conference, Nov.

Goertzel, Ben (1992). "Measuring Static Complexity," *Journal of Mathematics and Mathematical Sciences*

Goertzel, Ben (1992a). "Self-Organizing Evolution," *Journal of Social and Biological Structures* **15-1**

Goertzel, Ben (1992b). "Brain Function as Evolution," *Journal of Social and Biological Structures* **15-1**

Goertzel, Ben (1993). "Structural Complexity of Sequences, Images and Automata," in *Finite Fields, Coding Theory, and Advances in Communication and Computing*, ed. Shiue and Mullen, Marcel Dekker

Goertzel, Ben (1993a). *The Evolving Mind*, Gordon and Breach

Goertzel, Ben (1994). *Chaotic Logic*, Pergamon

Goswami, Amit (1990). "Consciousness in Quantum Physics and the Mind-Body Problem," *Journal of Mind and Behavior* **11**, 1

Grossberg (1987). *The Adaptive Brain*, North-Holland, NY

Gull, Steven (1989). "Developments in Maximum Entropy Data Analysis," in *Maximum Entropy and Bayesian Methods*, ed. Skilling, Kluwer Academic, Boston, MA

Hacking, Ian (1978). *The Emergence of Probability*, Oxford Press, NY

Hille, B. (1984). *Ionic Channels of Excitable Membranes*, Sinauer Associates, Sunderland M

Hochberg and McAlister (1953). *Journal of Experimental Psychology* **XLVI**, pp. 361–364

Honner, John (1987). *The Description of Nature*, Oxford Press, NY

Hubel, David (1988). *Eye, Brain and Vision*, Freeman, NY

Hume, David (1739). *A Treatise of Human Nature*

Hummel, Robert A., and Zucker, Steven W. (1983). "On the Foundations of Relaxation Labeling Processes." *IEEE TPAMI* 5, 3, p. 267

Indurkhya, Bipin (1988). *Analogical and Inductive Inference*, Springer-Verlag, NY

Jaynes, E.T. (1979). "Where Do We Stand on Maximum Entropy?" in *The Maximum Entropy Formalism*, ed. Levine and Tribus, MIT Press, Cambridge, MA

Jousselin, C. (1987). "Nouvelle arithmetique d'acces memoire," *Revue Annuelle LEP*

Kauffmann, Louis (1976). *Sign and Space*, privately distributed

Kohler, Wolfgang (1947). *Gestalt Psychology*, Meridian, NY

Kohonen, Teuvo (1984). *Self-Organization and Associative Memory*, Springer-Verlag, NY

Leibniz, Gottfried Wilhelm (1704/1898). *Leibniz--The Monadology and Other Essays*, Oxford University Press, Oxford

London and Bauer (1983). In *Quantum Theory and Measurement*, ed. Wheeler and Zurek, Princeton University Press, Princeton, NJ, pp. 217–259

Mandler (1985). *Cognitive Psychology: An Essay in Cognitive Science*, Erlbaum Press, Hillsdale, NJ

Marcel (1983a). "Conscious and Unconscious Perception: Experiments on Visual Masking and Word Recognition," *Cognitive Science* 15

Marcel (1983b). "Conscious and Unconscious Perception: An Approach to the Relation Between Phenomenal Experience and Perceptual Practice," *Cognitive Science* 15

Margeneau, H. (1984). *The Miracle of Existence*, Ox Bow Press, Woodbridge, CT

Maturana, Humberto (1981). In *Autopoeisis: A Theory of Living Organization*, ed. Zeleny, North-Holland, NY

McCulloch and Pitts (1943). "A Logical Calculus of the Ideas Immanent in Nervous Activity," *Bull. Math. Bio.* 5, pp. 115–133

Minsky, Marvin (1975). "A Framework for Representing Knowledge," in *The Psychology of Computer Vision*, ed. P.H. Winston, McGraw-Hill, NY

Mittelstaedt, Peter (1978). *Quantum Logic*, Dordrecht, Boston, MA

Nelson, J.J. (1985). "The Cellular Basis of Perception," in *Models of the Visual Cortex*, ed. Rose and Dobson, Wiley, NY

Nietszche, Friedrich (1968). *The Will to Power*, tr. Walter Kauffman, Random House, NY

Nietszche, Friedrich (1968a). "Beyond Good and Evil," in *Basic Writings of Nietszche*, tr. Walter Kauffman, Random House, NY, p. 216

Palm, Gunther (1980). "On Associative Memory." *Biological Cybernetics* 36, pp. 19–31

Peirce, Charles Sanders Santiago (1935). *Collected Works of Charles S. Peirce*, Vol. 5, Harvard University Press, Cambridge, MA, p. 139

Poetschke (1988). *Analogical and Inductive Inference*, Springer-Verlag, NY

Polya, G. (1981). *Mathematical Discovery*, Wiley, NY

Ruse and Dubose, eds. (1985). *Models of the Visual Cortex*, Wiley, NY

Segal et al. (1966). *The Influence of Culture on Visual Perception*, Indianapolis

Shore and Johnson (1980). "Axiomatic Derivation of the Principle of Maximum Entropy and the Principle of Minimum Cross-Entropy," *IEEE Transactions on Information Theory* **IT-26**, pp. 26–39, and **IT-29**, pp. 942–943

Simmel, Georg (1959). "The Face," in *Essays on Sociology, Philosophy, and Aesthetics by Georg Simmel, et al*, ed. Kurt H. Wolff, OSU Press, Columbus, OH

Simon, Herbert (1977). *Models of Thought*, Yale University Press, New Haven, CT

Skilling (1989). "Classic Maximum Entropy," in *Maximum Entropy and Bayesian Methods*, Kluwer Academic, Boston

Sommerhoff, Gerd (1990). *Life, Brain and Consciousness*, North-Holland, NY

Spencer-Brown, G. (1970). *Laws of Form*, Random House, NY

Spiller and Clark (1986). "SQUIDs: Macroscopic quantum objects," *New Scientist* **1537**, Dec. 4

Varela, Francisco (1979). *Principles of Biological Autonomy*, North-Holland, NY

von Foerster, Heinz (1981). *Observing Systems*, Intersystems, Seaside, CA

von Mises, Richard (1957). *Probability, Statistics, and Truth*, London

Whorf, Benjamin (1956). *Language, Thought and Reality*, MIT Press, Cambridge, MA

Wigner, E.P. (1962). *Symmetries and Reflections*, Indiana University Press, Bloomington, IN

Wilf, H.S. (1986). *Algorithms and Computation*, Prentice-Hall, Englewood Cliffs, NJ

Winkless and Browning (1976). *Robots on Your Doorstep*, Robotics Press, Bend, OR

Index

PROOF. The statement means that $p_k(\xi_1 \oplus \xi_2) = \sum_{i=0}^{k} p_i(\xi_1) \cup p_{k-i}(\xi_2)$. This follows from Lemma 4.2 by an argument similar to the one used for the Euler class of a Whitney sum.   □

EXERCISE 153. Use the results from this section to reprove that an oriented bundle which admits a nowhere-zero section has vanishing Euler class.

EXERCISE 154. A bundle ξ^n is said to be *stably trivial* if there exists a trivial bundle ϵ^k such that $\xi^n \oplus \epsilon^k = \epsilon^{n+k}$. For example, the tangent bundle of the sphere is stably trivial. Show that a stably trivial bundle has vanishing total Pontrjagin class.

5. Some Examples

In this section, we look at characteristic classes of vector bundles over low-dimensional spheres. It turns out that these classes determine the bundles up to "finite ambiguity." Since $H^k(S^n) = 0$ except when $k = 0$ or n, any characteristic class lives in $H^n(S^n)$; in fact, they can only exist when n is even, so if $n \leq 4$, we are left with bundles over S^2 and S^4. This leaves out only one bundle, for any bundle over S^3 is trivial, and there is exactly one nontrivial bundle over S^1.

By Theorem 15.2 in Chapter 1, the map

$$H^n(S^n) \longrightarrow \mathbb{R},$$

$$[\omega] \longmapsto \int_{S^n} \omega$$

is an isomorphism, so that the Euler class and appropriate Pontrjagin class may be identified with numbers. As noted earlier, these numbers are actually integers, and are called the *Euler and Pontrjagin numbers* of the bundle.

Recall that equivalence classes of rank k vector bundles over S^n are in bijective correspondence with $\pi_{n-1}(SO(k))$.

LEMMA 5.1. *Let α denote the Euler or Pontrjagin form corresponding to rank k bundles over S^n. Then the map*

$$\mathrm{Vect}_k(S^n) \cong \pi_{n-1}(SO(k)) \longrightarrow \mathbb{Z},$$

$$\xi \longmapsto \int_{S^n} \alpha(\xi)$$

is a homomorphism.

PROOF. Let $\tilde{G}_{k,l}$ be a classifying space for rank k bundles over S^n. If $f : S^n \to \tilde{G}_{k,l}$ is a classifying map for ξ, then ξ is equivalent to $f^*\tilde{\gamma}_{k,l}$, and by Theorem 4.1,

$$\int_{S^n} \alpha(\xi) = \int_{S^n} \alpha(f^*\tilde{\gamma}_{k,l}) = \int_{S^n} f^*\alpha(\tilde{\gamma}_{k,l}) = (\deg f) \int_{\tilde{G}_{k,l}} \alpha(\tilde{\gamma}_{k,l}).$$

But $\deg : \pi_n(\tilde{G}_{k,l}) \cong \pi_{n-1}(SO(k)) \to \mathbb{Z}$ is a homomorphism (cf. Examples and Remarks 2.1 in Chapter 3), and the statement follows.   □

5.1. Bundles over S^2. Rank k bundles over S^2 are classified by $\pi_1(SO(k))$. When $k = 2$, there exists, for each $n \in \mathbb{Z}$, precisely one bundle ξ_n with $C(\xi_n) = n$, according to the discussion in Section 5 of Chapter 3.

Letting R denote the curvature tensor of some Riemannian connection on ξ_n, the 2-form e_n on S^2 given by

$$e_n(p)(x,y) = \frac{1}{2\pi}\langle R(x,y)v, u\rangle$$

(for x, $y \in S_p^2$ and a positively oriented orthonormal basis u, v of $E(\xi_n)_p$) represents the Euler class of ξ_n by Examples and Remarks 3.1(i). In the case of the tangent bundle ξ_2 of the 2-sphere together with the canonical connection,

$$e_2(p)(x,y) = \frac{1}{2\pi}\langle R(x,y)y, x\rangle = \frac{1}{2\pi}$$

if x, y is a positively oriented orthonormal basis of S_p^2. Thus, e_2 equals $(1/2\pi)$ times the volume form ω of S^2, and the Euler number of ξ_2 is $\frac{1}{2\pi}\int_{S^2}\omega = 2$. By Lemma 5.1, the Euler number of ξ_n is n, and thus determines the bundle.

When $k > 2$, there is exactly one nontrivial rank k bundle over S^2; it cannot be distinguished from the trivial one by any characteristic class.

5.2. Bundles over S^4. Rank k bundles over S^4 are classified by $\pi_3(SO(k))$. When $k < 3$, any such bundle is trivial. For $k = 3$, there is one and only one rank 3 bundle ξ_n^3 over S^4 with $C(\xi_n^3) = n$ for each $n \in \mathbb{Z}$. We will shortly see that the rank 4 bundle $\epsilon^1 \oplus \xi_n^3$ has first Pontrjagin number $-4n$. Assuming this for the moment, we have

$$p(\epsilon^1 \oplus \xi_n^3) = p(\epsilon^1) \cup p(\xi_n^3) = p(\xi_n^3),$$

so that ξ_3^n is determined by its first Pontrjagin number $-4n$.

Rank 4 bundles over S^4 are classified by $\pi_3(SO(4)) \cong \pi_3(S^3) \oplus \pi_3(SO(3)) \cong \mathbb{Z} \oplus \mathbb{Z}$. Denote by $\xi_{m,n}^4$ the bundle corresponding to $(m[1_{S^n}], n[\rho]) \in \pi_3(S^3) \oplus \pi_3(SO(3))$, where $\rho : S^3 \to SO(3)$ is the covering homomorphism from Chapter 3. $\xi_{m,0}^4$ has structure group reducible to S^3, and $\xi_{0,n}^4$ to $SO(3)$. In fact, $\xi_{0,n}^4 \cong \epsilon^1 \oplus \xi_n^3$.

Insofar as the Pontrjagin class is concerned, we shall work in a slightly more general setting: Let M denote a 4-dimensional compact, oriented Riemannian manifold with volume form ω, and Hodge operator $\star : \Lambda_2^* M \to \Lambda_2^* M$, cf. Section 3. For $\alpha \in \Lambda_2^* M$, the identity $\alpha = \frac{1}{2}(\alpha + \star\alpha) + \frac{1}{2}(\alpha - \star\alpha)$ decomposes $\Lambda_2^* M$ into a direct sum $\Lambda^+ \oplus \Lambda^-$ of the $+1$ and -1 eigenspaces of $\star$. This decomposition is orthogonal, since $\star$ is norm-preserving:

$$\langle\star\alpha, \star\alpha\rangle\omega = \star\alpha \wedge \alpha = \alpha \wedge \star\alpha = \langle\alpha, \alpha\rangle\omega.$$

Furthermore, ω is parallel, so that $\star$ is a parallel section of the bundle $\text{End}(\Lambda_2^* M)$. There is a corresponding decomposition of the space $A_2(M) = A_2^+(M) \oplus A_2^-(M)$ of 2-forms on M. $\alpha \in A_2(M)$ is said be *self-dual* if $\star\alpha = \alpha$, *anti-self-dual* if $\star\alpha = -\alpha$.

For a vector bundle ξ over M, we have, as above, a splitting $A_2(M, \text{End}\,\xi) = A_2^+(M, \text{End}\,\xi) \oplus A_2^-(M, \text{End}\,\xi)$. The curvature tensor R of a connection on ξ decomposes as $R = R^+ + R^-$, and we say R is *self-dual* if $R = R^+$, *anti-self-dual* if $R = R^-$.

When the bundle ξ is Euclidean, the inner product on $\Lambda_k(M_p^*)$ extends to $\text{Hom}(\Lambda_k(M_p), E(\xi)_p) = \Lambda_k(M_p^*) \otimes E(\xi)_p$ by defining

$$\langle \alpha, \beta \rangle = \sum_{i_1 < \cdots < i_k} \langle \alpha(x_{i_1}, \ldots, x_{i_k}), \beta(x_{i_1}, \ldots, x_{i_k}) \rangle,$$

where x_i is an orthonormal basis of M_p. (When ξ is the trivial line bundle over M with the standard inner product on the $\mathbb{R}$-factor, this inner product coincides with the one on $\Lambda_k(M_p^*)$. In general, it induces a pointwise inner product on $A_k(M, \xi)$, which, when integrated over M, yields one on all of $A_k(M, \xi)$.)

In order to apply this to $R \in A_2(M, \mathfrak{o}(\xi))$, we introduce an inner product on $\mathfrak{o}(\xi)$ by defining

(5.1) $$\langle A, B \rangle = \frac{1}{2} \text{tr}(A^t \cdot B).$$

This inner product is in fact the one for which the equivalence

$$L : \Lambda_2(\xi) \longrightarrow \mathfrak{o}(\xi),$$

$$u \wedge v \longmapsto (w \mapsto \langle v, w \rangle u - \langle u, w \rangle v).$$

becomes a linear isometry, if $\Lambda_2(\xi)$ is endowed with the Euclidean metric induced by the one on ξ: It is straightforward to check that if u_i is an orthonormal basis of E_p, then $\{u_i \wedge u_j \mid i < j\}$ is one for $\Lambda_2(E_p)$.

PROPOSITION 5.1. *Let ξ be a Euclidean bundle over M^4 with curvature tensor R. The first Pontrjagin form of ξ is given by*

$$p_1 = \frac{1}{(2\pi)^2}(|R^+|^2 - |R^-|^2)\omega.$$

PROOF. Let R^{ij} denote as before the local 2-form on M given by $R^{ij}(p)(x, y)$ $\langle R(x, y)U_j(p), U_i(p) \rangle$, where $\{U_i\}$ is a local orthonormal basis of sections of the bundle. Given an orthonormal basis x_i of M_p, we have

$$|R|^2(p) = \sum_{k<l} \frac{1}{2} \text{tr} \, R^t(x_k, x_l) \cdot R(x_k, x_l) = \frac{1}{2} \sum_{i<j, k<l} R^{ij2}(x_k, x_l) = \sum_{i<j} |R^{ij}|^2(p).$$

In particular, $|R^\pm|^2 = \sum_{i<j} |R^{ij\pm}|^2$. Now, $R^{ij+} \wedge R^{ij+} = R^{ij+} \wedge \star R^{ij+} = |R^{ij+}|^2 \omega$, whereas $R^{ij+} \wedge R^{ij-} = -R^{ij+} \wedge \star R^{ij-} = -\langle R^{ij+}, R^{ij-} \rangle \omega = 0$. Similarly, $R^{ij-} \wedge R^{ij-} = -R^{ij-} \wedge \star R^{ij-} = -|R^{ij-}|^2 \omega$. Thus,

$$p_1 = \frac{1}{(2\pi)^2} \sum_{i<j} R^{ij} \wedge R^{ij} = \frac{1}{(2\pi)^2} \sum_{i<j} (|R^{ij+}|^2 - |R^{ij-}|^2)\omega$$

$$= \frac{1}{(2\pi)^2}(|R^+|^2 - |R^-|^2)\omega.$$

$\square$

Next, we derive an analogous formula for the Euler form of ξ, where ξ is now assumed to be oriented, of rank 4. The Hodge operator $\star_\xi : \Lambda_2(\xi) \to \Lambda_2(\xi)$ is a parallel section of $\text{End}(\Lambda_2(\xi))$, and induces an orthogonal, parallel splitting $\Lambda_2(\xi) = \Lambda_2^+(\xi) \oplus \Lambda_2^-(\xi)$ of Λ_2 into a direct sum of the ± 1-eigenspaces of $\star_\xi$. Given $p \in M$, $x, y \in M_p$, $R(x, y) \in \Lambda_2(E_p)$, and we write $R = R_+ + R_-$ for the corresponding decomposition of the curvature tensor. By (3.3) and arguing as above, the Euler form e of ξ is given by

$$e = \frac{1}{8\pi^2}\langle R_+ \wedge_\xi R_+, \omega_\xi\rangle + \langle R_- \wedge_\xi R_-, \omega_\xi\rangle.$$

Now,

$$R_\pm(x,y) \wedge_\xi R_\pm(z,w) = \pm\langle R_\pm(x,y), R_\pm(z,w)\rangle\omega_\xi,$$

so that

$$
\begin{aligned}
e(x_1,\ldots,x_4) &= \frac{1}{(8\pi^2)}\frac{1}{4}\sum_{\sigma\in P_4}(\operatorname{sgn}\sigma)\frac{1}{2}(\operatorname{tr} R_+^t(x_{\sigma(1)},x_{\sigma(2)})R_+(x_{\sigma(3)},x_{\sigma(4)}) \\
&\quad - \operatorname{tr} R_-^t(x_{\sigma(1)},x_{\sigma(2)})R_-^t(x_{\sigma(3)},x_{\sigma(4)})) \\
&= \frac{1}{8\pi^2}\frac{1}{4}\sum_{\sigma\in P_4}(\operatorname{sgn}\sigma)\sum_{i<j}(R_+^{ij}(x_{\sigma(1)},x_{\sigma(2)})R_+^{ij}(x_{\sigma(3)},x_{\sigma(4)}) \\
&\quad - R_-^{ij}(x_{\sigma(1)},x_{\sigma(2)})R_-^{ij}(x_{\sigma(3)},x_{\sigma(4)})) \\
&= \frac{1}{8\pi^2}\sum_{i<j}(R_+^{ij}\wedge R_+^{ij} - R_-^{ij}\wedge R_-^{ij})(x_1,\ldots,x_4).
\end{aligned}
$$

This may be rewritten as

$$
\begin{aligned}
e &= \frac{1}{8\pi^2}\sum_{i<j}R_+^{ij+}\wedge R_+^{ij+} + R_+^{ij-}\wedge R_+^{ij-} - R_-^{ij+}\wedge R_-^{ij+} - R_-^{ij-}\wedge R_-^{ij-} \\
&= \frac{1}{8\pi^2}\sum_{i<j}(|R_+^{ij+}|^2 - |R_+^{ij-}|^2 - |R_-^{ij+}|^2 + |R_-^{ij-}|^2)\omega.
\end{aligned}
$$

Summarizing, we have proved:

PROPOSITION 5.2. *Let ξ be an oriented rank 4 Euclidean bundle over M^4. The Euler form e of ξ is given by*

$$e = \frac{1}{8\pi^2}(|R_+^+|^2 - |R_+^-|^2 - |R_-^+|^2 + |R_-^-|^2)\omega.$$

It turns out that the rank 4 bundle ξ is determined by the two rank 3 bundles $\Lambda_2^\pm(\xi)$: Let $\phi : S^3 \times S^3 \to SO(4)$ denote the covering homomorphism given by $\phi(q_1,q_2)u = q_1 u q_2^{-1}$, $q_i \in S^3$, $u \in \mathbb{H} = \mathbb{R}^4$. Denote by S_+^3 (resp. S_-^3) the subgroup $\phi(S^3 \times 1)$ (resp. $\phi(1 \times S^3)$) of $SO(4)$. Since these are normal subgroups, Exercise 155 below implies that the bundles

$$P_\mp := P \times_{SO(4)} (SO(4)/S_\pm^3) = P/S_\pm^3 \longrightarrow M$$

associated to the orthonormal frame bundle $SO(\xi) = P \to M$ of ξ are in fact principal bundles over M with group $SO_\mp(3) = SO(4)/S_\pm^3$ isomorphic to $SO(3)$.

LEMMA 5.2. *$P_\pm \to M$ is the principal $SO(3)$-bundle of $\Lambda_2^\pm(\xi)$.*

PROOF. An orthonormal basis $e_1,\ldots,e_4$ of $\mathbb{R}^4$ induces an orthonormal basis $\frac{1}{\sqrt{2}}(e_1\wedge e_2 + e_3\wedge e_4), \frac{1}{\sqrt{2}}(e_1\wedge e_3 + e_4\wedge e_2), \frac{1}{\sqrt{2}}(e_1\wedge e_4 + e_2\wedge e_3)$ of $\Lambda_2^+(\mathbb{R}^4)$ and a corresponding one for $\Lambda_2^-(\mathbb{R}^4)$ (obtained by changing the sign of the second term in each basis element of Λ^+). Any $g \in SO(4)$ extends to a linear isometry (also denoted by) $g : \Lambda_2(\mathbb{R}^4) \to \Lambda^2(\mathbb{R}^4)$, by setting $g(u\wedge v) := gu \wedge gv$

and extending linearly. This action leaves $\Lambda_2^{\pm}$ invariant since $(ge_1, \ldots, ge_4)$ is positively oriented whenever $(e_1, \ldots, e_4)$ is. Given $q \in S^3$,

$$(1 \wedge i + j \wedge k)q = q \wedge iq + jq \wedge kq = 1 \wedge i + j \wedge k,$$

and the same is true for the other basis elements of Λ_2^+. Thus, S_-^3 is the kernel of the representation $SO(4) \to SO(\Lambda_2^+\mathbb{R}^4)$, and similarly, S_+^3 is the kernel of $SO(4) \to SO(\Lambda_2^-\mathbb{R}^4)$; i.e., the special orthogonal group $SO(\Lambda_2^{\pm}\mathbb{R}^4)$ is $SO_{\pm}(3)$. Since the map $P_{\pm} \to SO(\Lambda_2^{\pm}\xi)$ which takes $bS_{\mp}^3$ (where $b : \mathbb{R}^4 \to E_p$ is a linear isometry) to the orthonormal basis $\frac{1}{\sqrt{2}}b(e_1 \wedge e_2 \pm e_3 \wedge e_4)$, $\frac{1}{\sqrt{2}}b(e_1 \wedge e_3 \pm e_4 \wedge e_2)$, $\frac{1}{\sqrt{2}}b(e_1 \wedge e_4 \pm e_2 \wedge e_3)$ of $\Lambda_2^{\pm}(E_p)$ is $SO_{\pm}(3)$-equivariant, it is an equivalence by Theorem 3.1 in Chapter 2. $\square$

Our next objective is to relate the first Pontrjagin numbers $p_{\pm}$ of $\Lambda_2^{\pm}(\xi)$ to the Euler and first Pontrjagin numbers of ξ. Recall that if ∇ is a covariant derivative operator on ξ, then the one induced on $\Lambda_2(\xi)$ is given by

$$\tilde{\nabla}_x(U_1 \wedge U_2) = (\nabla_x U_1) \wedge U_2(p) + U_1(p) \wedge (\nabla_x U_2), \quad p \in M, \quad x \in M_p, \quad U_i \in \Gamma\xi.$$

This implies that the corresponding curvature tensor $\tilde{R}$ of $\Lambda_2(\xi)$ is related to the one on ξ by

$$\tilde{R}(x,y)(u_1 \wedge u_2) = (R(x,y)u_1) \wedge u_2 + u_1 \wedge (R(x,y)u_2).$$

The equivalence $L : \Lambda_2(\xi) \to \mathfrak{o}(\xi)$ induces a Lie algebra structure on each fiber of $\Lambda_2(\xi)$, see also Exercise 156 below; the corresponding Lie bracket is the one used in the following:

PROPOSITION 5.3. *The subbundles $\Lambda_2^{\pm}(\xi)$ are parallel under the induced connection; i.e., $\tilde{R} = \tilde{R}_+ + \tilde{R}_-$, with $\tilde{R}_{\pm} \in A_2(M, \operatorname{End}\Lambda_2^{\pm}(\xi))$. Given $x, y \in M_p$, and $\alpha, \beta \in \Lambda_2^{\pm}(E_p)$,*

$$\langle \tilde{R}(x,y)\alpha, \beta \rangle = \langle \tilde{R}_{\pm}(x,y)\alpha, \beta \rangle = \langle R_{\pm}(x,y), [\alpha, \beta] \rangle,$$

where $R(x,y) = R_+(x,y) + R_-(x,y) \in \Lambda_2^+(E_p) \oplus \Lambda_2^-(E_p)$.

PROOF. By Exercise 157, $\tilde{R}(x,y)\alpha = [R(x,y), \alpha]$. Since $\Lambda_2(E_p)$ is a direct sum of the ideals $\Lambda_2^{\pm}(E_p)$, the first statement is clear. The inner product on $\mathfrak{o}(E_p) = \Lambda_2(E_p)$ is Ad-invariant, so that ad is skew-adjoint. Thus,

$$\langle \tilde{R}_{\pm}(x,y)\alpha, \beta \rangle = \langle [R_{\pm}(x,y), \alpha], \beta \rangle = -\langle \operatorname{ad}_\alpha R_{\pm}(x,y), \beta \rangle = \langle R_{\pm}(x,y), \operatorname{ad}_\alpha \beta \rangle$$
$$= \langle R_{\pm}(x,y), [\alpha, \beta] \rangle.$$

$\square$

PROPOSITION 5.4. *Let $p_{\pm}$, p_1 denote the first Pontrjagin forms of $\Lambda_2^{\pm}(\xi)$, ξ, and e the Euler form of ξ. Then*

(1) $p_+ = \frac{2}{(2\pi)^2}(|R_+^+|^2 - |R_+^-|^2)\omega$, $\quad p_- = \frac{2}{(2\pi)^2}(|R_-^+|^2 - |R_-^-|^2)\omega$; *and*

(2) $2p_1 = p_+ + p_-$, $\quad 4e = p_+ - p_-$.

PROOF. Consider a positively oriented orthonormal basis $u_1, \ldots, u_4$ of E_q, and denote by $I^{\pm}$, $J^{\pm}$, $K^{\pm}$ the induced orthonormal bases of $\Lambda_2^{\pm}(E_q)$; i.e.,

$I^{\pm} = (1/\sqrt{2})(u_1 \wedge u_2 \pm u_3 \wedge u_4)$, etc. The first Pontrjagin form of $\Lambda_2^+(\xi)$ is given at q by

$$\frac{1}{(2\pi)^2}(\tilde{R}_+^{IJ} \wedge \tilde{R}_+^{IJ} + \tilde{R}_+^{JK} \wedge \tilde{R}_+^{JK} + \tilde{R}_+^{IK} \wedge \tilde{R}_+^{IK}),$$

where we have omitted the superscripts in I, J, K for simplicity of notation. By Proposition 5.3,

$$\tilde{R}_+^{IJ}(x,y) = \langle R_+(x,y), [J,I]\rangle = -\sqrt{2}\langle R_+(x,y), K\rangle,$$

and similarly, $\tilde{R}_+^{JK}(x,y) = -\sqrt{2}\langle R_+(x,y), I\rangle$, $\tilde{R}_+^{IK}(x,y) = \sqrt{2}\langle R_+(x,y), J\rangle$. Thus,

$$p_+ = \frac{1}{(2\pi^2)}\frac{1}{4}\sum_{\sigma \in P_4}(\operatorname{sgn}\sigma)\sum_{\alpha \in \{I,J,K\}} 2\langle R_+(x_{\sigma(1)}, x_{\sigma(2)}), \alpha\rangle\langle R_+(x_{\sigma(3)}, x_{\sigma(4)}), \alpha\rangle$$

$$= \frac{1}{(2\pi^2)}\frac{1}{4}\sum_{\sigma \in P_4}(\operatorname{sgn}\sigma)2\langle R_+(x_{\sigma(1)}, x_{\sigma(2)}), R_+(x_{\sigma(3)}, x_{\sigma(4)})\rangle.$$

Referring to Exercise 147, we see that p_+ equals two times the first Pontrjagin form of ξ with R replaced by R_+. Proposition 5.1 then implies part (1). Comparing the expressions in (1) with Propositions 5.1 and 5.2 yields (2).   □

Thus, for example, if the structure group of the bundle reduces to $SO(3)$, then $e = 0$, and $p_+ = p_-$. In order to see what happens when the group reduces to $S_{\pm}^3$, we use the following:

LEMMA 5.3. *A principal G-bundle $P \to M$ admits a reduction to a subgroup H of G iff the associated bundle $P \times_G (G/H) \to M$ with fiber G/H admits a cross-section.*

PROOF. Suppose $\pi_Q : Q \to M$ is an H-reduction of $\pi_P : P \to M$. Then there exists a fiber-preserving diffeomorphism $F : Q \times_H (G/H) \to P \times_G (G/H)$ between the associated bundles with fiber G/H. Define $s : M \to P \times_G (G/H)$ by $s(m) := F[q, H]$, where q is any point in $\pi_Q^{-1}(m)$. s is a well-defined section, since $[qh, H] = [q, H]$ for $h \in H$.

Conversely, let $s : M = P/G \to P/H = P \times_G (G/H)$ be a section; i.e., for $m \in M$, $s(m)$ equals the H-orbit of some $p \in \pi_P^{-1}(m)$. Define $Q := \cup_{m \in M} s(m) \subset P$. H acts on Q by restriction, and $\pi_Q : Q \to M$ is a principal H-bundle equivalent to $s^*(P \to P/H)$. It is also clearly a subbundle of π_P.   □

Notice that Lemma 5.3 generalizes Theorem 4.2 in Chapter 2: When $H = \{e\}$, the statement says that a principal bundle is trivial if and only if it admits a cross section.

COROLLARY 5.1. *An oriented rank 4 bundle ξ over S^4 admits a reduction to $S_{\pm}^3$ iff $\Lambda_2^{\pm}(\xi)$ is trivial; i.e., iff $p_1 = \pm 2e$.*

PROOF. The first assertion is an immediate consequence of the lemma, since in our case, H is normal in G, so that $P \times_G (G/H) \to M$ is principal by Exercise 155 below, and thus admits a section iff it is trivial. The second assertion follows from Proposition 5.4(2), together with the fact (which will be proved shortly) that a rank 3 bundle over S^4 is determined by its Pontrjagin class, so that $\Lambda_2^{\pm}(\xi)$ is trivial iff $p_{\pm} = 0$. ☐

The Hopf bundle, for example, is a principal S^3-bundle. As such, it is the reduction of a principal $SO(4)$-bundle to a subgroup isomorphic to S^3. In order to determine which subgroup, we use the following:

LEMMA 5.4. *If $Q \to M$ is a principal H-bundle, where H is a subgroup of G, then $Q \times_H G \to M$ is a principal G-bundle which reduces to the original H-bundle $Q \to M$.*

PROOF. There is a well-defined action by right multiplication of G on $Q \times_H G$, $[q, g]a := [q, ga]$ for $a \in G$, and the quotient is M. In order to exhibit a principal bundle atlas, consider a principal bundle chart $\phi : \pi_Q^{-1}(U) \to H$ of $\pi_Q : Q \to M$. By the proof of Theorem 2.1 in Chapter 2, the induced chart $\bar{\phi} : \pi^{-1}(U) \to G$ on the associated bundle $\pi : Q \times_H G \to M$ is given by $\bar{\phi} : \pi^{-1}(U) \to G$, where $\bar{\phi}[q, g] = \phi(q)g$. But then for $a \in G$,

$$\bar{\phi}([q, g]a) = \bar{\phi}[q, ga] = \phi(q)ga = (\bar{\phi}[q, g])a,$$

so that $\bar{\phi}$ is a principal bundle chart. Clearly, $Q = Q \times_H H \to M$ is a reduction of $Q \times_H G \to M$. ☐

Consider the subgroup S^3 of $SO(4)$. It acts on $\mathbb{H}$ *from the left* via $\mu :$ $S_-^3 \times \mathbb{H} \to \mathbb{H}$, where $\mu(q, u) = uq^{-1}$ for $q \in S_-^3$, $u \in \mathbb{H}$. Define a right action $\bar{\mu}$ of S_-^3 on $\mathbb{H}$ by $\bar{\mu}(u, q) = \mu(q^{-1}, u) = uq$. This action extends to $\mathbb{H} \times \mathbb{H}$, and its restriction to S^7 is the Hopf fibration. By the above lemma, the bundle $S^7 \times_{S^3} SO(4) \to S^4$, with S_-^3 acting on S^7 via $\bar{\mu}$, is a principal $SO(4)$-bundle which reduces to the Hopf fibration with group S_-^3. Corollary 5.1 then implies that the associated rank 4 bundle $\xi_{-1,0}$ has first Pontrjagin form $p_1 = -2e$.

On the other hand, the tangent bundle $\xi_{2,-1}$ of S^4 has Euler number 2 (see Exercise 151), and by Lemma 5.1, $e(\xi_{2,-1}) = e(\xi_{2,0}) + e(\xi_{0,-1}) = 2$. But $\xi_{0,-1}$ admits a nowhere-zero section, so that its Euler number vanishes, and $e(\xi_{2,0}) = 2$, or more generally, $e(\xi_{k,0}) = k$. For $k = -1$, this implies that the Hopf bundle has Pontrjagin number $p_1(\xi_{-1,0}) = -2e(\xi_{-1,0}) = 2$. More generally, $p_1(\xi_{k,0}) = -2k$. Finally, since $p_1(\xi_{2,-1}) = 0$, $p_1(\xi_{2,0}) = p_1(\xi_{0,1})$, and $p_1(\xi_{0,k}) = p_1(\xi_{2k,0}) = -4k$. Summarizing, we have:

THEOREM 5.1. *Oriented rank 4 bundles over S^4 are determined by their Pontrjagin and Euler numbers. Specifically, $p_1(\xi_{m,n}) = -2m - 4n$, $e(\xi_{m,n}) = m$.*

Bundles over S^n with rank larger than n are in general not classified by their characteristic numbers. This can clearly be seen in the cases $n = 2$ and $n = 4$ that we discussed: According to Proposition 5.1 in Chapter 3, such a bundle is equivalent to a Whitney sum of a rank n bundle with a trivial bundle, so that by Theorem 4.2, it must have zero Euler class.

As a final application, consider a vector bundle ξ over a compact manifold M, with structure group a compact subgroup G of $GL(k)$. If $\mathcal{C}$ denotes the affine space of connections ∇ on ξ with holonomy group G, the *Yang-Mills functional* on $\mathcal{C}$ is defined by

$$\mathcal{YM}(\nabla) = \frac{1}{2} \int_M |R|^2,$$

where R is the curvature tensor of ∇. A critical point of this functional is called a *Yang-Mills connection*. Such a connection is said to be *stable* if it is a local minimum of the functional.

Simons [7] showed that there are no stable Yang-Mills connections on bundles over S^n if $n > 4$. Bourguignon and Lawson studied the four-dimensional case, which turns out to be quite different: Let ξ be an oriented rank 4 bundle over S^4 with Pontrjagin number p and Euler number e. By Propositions 5.1 and 5.2, the Yang-Mills functional for $SO(4)$-connections satisfies

$$\mathcal{YM}(\nabla) \geq 2\pi^2|p|, 4\pi^2|e|.$$

For example, when ξ is the tangent bundle of the 4-sphere, the curvature R of the canonical connection ∇ is the identity on Λ_2, so that $R_-^+ = R_+^- = 0$. Thus, $\mathcal{YM}(\nabla) = 4\pi^2 e$, and since the tangent bundle has vanishing Pontrjagin class, the Levi-Civita connection is an absolute minimum of the Yang-Mills functional. Similarly, for a bundle with structure group S_-^3,

$$p = \frac{1}{4\pi^2} \int_{S^4} |R_+^+|^2 - |R_+^-|^2.$$

It is know that such a bundle admits connections the curvature tensor of which is self-dual or anti-self-dual depending on whether p is positive or negative. Any such connection is therefore stable. The reader is referred to [6] for further details.

EXERCISE 155. Consider a principal G-bundle $P \to M$. Show that if H is a normal subgroup of G, then the associated bundle with fiber G/H is principal. (Identify P/H with $P \times_G (G/H)$ via $pH \mapsto [p, H]$. The action of G/H on P/H is then given by $(pH)(aH) := paH$, for $p \in P$, $a \in G$).

EXERCISE 156. Let $\phi : S^3 \times S^3 \to SO(4)$ denote the covering homomorphism, $\phi(q_1, q_2)u = q_1 u \bar{q}_2^{-1}$, $q_i \in S^3$, $u \in \mathbb{H} = \mathbb{R}^4$. Define $\phi_\pm : S^3 \to SO(4)$ by $\phi_\pm = \phi \circ \imath_\pm$, where $\imath_\pm : S^3 \to S^3 \times S^3$ are the inclusion homomorphisms $\imath_+(q) = (q, 1)$, $\imath_-(q) = (1, q)$.

(a) Prove that the Lie algebra $\mathfrak{o}(4)$ is isomorphic to $\phi_{+*}\mathfrak{o}(3) \times \phi_{-*}\mathfrak{o}(3)$ (recall that the Lie algebra of S^3 is isomorphic to $\mathfrak{o}(3)$).

(b) Let $L^{-1} : \mathfrak{o}(4) \to \Lambda_2(\mathbb{R}^4) = \Lambda_2^+ \oplus \Lambda_2^-$ denote the usual isometry. Show that $L^{-1} \circ \phi_{\pm*}$ maps the Lie algebra $\mathfrak{o}(3)$ isomorphically onto $\Lambda_2^\pm$.

EXERCISE 157. Given $A \in \mathfrak{o}(n)$, define $\tilde{A} : \Lambda_2(\mathbb{R}^n) \to \Lambda_2(\mathbb{R}^n)$ by

$$\tilde{A}(v \wedge w) = (Av) \wedge w + v \wedge (Aw)$$

on decomposable elements, and extending linearly.

(a) Prove that $\tilde{A}(v \wedge w) = [L^{-1}A, v \wedge w]$, where $L : \Lambda_2(\mathbb{R}^n) \to \mathfrak{o}(n)$ is the canonical isomorphism.

(b) Let R be the curvature tensor of some connection on the bundle ξ over M, and $\tilde{R}$ the induced curvature tensor of $\Lambda_2\xi$. Show that for $\alpha \in \Lambda_2(E(\xi)_p)$,

$$\tilde{R}(x, y)\alpha = [R(x, y), \alpha], \qquad x, y \in M_p,$$

after identifying $R(x, y)$ with an element of $\Lambda_2(E(\xi)_p)$ via L^{-1}.

6. The Unit Sphere Bundle and the Euler Class

Consider an oriented rank $n = 2k$ Euclidean bundle $\xi = \pi : E \to M$ and its unit sphere bundle $\xi^1 = \pi_{|E^1} : E^1 \to M$, where $E^1 = \{u \in E \mid |u| = 1\}$. Our goal in this section is to show that the pullback of the Euler form of ξ to E^1 is exact, a fact that will be needed in the proof of the generalized Gauss-Bonnet theorem in the next section.

Recall that for $u \in E$, $\mathcal{J}_u$ denotes the canonical isomorphism of the fiber $E_{\pi(u)}$ of ξ through u with its tangent space at u. For convenience of notation, the latter will be identified with a subspace of $T_u E$ via the derivative of the inclusion $E_{\pi(u)} \hookrightarrow E$, so that $\mathcal{J}_u : E_{\pi(u)} \to (\mathcal{V}E)_u \subset T_u E$.

LEMMA 6.1. *There is a canonical isomorphism $\mathcal{J} : \Gamma_\pi \xi \to \Gamma \mathcal{V}\xi$ of the space $\Gamma_\pi \xi$ of sections of ξ along π with the space $\Gamma \mathcal{V}\xi$ of sections of the vertical bundle $\mathcal{V}\xi$ over E. A Riemannian connection $\tilde\nabla$ on ξ induces a Riemannian connection ∇ on $\mathcal{V}\xi$ given by*

$$\nabla_x \mathcal{J}U = \mathcal{J}_u \tilde\nabla_x U, \qquad U \in \Gamma_\pi \xi, \quad x \in T_u E, \quad u \in E.$$

($\tilde\nabla$ in the above identity denotes the covariant derivative along $\pi : E \to M$.)

PROOF. The equivalence

$$\pi^* \xi \longrightarrow \mathcal{V}\xi,$$
$$(u, v) \longmapsto \mathcal{J}_u v$$

induces an isomorphism between $\Gamma \pi^* \xi$ and $\Gamma \mathcal{V}\xi$. On the other hand, the map $\Gamma \pi^* \xi \to \Gamma_\pi \xi$ that takes U to $\pi_2 U$ is an isomorphism with inverse $V \mapsto (1_E, V)$, where $(1_E, V)(u) = (u, V(u))$. Combining the two, we obtain an isomorphism $\mathcal{J} : \Gamma_\pi \xi \to \Gamma \mathcal{V}\xi$ given by $(\mathcal{J}U)(v) = \mathcal{J}_v U(v)$. This establishes the first part of the lemma.

A Riemannian connection $\tilde\nabla$ on ξ induces a connection $\bar\nabla$ on $\pi^* \xi$, where

$$\bar\nabla_x (1_E, U) = (u, \tilde\nabla_x U), \qquad U \in \Gamma_\pi \xi, \quad x \in T_u E, \quad u \in E.$$

The above equivalence $\pi^* \xi \cong \mathcal{V}\xi$ then yields a connection ∇ on $\mathcal{V}\xi$, and $\nabla_x \mathcal{J}U = \mathcal{J}_u \tilde\nabla_x U$, as claimed; ∇ is Riemannian because $\tilde\nabla$ is, and because $\mathcal{J}_u$ is isometric. $\qquad\square$

Denoting by $\tilde R$, R the corresponding curvature tensors, the structure equation (Lemma 3.1 in Chapter 4) implies

(6.1)
$$R(x, y)\mathcal{J}_u v = \mathcal{J}_u \tilde R(\pi_* x, \pi_* y)v, \qquad x, y \in T_u E, \quad u, v \in E, \quad \pi(u) = \pi(v).$$

(Equivalently, in the bundle $\pi^* \xi$, $\bar R(x, y)(u, v) = (u, \tilde R(\pi_* x, \pi_* y)v)$.)

There is a canonical section of ξ along π, namely the identity 1_E. Under the isomorphism of Lemma 6.1, it corresponds to the position vector field P on the manifold TE; i.e., P is the section of $\mathcal{V}\xi$ defined by $P(u) = \mathcal{J}_u u$ for $u \in E$. Notice that

(6.2)
$$d^\nabla P(x) = \nabla_x P = x^v, \qquad x \in TE.$$

To see this, observe that if κ denotes the connection map of ∇ and $x \in T_u E$, then

$$\nabla_x P = \nabla_x \mathcal{J} 1_E = \mathcal{J}_u \tilde{\nabla}_x 1_E = \mathcal{J}_u \kappa 1_{E_*} x = \mathcal{J}_u \kappa x = x^v.$$

By Theorem 3.1 in Chapter 4, $d^{\nabla^2} P(x,y) = R(x,y)P$, which together with (6.1) implies

(6.3) $d^{\nabla^2} P(x,y) = \mathcal{J}_u \tilde{R}(\pi_* x, \pi_* y) u, \qquad x, y \in T_u E, \quad u \in E.$

The following observations will be used throughout the section:

REMARK 6.1. (i) The wedge product from (3.4) extends to all of $A(M, \Lambda\xi)$: For $\alpha \in A_p(M, \Lambda_q \xi)$, $\beta \in A_r(M, \Lambda_s \xi)$, define $\alpha \wedge_\xi \beta \in A_{p+r}(M, \Lambda_{q+s}\xi)$ by

$$(\alpha \wedge_\xi \beta)(X_1, \ldots, X_{p+r}) = \frac{1}{p! r!} \sum_{\sigma \in P_{p+r}} (\mathrm{sgn}\,\sigma) \alpha(X_{\sigma(1)}, \ldots, X_{\sigma(p)})$$
$$\wedge \beta(X_{\sigma(p+1)}, \ldots, X_{\sigma(p+r)}).$$

(The wedge product in the right side is of course the one in $\Lambda\xi$). Then $\alpha \wedge_\xi \beta = (-1)^{pr+qs} \beta \wedge_\xi \alpha$, and $d^\nabla(\alpha \wedge_\xi \beta) = (d^\nabla \alpha) \wedge_\xi \beta + (-1)^p \alpha \wedge_\xi d^\nabla \beta$. Notice that $\tilde{R} \in A_2(M, \Lambda_2 \xi)$ commutes with any other $\Lambda\xi$-valued form.

(ii) Since $\star_\xi$ is parallel, (0.1) implies

$$d(\star_\xi \alpha) = \star_\xi d^\nabla \alpha, \qquad \alpha \in A(M, \Lambda_n \xi).$$

(iii) If u_i is an orthonormal basis of $E_{\pi(u)}$, then $\mathcal{J}_u u_i$ is an orthonormal basis of $(\mathcal{V}E)_u$. Thus, by (6.1), $\star_{\mathcal{V}} R^k = \pi^* \star_\xi \tilde{R}^k$.

(iv) Let $U_1, \ldots, U_n$ denote a local orthonormal basis of sections of ξ. If α, β are sections of $\Lambda_p \xi$, $\Lambda_{n-p}\xi$, respectively, then locally,

$$\alpha = \sum_{i_1 < \cdots < i_p} \langle \alpha, U_{i_1} \wedge \cdots \wedge U_{i_p} \rangle U_{i_1} \wedge \cdots \wedge U_{i_p}.$$

A similar expression holds for β, so that

$$\langle \alpha \wedge \beta, U_1 \wedge \cdots \wedge U_n \rangle = \sum_{\substack{i_1 < \cdots < i_p \\ j_1 < \cdots < j_{n-p}}} \epsilon^{i_1 \ldots i_p j_1 \ldots j_{n-p}} \langle \alpha, U_{i_1} \wedge \cdots \wedge U_{i_p} \rangle$$
$$\langle \beta, U_{j_1} \wedge \cdots \wedge U_{j_{n-p}} \rangle$$
$$= \frac{1}{p!} \frac{1}{(n-p)!} \sum_{\sigma \in P_n} (\mathrm{sgn}\,\sigma) \langle \alpha, U_{\sigma(1)} \wedge \cdots \wedge U_{\sigma(p)} \rangle$$
$$\langle \beta, U_{\sigma(p+1)} \wedge \cdots \wedge U_{\sigma(n)} \rangle.$$

This identity also holds when α, β are $\Lambda\xi$-valued forms on M as in (i).

From now on we will work in E^1, so let $\mathcal{V}\xi$ denote the restriction $\imath^* \mathcal{V}\xi$ of the vertical bundle to E^1, where $\imath : E^1 \hookrightarrow E$ is inclusion. Similarly, P will denote the restriction $P \circ \imath$ of the position vector field, R the pullback $\imath^* R \in A_2(E^1, \Lambda_2 \mathcal{V}\xi)$ of R, and $\pi : E^1 \to M$ the projection. For $i = 1, \ldots, k$, define $\omega_i \in A_{n-1}(E^1, \Lambda_n \mathcal{V}\xi)$ by

$$\omega_i = P \wedge_{\mathcal{V}} (d^\nabla P)^{2i-1} \wedge_{\mathcal{V}} R^{k-i},$$

with the wedge product as defined in Remark 6.1(i).

LEMMA 6.2.

$$d^\nabla \omega_i = (d^\nabla P)^{2i} \wedge_\nu R^{k-i} - \frac{2i-1}{k-i+1}(d^\nabla P)^{2i-2} \wedge_\nu R^{k-i+1}.$$

PROOF. By the Bianchi identity,

$$d^\nabla \omega_i = (d^\nabla P)^{2i} \wedge_\nu R^{k-i} + (2i-1)P \wedge_\nu d^{\nabla 2}P \wedge_\nu (d^\nabla P)^{2i-2} \wedge R^{k-i}$$

$$= (d^\nabla P)^{2i} \wedge_\nu R^{k-i} + (2i-1)(d^\nabla P)^{2i-2} \wedge_\nu P \wedge_\nu d^{\nabla 2}P \wedge_\nu R^{k-i}.$$

In order to evaluate the second summand, consider a positively oriented orthonormal basis U_j of local sections of $\mathcal{V}\xi$ with $U_{2i-1} = P$. Then

$$\langle (d^\nabla P)^{2i-2} \wedge_\nu P \wedge_\nu d^{\nabla 2}P \wedge_\nu R^{k-i}, U_1 \wedge \cdots \wedge U_n \rangle$$

$$= \frac{1}{2^{k-i}} \sum_{\sigma \in P_n} (\operatorname{sgn}\sigma)\langle d^\nabla P, U_{\sigma(1)} \rangle \wedge \cdots \wedge \langle d^\nabla P, U_{\sigma(2i-2)} \rangle \wedge \langle P, U_{\sigma(2i-1)} \rangle$$

$$\wedge \langle d^{\nabla 2}P, U_{\sigma(2i)} \rangle \wedge \langle R, U_{\sigma(2i+1)} \wedge U_{\sigma(2i+2)} \rangle \wedge \cdots$$

$$\wedge \langle R, U_{\sigma(n-1)} \wedge U_{\sigma(n)} \rangle$$

$$= -\frac{1}{2^{k-i}} \sum_{\{\sigma | \sigma(2i-1)=2i-1\}} (\operatorname{sgn}\sigma)\langle d^\nabla P, U_{\sigma(1)} \rangle \wedge \cdots \wedge \langle d^\nabla P, U_{\sigma(2i-2)} \rangle$$

$$\wedge \langle R, U_{\sigma(2i-1)} \wedge U_{\sigma(2i)} \rangle \wedge \cdots \wedge \langle R, U_{\sigma(n-1)} \wedge U_{\sigma(n)} \rangle$$

by (6.3) and (6.1). Fix any $\sigma \in P_n$ with $\sigma(2i-1) \neq 2i-1$, so that $P = U_{\sigma(l)}$ for some $l \neq 2i-1$. If $l < 2i-1$, the corresponding expression in the last equality vanishes, because $\langle d^\nabla P, U_{\sigma(l)} \rangle = \langle d^\nabla P, P \rangle$, and $\langle d^\nabla P(x), P \rangle = \langle \nabla_x P, P \rangle = \frac{1}{2}x\langle P, P \rangle = 0$ on E^1 where P has constant norm 1. If $l > 2i-1$, then the corresponding expression is the same as in the case $\sigma(2i-1) = 2i-1$: In fact, $(\operatorname{sgn}\sigma)\langle R, U_{\sigma(2i-1)} \wedge U_{\sigma(2i)} \rangle \wedge \cdots \wedge \langle R, U_{\sigma(n-1)} \wedge U_{\sigma(n)} \rangle$ remains unchanged when switching pairs $(\sigma(2p-1), \sigma(2p))$ and $(\sigma(2q-1), \sigma(2q))$. Similarly, this expression undergoes a sign change twice when interchanging $\sigma(2p-1)$ and $\sigma(2p)$ (once in $\langle R, U_{\sigma(2p-1)} \wedge U_{\sigma(2p)} \rangle$ and again in $(\operatorname{sgn}\sigma)$). Thus,

$$\langle (d^\nabla P)^{2i-2} \wedge_\nu P \wedge_\nu d^{\nabla 2}P \wedge_\nu R^{k-i}, U_1 \wedge \cdots \wedge U_n \rangle$$

$$= -\frac{1}{2^{k-i}2(k-i+1)} \sum_{\sigma \in P_n} (\operatorname{sgn}\sigma)\langle d^\nabla P, U_{\sigma(1)} \rangle \wedge \cdots \wedge \langle d^\nabla P, U_{\sigma(2i-2)} \rangle$$

$$\wedge \langle R, U_{\sigma(2i-1)} \wedge U_{\sigma(2i)} \rangle \wedge \cdots \wedge \langle R, U_{\sigma(n-1)} \wedge U_{\sigma(n)} \rangle$$

$$= -\frac{2^{k-i+1}}{2^{k-i}2(k-i+1)}\langle (d^\nabla P)^{2i-2} \wedge_\nu R^{k-i+1}, U_1 \wedge \cdots \wedge U_n \rangle,$$

so that

$$(d^\nabla P)^{2i-2} \wedge_\nu P \wedge_\nu d^{\nabla 2}P \wedge_\nu R^{k-i} = -\frac{1}{k-i+1}(d^\nabla P)^{2i-2} \wedge_\nu R^{k-i+1}.$$

Substituting into the original expression for $d^\nabla \omega_i$ then yields the result. $\square$

THEOREM 6.1. *Consider an oriented Euclidean bundle* $\xi = E \to M$ *of rank* $n = 2k$, *with Riemannian connection and corresponding Euler form* e. *If* $\xi^1 = \pi : E^1 \to M$ *denotes the unit sphere bundle of* ξ, *then the pullback* $\pi^*e \in A_n(E^1)$ *of the Euler form is exact. Specifically, there exists* $\Omega \in A_{n-1}(E^1)$ *such that*

(1) $\pi^* e = d\Omega$; and

(2) for $p \in M$, $\int_{(E^1)_p} \jmath^* \Omega = -1$, where $\jmath : (E^1)_p \hookrightarrow E^1$ denotes inclusion.

PROOF. Set $\Omega_i := \star_V \omega_i \in A_{n-1}(E^1)$. We seek constants $a_i \in \mathbb{R}$ so that $\Omega = \sum a_i \Omega_i$ satisfies (1) and (2). We begin with (2): Given $u \in (E^1)_p$, $p \in M$, consider a local positively oriented orthonormal basis U_i of sections of $\mathcal{V}\xi$ in a neighborhood of u with $U_1 = P$. Since P is orthogonal to the unit sphere $S^{n-1} = (E^1)_p$, the volume form of $(E^1)_p$ is given locally by $(U_2 \wedge \cdots \wedge U_n)^\flat \circ \jmath$. Now, $\jmath^* \Omega$ is vertical, whereas R is horizontal by (6.1), so that

$$\jmath^* \Omega = a_k \jmath^* \Omega_k = a_k \langle \jmath^* \omega_k, U_1 \wedge \cdots \wedge U_n \rangle$$

$$= a_k \sum_{\sigma \in P_n} (\operatorname{sgn} \sigma) \jmath^* (\langle P, U_{\sigma(1)} \rangle \wedge \langle d^\nabla P, U_{\sigma(2)} \rangle \wedge \cdots \wedge \langle d^\nabla P, U_{\sigma(n)} \rangle)$$

$$= a_k \sum_{\{\sigma | \sigma(1) = 1\}} (\operatorname{sgn} \sigma) \jmath^* (\langle d^\nabla P, U_{\sigma(2)} \rangle \wedge \cdots \wedge \langle d^\nabla P, U_{\sigma(n)} \rangle)$$

$$= a_k \sum_{\tau \in P_{n-1}} (\operatorname{sgn} \tau) \jmath^* (\langle d^\nabla P, U_{1+\tau(1)} \rangle \wedge \cdots \wedge \langle d^\nabla P, U_{1+\tau(n-1)} \rangle)$$

$$= a_k (n-1)! \jmath^* (\langle d^\nabla P, U_2 \rangle \wedge \cdots \wedge \langle d^\nabla P, U_n \rangle).$$

Now, for x_i in the tangent space at u of the fiber $(E^1)_p$ over p, $\jmath_* x_i$ is vertical, and $\jmath^* d^\nabla P(x_i) = \jmath_* x_i$ by (6.2). Thus,

$$\jmath^* \Omega(x_1, \ldots, x_{n-1}) = a_k (n-1)! \sum_{\sigma \in P_{n-1}} (\operatorname{sgn} \sigma) \langle \jmath_* x_{\sigma(1)}, U_2(u) \rangle \cdots$$

$$\langle \jmath_* x_{\sigma(n-1)}, U_n(u) \rangle$$

$$= a_k (n-1)! \det \langle \jmath_* x_i, U_j(u) \rangle$$

$$= a_k (n-1)! \langle \jmath_* x_1 \wedge \cdots \wedge \jmath_* x_{n-1}, U_2(u) \wedge \cdots \wedge U_n(u) \rangle$$

$$= a_k (n-1)! \omega(x_1, \ldots, x_{n-1}),$$

where ω denotes the volume form of $(E^1)_p$. Since the latter is isometric to S^{n-1},

$$\int_{(E^1)_p} \jmath^* \Omega = a_k (n-1)! \operatorname{vol}(S^{n-1}) = a_k (n-1)! \frac{2\pi^k}{(k-1)!} = -1,$$

if we set $a_k = -(k-1)!/2\pi^k(2k-1)!$.

Next, we determine a_i for $i < k$ so that Ω satisfies (1):

$$d^\nabla \left(\sum a_i \omega_i \right) = \sum a_i \left((d^\nabla P)^{2i} \wedge_V R^{k-i} - \frac{2i-1}{k-i+1} (d^\nabla P)^{2i-2} \wedge_V R^{k-i+1} \right)$$

$$= -\frac{a_1}{k} R^k + a_k (d^\nabla P)^{2k} + \sum_{i=1}^{k-1} \left(a_i - \frac{2i+1}{k-i} a_{i+1} \right) (d^\nabla P)^{2i}$$

$$\wedge_V R^{k-i}.$$

With a_k as above, define $a_i = (2i + 1/k - i) a_{i+1}$ inductively; then

$$a_i = -\frac{(i-1)!}{2^{k-i+1} \pi^k (k-i)! (2i-1)!},$$

and

$$d^\nabla \left(\sum a_i \omega_i \right) = \frac{1}{(2\pi)^k} R^k + a_k (d^\nabla P)^{2k},$$

so that

$$d\Omega = d \left(\star_\nabla \sum a_i \omega_i \right) = \star_\nabla d^\nabla \left(\sum a_i \omega_i \right) = \frac{1}{(2\pi)^k} \star_\nabla R^k + a_k \star_\nabla (d^\nabla P)^{2k}.$$

Finally, $\star_\nabla (d^\nabla P)^{2k} = 0$ by (6.2), and $\star_\nabla R^k = \pi^* \star_\xi \tilde{R}^k$. Thus, $d\Omega = \pi^* e$, as claimed. □

EXERCISE 158. Use Theorem 6.1 to show once again that the Euler class of a vector bundle vanishes if the bundle admits a nowhere-zero section.

7. The Generalized Gauss-Bonnet Theorem

Let M be a compact, oriented, n-dimensional manifold. The *Euler characteristic* of M is defined to be $\chi(M) = \sum_{k=0}^n (-1)^k \dim H^k(M)$. It turns out that this number can be computed by looking at the behavior of any vector field X on M with finitely many zeros. We shall only explain the procedure and concepts involved. For a proof, the reader is referred to [25]. Let p be a zero of X, choose $\epsilon \in (0, \text{inj}_p)$ (for some Riemannian metric on M) so that the ball $B_\epsilon(p)$ of radius ϵ centered at p contains no other zeros of X, and denote by S^{n-1} the unit sphere centered at 0 in M_p. Consider the maps $\iota_t : S^{n-1} \to S^{n-1} \times [0, \epsilon]$, $t \in [0, \epsilon]$, $\iota_t(v) = (v, t)$, and $H : S^{n-1} \times [0, \epsilon] \to M$, $H(v, t) = \exp_p(tv)$. The *index* $\text{ind}_p X$ of X at p is the degree of the map $f_\epsilon := \Phi_\epsilon \circ (X/|X|) \circ H \circ \iota_\epsilon : S^{n-1} \to S^{n-1}$. Here, $\Phi_\epsilon : T^1 M_{\partial B_\epsilon(p)} \to S^{n-1}$ maps $u \in T^1 M \cap M_{\exp_\epsilon v}$ to the parallel translate of u along the geodesic $t \mapsto \exp_p((\epsilon - t)v)$, $0 \le t \le \epsilon$.

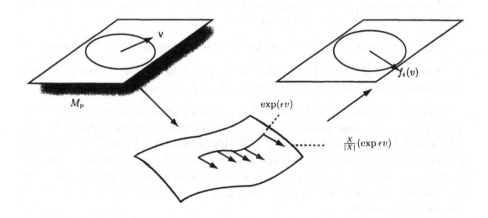

FIGURE 1

Thus, to obtain the value of f_ϵ at a point $v \in S^{n-1}$, one goes out at distance ϵ along the geodesic in direction v, evaluates the normalized vector field $X/|X|$ at that point, and parallel translates it back to p along the same geodesic. The index of X at p is well-defined, for if $\delta \in (0, \mathrm{inj}_p)$, then f_δ and f_ϵ are homotopic via $(v, t) \mapsto f_{t\delta + (1-t)\epsilon}(v)$.

FIGURE 2

The proof of the following theorem can be found, for example, in [**25**]:

THEOREM 7.1 (Poincaré-Hopf). *Let X be a vector field with finitely many zeros on a compact, oriented manifold M (such an X always exists). Then the Euler characteristic $\chi(M)$ of M equals the index sum over all zeros of X.*

The next theorem is known as the generalized Gauss-Bonnet theorem:

THEOREM 7.2 (Allendoerfel-Weil, Chern). *If M^{2k} is a compact, oriented Riemannian manifold with Euler form e, then $\int_M e = \chi(M)$.*

PROOF. Consider a vector field X on M with finite zero set $N = \{p \in M \mid X(p) = 0\}$, and choose some $0 < \epsilon < \mathrm{inj}_M$ such that $\epsilon < \min\{\frac{1}{2} d(p, q) \mid p, q \in N\}$. Let Z be a vector field on $M \setminus N$ that equals $X/|X|$ on $M \setminus B_{2\epsilon/3}(N)$, and such that for each $p \in N$, and unit $v \in M_p$, $Z \circ c_v$ is parallel along the geodesic $c_v : (0, \epsilon/3) \to M$, $c_v(t) = \exp(tv)$. If π denotes the projection of the unit tangent bundle $\tau^1 M$, then $\pi \circ Z = 1_{M \setminus N}$, and the restriction of e to $M \setminus N$ may be expressed as

$$e = (\pi \circ Z)^* e = Z^* \pi^* e = Z^* d\Omega = dZ^* \Omega,$$

with Ω denoting the $(2k - 1)$-form on $T^1 M$ from Theorem 6.1. Let $p \in N$, and $H : S^{n-1} \times [0, \epsilon] \to M$ as above. Although Z does not extend continuously to $B_\epsilon(p)$, we obtain a differentiable vector field Y along H by setting

$$Y(v, t) = Z \circ H(v, t) \text{ for } t > 0, \text{ and } Y(v, 0) = \lim_{t \to 0^+} Z \circ H(v, t).$$

Stokes' theorem then implies

$$\int_{\overline{B_\epsilon}(p)} e = \int_{H(S^{n-1}\times[0,\epsilon])} dZ^*\Omega = \int_{S^{n-1}\times[0,\epsilon]} H^*dZ^*\Omega = \int_{S^{n-1}\times[0,\epsilon]} dH^*Z^*\Omega$$

$$= \int_{S^{n-1}\times\epsilon} H^*Z^*\Omega - \int_{S^{n-1}\times 0} H^*Z^*\Omega$$

$$= \int_{\partial B_\epsilon(p)} Z^*\Omega \quad - \int_{S^{n-1}\times 0} H^*Z^*\Omega.$$

Since the degree of $Y \circ \imath_0$ equals the index of X at p, we have

$$\int_{S^{n-1}\times 0} H^*Z^*\Omega = \int_{S^{n-1}} (Y \circ \imath_0)^*\Omega = \mathrm{ind}_p X \int_{S^{n-1}} \Omega = -\mathrm{ind}_p X.$$

Thus,

$$\int_M e = \int_{M\setminus\cup_{p\in N} B_\epsilon(p)} e + \sum_{p\in N} \int_{\overline{B_\epsilon}(p)} e$$

$$= \int_{M\setminus\cup_{p\in N} B_\epsilon(p)} dZ^*\Omega + \sum_{p\in N} \left(\int_{\partial B_\epsilon(p)} Z^*\Omega + \mathrm{ind}_p X \right)$$

$$= -\sum_{p\in N} \int_{\partial B_\epsilon(p)} Z^*\Omega + \sum_{p\in N} \int_{\partial B_\epsilon(p)} Z^*\Omega + \sum_{p\in N} \mathrm{ind}_p X$$

$$= \chi(M).$$

$\square$

EXAMPLES AND REMARKS 7.1. (i) For an oriented surface M^2, the Euler form at $p \in M$ is given by $e(x,y) = \frac{1}{2\pi}\langle R(x,y)v, u\rangle$, where u, v is a positively oriented orthonormal basis of M_p. Thus, $e = \frac{1}{2\pi}K\omega$, with K the sectional curvature, and ω the volume form of M. The 2-dimensional case then reduces to the classical Gauss-Bonnet theorem:

$$\int_M K\omega = 2\pi\chi(M).$$

(ii) A Riemannian manifold is said to be *Einstein* if the Ricci curvature $\mathrm{Ric} = \kappa\langle,\rangle$ of M equals a constant multiple κ of the metric, $\kappa \in \mathbb{R}$. Any space of constant curvature is Einstein of course, but so is for example $S^2 \times S^2$ with the product metric.

Consider a compact, oriented 4-dimensional Einstein manifold. Given $p \in M$, let $e_1, \ldots, e_4$ denote a positively oriented orthonormal basis of M_p. If

$$\alpha_2 = \frac{1}{\sqrt{2}}e_1 \wedge e_2, \qquad \alpha_3 = \frac{1}{\sqrt{2}}e_1 \wedge e_3, \qquad \alpha_4 = \frac{1}{\sqrt{2}}e_1 \wedge e_4,$$

then $\alpha_i \pm \star\alpha_i$ $i = 2, 3, 4$, is an orthonormal basis of $\Lambda_2^\pm(M_p)$. We claim that $\langle R\alpha, \beta\rangle = 0$ for all $\alpha \in \Lambda_2^+(M_p)$ and $\beta \in \Lambda_2^-(M_p)$. To see this, notice first that

$$0 = \mathrm{Ric}(e_2, e_3) = \langle R(e_1, e_2)e_3, e_1\rangle + \langle R(e_4, e_2)e_3, e_4\rangle$$

$$= \langle Re_1 \wedge e_2, e_1 \wedge e_3\rangle - \langle Re_4 \wedge e_2, e_3 \wedge e_4\rangle$$

$$= 2\langle R\alpha_2, \alpha_3\rangle - 2\langle R \star \alpha_3, \star\alpha_2\rangle.$$

Similarly,

$$0 = \mathrm{Ric}(e_1, e_4) = \langle R(e_2, e_1)e_4, e_2 \rangle + \langle R(e_3, e_1)e_4, e_3 \rangle$$
$$= 2\langle R\alpha_2, \star\alpha_3 \rangle - 2\langle R\alpha_3, \star\alpha_2 \rangle.$$

Thus,

$$\langle R(\alpha_2 + \star\alpha_2), \alpha_3 - \star\alpha_3 \rangle = \frac{1}{2}(\mathrm{Ric}(e_2, e_3) - \mathrm{Ric}(e_1, e_4)) = 0.$$

A similar computation shows that $\langle R(\alpha_i + \star\alpha_i), \alpha_j - \star\alpha_j \rangle = 0$ whenever $i \neq j$. When $i = j$,

$$\langle R(\alpha_i + \star\alpha_i), \alpha_i - \star\alpha_i) \rangle = \langle R\alpha_i, \alpha_i \rangle - \langle R \star \alpha_i, \star\alpha_i \rangle = K_{\alpha_i} - K_{\star\alpha_i},$$

with K_{α_i} denoting the sectional curvature of the plane spanned by e_1 and e_i. This expression is always zero: For example,

$$K_{\alpha_2} - K_{\star\alpha_2} = K_{e_1, e_2} - K_{e_3, e_4}$$
$$= \frac{1}{2}(\mathrm{Ric}(e_1, e_1) + \mathrm{Ric}(e_2, e_2) - \mathrm{Ric}(e_3, e_3) - \mathrm{Ric}(e_4, e_4)) = 0.$$

This establishes our claim that the curvature tensor R of an oriented 4-dimensional Einstein manifold leaves the subspaces $\Lambda_2^\pm(M_p)$ invariant; i.e., $R_-^+ = R_+^- = 0$ in the notation of Section 4. By Proposition 5.2, the Euler form of M equals

$$e = \frac{1}{8\pi^2}(|R_+^+|^2 + |R_-^-|^2).$$

According to the Gauss-Bonnet theorem, the Euler characteristic of M is then nonnegative, and is zero iff M is flat.

(iii) One large class of Einstein manifolds is the one consisting of so-called semi-simple Lie groups: The *Killing form* $B : \mathfrak{g} \times \mathfrak{g} \to \mathbb{R}$ of a Lie algebra $\mathfrak{g}$ is the symmetric bilinear form given by $B(X, Y) = \mathrm{tr} \, \mathrm{ad}_X \circ \mathrm{ad}_Y$. A Lie group G is said to be *semi-simple* if the Killing form of its Lie algebra is nondegenerate.

It turns out that a compact Lie group is semi-simple iff it has discrete center $Z(G) = \{g \in G \mid gh = hg \text{ for all } h \in G\}$. To see this, assume first that G is compact and semi-simple. By compactness, there exists an inner product on $\mathfrak{g}$ for which $\mathrm{ad}_X : \mathfrak{g} \to \mathfrak{g}$ is skew-adjoint for each $X \in \mathfrak{g}$, cf. Examples and remarks 1.1(ii) in Chapter 5. If (a_{ij}) denotes the matrix of ad_X with respect to some orthonormal basis of $\mathfrak{g}$, then

$$B(X, X) = \mathrm{tr} \, \mathrm{ad}_X^2 = \sum_{i,j} a_{ij} a_{ji} = -\sum_{i,j} a_{ij}^2 \leq 0,$$

and equals zero iff $\mathrm{ad}_X = 0$. Thus, the kernel of $\mathrm{ad} = \mathrm{Ad}_{\star e}$ is trivial (see the observation in Section 5 of Chapter 4), so that $Z(G) \subset \ker \mathrm{Ad}$ has trivial Lie algebra, and must be discrete. Notice that in fact, $Z(G) = \ker \mathrm{Ad}$: If $g \in \ker \mathrm{Ad}$, then for any $X \in \mathfrak{g}$, $X(g) = R_{g*}X(e)$. Thus, the curve c, where $c(t) = R_g(\exp tX)$, is an integral curve of X which passes through g when $t = 0$. By uniqueness of integral curves, it must equal $t \mapsto L_g(\exp tX)$. Since the exponential map is onto (we are implicitly assuming G is connected), g belongs to the center. This also implies that conversely, if $Z(G)$ is discrete, then its Lie algebra is trivial, and B is nondegenerate.

Suppose then that G is compact and semi-simple, so that its Killing form is nondegenerate. Then $-B$ is an inner product on $\mathfrak{g}$ for which ad_Y is skew-adjoint, $Y \in \mathfrak{g}$:

$$
\begin{aligned}
-B(\mathrm{ad}_Y X, Z) = B(\mathrm{ad}_X Y, Z) &= \mathrm{tr}(\mathrm{ad}_{[X,Y]} \circ \mathrm{ad}_Z) \\
&= \mathrm{tr}(\mathrm{ad}_X \circ \mathrm{ad}_Y \circ \mathrm{ad}_Z - \mathrm{ad}_Y \circ \mathrm{ad}_X \circ \mathrm{ad}_Z) \\
&= \mathrm{tr}(\mathrm{ad}_X \circ \mathrm{ad}_Y \circ \mathrm{ad}_Z - \mathrm{ad}_X \circ \mathrm{ad}_Z \circ \mathrm{ad}_Y) \\
&= \mathrm{tr}(\mathrm{ad}_X \circ \mathrm{ad}_{[Y,Z]}) = B(X, \mathrm{ad}_Y Z).
\end{aligned}
$$

Thus, $-B$ induces a so-called *canonical bi-invariant metric* on G. (2.4) in Chapter 5 implies that G with the canonical metric is an Einstein manifold with $\kappa = \frac{1}{4}$: Given $X, Y \in \mathfrak{g}$, and an orthonormal basis Z_i of $\mathfrak{g}$,

$$
\begin{aligned}
\mathrm{Ric}(X, Y) = \sum_i \langle R(Z_i, X)Y, Z_i \rangle &= -\frac{1}{4} \sum_i \langle [[Z_i, X], Y], Z_i \rangle \\
&= -\frac{1}{4} \mathrm{tr}(\mathrm{ad}_X \circ \mathrm{ad}_Y) = \frac{1}{4} \langle X, Y \rangle.
\end{aligned}
$$

EXERCISE 159. Prove that a compact, oriented 4-dimensional Riemannian manifold M with constant curvature κ has Euler characteristic $\chi(M) = \frac{3\kappa^2}{4\pi^2} \mathrm{vol}(M)$.

EXERCISE 160. Let G be a compact, connected, semi-simple Lie group with its canonical metric, $L : \Lambda_2\mathfrak{g} \to \mathfrak{g}$ the linear map which on decomposable elements is given by $L(X \wedge Y) = [X, Y]$. Show that for any $\alpha \in \Lambda_2\mathfrak{g}$, $\langle R\alpha, \alpha \rangle = \frac{1}{4}|T\alpha|^2$. Thus, G has nonnegative-definite curvature operator. The Gauss-Bonnet theorem can be used to show that any Riemannian manifold with nonnegative curvature operator has nonnegative Euler characteristic.

8. Complex and Symplectic Vector Spaces

There is yet another characteristic class, called the Chern class, that can be defined on certain bundles possessing additional structure. Before introducing it, we review some basic notions from complex linear algebra. The reader familiar with the material may proceed to Theorem 8.1 below without loss of continuity.

A *complex vector space* $(V, +, \cdot)$ is a set V together with two operations $+$, $\cdot$, satisfying the usual vector space axioms, but taking $\mathbb{C}$ as the scalar field instead of $\mathbb{R}$. A (complex) linear transformation $L : V \to W$ between complex spaces V, W is a map that satisfies $L(v + w) = Lv + Lw$, $L(\alpha v) = \alpha Lv$, for $v, w \in V$, $\alpha \in \mathbb{C}$. The standard example of a complex vector space is $(\mathbb{C}^n, +, \cdot)$ where for $v = (\alpha_1, \ldots, \alpha_n)$, $w = (\beta_1, \ldots, \beta_n) \in \mathbb{C}^n$, and $\alpha \in \mathbb{C}$, $v + w = (\alpha_1 + \beta_1, \ldots, \alpha_n + \beta_n)$, $\alpha \cdot v = (\alpha\alpha_1, \ldots, \alpha\alpha_n)$. All standard notions from real linear algebra, such as linear independence, bases, etc., carry over. If $\mathbf{e}_j$ denotes the n-tuple with 1 in the j-th slot and 0 elsewhere, then any n-dimensional complex vector space is isomorphic to $\mathbb{C}^n$ by mapping a basis $v_1, \ldots, v_n$ of V pointwise to $\mathbf{e}_1, \ldots, \mathbf{e}_n$ and extending linearly.

DEFINITION 8.1. The *realification* $V_\mathbb{R}$ of a complex vector space $(V, +, \cdot)$ is the real vector space $(V, +, \cdot_{|\mathbb{R}})$ with scalar multiplication restricted to the reals.

An endomorphism J of a real vector space V is said to be a *complex structure* on V if $J^2 = -1_V$, cf. Exercise 57 in Chapter 2. The realification $V_{\mathbb{R}}$ of a complex space V admits a canonical complex structure given by $Jv = iv$ for $v \in V$. Conversely, any real space with a complex structure J becomes a complex space when defining $(a + ib)v = av + bJv$.

DEFINITION 8.2. The *complexification* $V_{\mathbb{C}}$ of a real vector space V is the complex space determined by the (real) space $V \oplus V$ together with the complex structure J given by $J(v, w) = (-w, v)$.

Thus, the isomorphism $(V_{\mathbb{C}})_{\mathbb{R}} \cong V \oplus V$ maps $u + iv$ to (u, v). One customarily thinks of $\mathbb{C}^n$ as the complexification of $\mathbb{R}^n$, so that the identification between the underlying real spaces is given by

$$h : (\mathbb{C}^n)_{\mathbb{R}} \longrightarrow (\mathbb{R}^n_{\mathbb{C}})_{\mathbb{R}} = \mathbb{R}^n \times \mathbb{R}^n,$$
$$v \longmapsto (\operatorname{Re} v, \operatorname{Im} v).$$

The isomorphism h induces a linear map $h : M_{n,n}(\mathbb{C}) \to M_{2n,2n}(\mathbb{R})$ from the space of $n \times n$ complex matrices to the space of $2n \times 2n$ real ones determined by $h(Mv) = h(M)h(v)$, for $M \in M_{n,n}(\mathbb{C})$ and $v \in \mathbb{C}^n$. Writing $M = A + iB$ with $A, B \in M_{n,n}(\mathbb{R})$, we have for $v = x + iy \in \mathbb{C}^n$,

$$h(M)(x, y) = h(Mv) = h((A + iB)(x + iy)) = h(Ax - By + i(Bx + Cy))$$
$$= (Ax - By, By + Ax).$$

Thus,

$$(8.1) \qquad h(M) = \begin{pmatrix} \operatorname{Re} M & -\operatorname{Im} M \\ \operatorname{Im} M & \operatorname{Re} M \end{pmatrix} \in M_{2n,2n}(\mathbb{R}).$$

If we denote by $GL(n, \mathbb{C})$ the group of all invertible $n \times n$ complex matrices, then $h : GL(n, \mathbb{C}) \to GL(2n, \mathbb{R})$ is a group homomorphism. Identifying $GL(n, \mathbb{C})$ with its image shows that it is a Lie subgroup of $GL(2n, \mathbb{R})$ of dimension $2n^2$.

DEFINITION 8.3. A *Hermitian inner product* on a complex vector space V is a map $\langle , \rangle : V \times V \to \mathbb{C}$ satisfying

    (1) $\langle \alpha v_1 + v_2, v \rangle = \alpha \langle v_1, v \rangle + \langle v_2, v \rangle$,
    (2) $\overline{\langle v_1, v_2 \rangle} = \langle v_2, v_1 \rangle$, and
    (3) $\langle v, v \rangle > 0$ if $v \neq 0$,

for all $\alpha \in \mathbb{C}$, $v, v_i \in V$.

By (1) and (2), $\langle v, \alpha w \rangle = \overline{\alpha} \langle v, w \rangle$. For example, the *standard Hermitian inner product* on $\mathbb{C}^n$ is given by

$$\langle v, w \rangle = \sum_j \alpha_j \overline{\beta_j}, \qquad v = (\alpha_1, \ldots, \alpha_n), \quad w = (\beta_1, \ldots, \beta_n).$$

If J denotes a complex structure on a real space V, there is always a (real) inner product on V for which J is skew-adjoint: Let v_1 be any nonzero vector, and set $v_{n+1} := Jv_1$, $W_1 = \operatorname{span}\{v_1, v_{n+1}\}$. Since J^2 equals minus the identity, W_1 is invariant under J. Arguing inductively, V decomposes as a direct sum $\oplus_k W_k$ of J-invariant planes $W_k = \operatorname{span}\{v_k, v_{n+k} = Jv_k\}$, $k = 1, \ldots, n$. If $\langle , \rangle$

denotes that inner product for which the basis $v_1, \ldots, v_{2n}$ is orthonormal, then the matrix of J with respect to this basis is

$$\begin{pmatrix} 0 & -I_n \\ I_n & 0 \end{pmatrix} \in M_{2n,2n}(\mathbb{R}).$$

This shows that J is skew-adjoint, and in fact isometric: $\langle Jv, Jw \rangle = -\langle J^2 v, w \rangle = \langle v, w \rangle$.

PROPOSITION 8.1. *Let V be a complex vector space, J the induced complex structure on the underlying real space $V_{\mathbb{R}}$. Given any inner product $\langle, \rangle$ on $V_{\mathbb{R}}$ for which J is skew-adjoint, the formula*

$$(8.2) \qquad \langle v, w \rangle_{\mathbb{C}} := \langle v, w \rangle + i \langle v, Jw \rangle$$

defines a Hermitian inner product $\langle, \rangle_{\mathbb{C}}$ on V. Conversely, if $\langle, \rangle_{\mathbb{C}}$ is a Hermitian inner product on V, then the real part of $\langle, \rangle_{\mathbb{C}}$ is an inner product on $V_{\mathbb{R}}$ with respect to which J is skew-adjoint, and $\langle, \rangle_{\mathbb{C}}$ is given by (8.2).

PROOF. Given a real inner product on $V_{\mathbb{R}}$, (8.2) defines a complex-valued function on $V \times V$ that is clearly additive in the first variable. Given $\alpha = a + ib \in \mathbb{C}$,

$$\begin{aligned} \langle \alpha v, w \rangle_{\mathbb{C}} &= \langle (a+ib)v, w \rangle + i \langle (a+ib)v, Jw \rangle \\ &= a \langle v, w \rangle + b \langle iv, w \rangle + ia \langle v, Jw \rangle + ib \langle iv, Jw \rangle \\ &= a \langle v, w \rangle - b \langle v, Jw \rangle + ia \langle v, Jw \rangle + ib \langle v, w \rangle \\ &= (a+ib)(\langle v, w \rangle + i \langle v, Jw \rangle) = \alpha \langle v, w \rangle_{\mathbb{C}}. \end{aligned}$$

The second axiom follows from $\overline{\langle v, w \rangle_{\mathbb{C}}} = \langle v, w \rangle - i \langle v, Jw \rangle = \langle w, v \rangle + i \langle w, Jv \rangle = \langle w, v \rangle_{\mathbb{C}}$ by the skew-adjoint property of J. For the same reason $\langle v, Jv \rangle = 0$, so that $\langle v, v \rangle_{\mathbb{C}} = \langle v, v \rangle > 0$ if $v \neq 0$. Thus, $\langle, \rangle$ is Hermitian. Conversely, if $\langle, \rangle_{\mathbb{C}}$ is a Hermitian inner product on V, it is elementary to check that its real part $\langle, \rangle$ is an inner product on $V_{\mathbb{R}}$. Furthermore,

$$\operatorname{Im} \langle v, w \rangle_{\mathbb{C}} = \operatorname{Re}(-i \langle v, w \rangle_{\mathbb{C}}) = \operatorname{Re} \langle v, iw \rangle_{\mathbb{C}} = \langle v, Jw \rangle,$$

so that (8.2) holds. Finally,

$$\langle Jv, w \rangle = \operatorname{Re} \langle iv, w \rangle_{\mathbb{C}} = \operatorname{Re}(i \langle v, w \rangle_{\mathbb{C}}) = -\operatorname{Im} \langle v, w \rangle_{\mathbb{C}} = -\langle v, Jw \rangle,$$

where the last equality follows from the previous equation, so that J is skew-adjoint. $\qquad \square$

There is an alternative way of describing complex structures:

DEFINITION 8.4. A *symplectic form* on a real vector space V is a nondegenerate, skew-symmetric, bilinear form σ on V. (V, σ) is then called a *symplectic vector space*.

For example, the *canonical symplectic form* on $\mathbb{R}^{2n}$ is $\sigma_0 = \sum_{k=1}^{n} u^k \wedge u^{n+k}$. It is the bilinear form associated to the canonical complex structure J_0 on $\mathbb{R}^{2n}$, in the sense that $\sigma_0(v, w) = \langle J_0 v, w \rangle$; this follows for instance from the fact that the matrix of σ_0 with respect to the standard basis is given by

$$\begin{pmatrix} 0 & I_n \\ -I_n & 0 \end{pmatrix},$$

so that $\sigma_0(\mathbf{e}_i, \mathbf{e}_j) = -\langle J_0\mathbf{e}_j, \mathbf{e}_i \rangle = \langle J_0\mathbf{e}_i, \mathbf{e}_j \rangle$. Notice also that

$$\sigma_0(J_0 v, J_0 w) = \langle J_0^2 v, J_0 w \rangle = -\langle v, J_0 w \rangle = \langle J_0 v, w \rangle = \sigma_0(v, w).$$

Up to isomorphism, σ_0 is the only symplectic form: For any symplectic vector space (V, σ), there exists an isomorphism $L : V \to \mathbb{R}^{2n}$ such that $\sigma_0(Lv, Lw) = \sigma(v, w)$ for all $v, w \in V$ (and in particular, V is even-dimensional). This is the essence of the following:

PROPOSITION 8.2. *For any symplectic vector space (V, σ), there exists a basis $\alpha_1, \dots, \alpha_{2n}$ of the dual V^* such that $\sigma = \sum_{k=1}^{n} \alpha_k \wedge \alpha_{n+k}$.*

PROOF. Let v_1 be any nonzero vector in V. Since σ is nondegenerate, there exists some $w \in V$ with $\sigma(v_1, w) = 1$. Set $v_{n+1} := w$, $W := \mathrm{span}\{v_1, v_{n+1}\}$, and $Z := \{v \in V \mid \sigma(v, v_1) = \sigma(v, v_{n+1}) = 0\}$. Any $v \in V$ can then be written as $v = w + (v - w) \in W + Z$, where $w = \sigma(v, v_{n+1}) v_1 - \sigma(v, v_1) v_{n+1}$. If $u \in W \cap Z$, then $u = av_1 + bv_{n+1}$ for some $a, b \in \mathbb{R}$, and since u also belongs to Z, $0 = \sigma(u, v_1) = b\sigma(v_{n+1}, v_1) = -b$. Similarly, $0 = \sigma(u, v_{n+1}) = a\sigma(v_1, v_{n+1}) = a$. Thus, $W \cap Z = \{0\}$, so that $V = W \oplus Z$, and the restriction of σ to Z is symplectic. Arguing inductively, we obtain a basis $v_1, \dots, v_{2n}$ of V, with dual basis $\alpha_1, \dots, \alpha_{2n}$, such that $\sigma = \sum \alpha_k \wedge \alpha_{n+k}$. $\square$

A symplectic form σ and a complex structure J on V are said to be *compatible* if $\sigma(Jv, Jw) = \sigma(v, w)$ for all $v, w \in V$.

PROPOSITION 8.3. *If a real vector space has a complex structure J, then it admits a compatible symplectic form σ. Conversely, any symplectic form σ on V induces a compatible complex structure J. In each case, there exists an inner product on V such that $\sigma(v, w) = \langle Jv, w \rangle$, and J is an isometry.*

PROOF. Given a complex structure J on V, choose an inner product for which J is skew-adjoint, and hence also isometric. Then σ, where $\sigma(v, w) := \langle Jv, w \rangle$ is symplectic. Furthermore,

$$\sigma(Jv, Jw) = \langle J^2 v, Jw \rangle = -\langle v, Jw \rangle = \langle Jv, w \rangle = \sigma(v, w).$$

Conversely, if σ is a symplectic form on V, choose a basis v_k such that $\sigma = \sum \alpha_k \wedge \alpha_{n+k}$, where α_k denotes the basis dual to v_k, see Proposition 8.2. Consider the inner product on V for which v_k is orthonormal, and define $Jv := (\iota_v \sigma)^{\#}$; i.e., $\langle Jv, w \rangle = \sigma(v, w)$. The matrix of J with respect to the basis v_k has as (k, l)-th entry $\langle Jv_l, v_k \rangle = \sigma(v_l, v_k)$, and is thus given by

$$\begin{pmatrix} 0 & -I_n \\ I_n & 0 \end{pmatrix}.$$

This clearly implies that J is a complex structure and an isometry. Compatibility of J and σ follows as before. $\square$

PROPOSITION 8.4. *If V is a complex vector space, then its realification $V_{\mathbb{R}}$ inherits a canonical orientation.*

PROOF. An arbitrary basis $\{v_1, \dots, v_n\}$ of V induces an element

$$v_1 \wedge \cdots \wedge v_n \wedge Jv_1 \wedge \cdots \wedge Jv_n \in (\Lambda_{2n} V_{\mathbb{R}}) \setminus \{0\}.$$

The component of $(\Lambda_{2n} V_{\mathbb{R}}) \setminus \{0\}$ containing it is independent of the original basis: If $w_1, \ldots, w_n$ is another basis of V, and $\langle , \rangle$ is an inner product on $V_{\mathbb{R}}$ for which J is skew-adjoint, then

$$\langle v_1 \wedge \cdots \wedge v_n \wedge J v_1 \wedge \cdots \wedge J v_n, w_1 \wedge \cdots \wedge w_n \wedge J w_1 \wedge \cdots \wedge J w_n \rangle = \det \begin{pmatrix} A & -B \\ B & A \end{pmatrix},$$

where the components a_{ij}, b_{ij}, of A, B, are given by $a_{ij} = \langle v_i, w_j \rangle = \langle J v_i, J w_j \rangle$, and $b_{ij} = \langle J v_i, w_j \rangle = -\langle v_i, J w_j \rangle$. The matrix above is the image via h of $M = A + iB \in M_{n,n}(\mathbb{C})$. The claim now follows from: $\qquad\square$

LEMMA 8.1. *For* $M \in M_{n,n}(\mathbb{C})$, $\det h(M) = |\det M|^2$.

PROOF. The claim is easily seen to be true for diagonalizable matrices. But the latter are dense in $M_{n,n}(\mathbb{C})$; in fact, we may assume that $M \in M_{n,n}(\mathbb{C})$ is in Jordan canonical form. If not all the diagonal terms are distinct, then modifying them appropriately yields a matrix arbitrarily close to M with n distinct eigenvalues. The latter is then diagonalizable. $\qquad\square$

REMARK 8.1. There is another orientation on $V_{\mathbb{R}}$ that is commonly used, namely the one induced by $v_1 \wedge J v_1 \wedge \cdots \wedge v_n \wedge J v_n$, where v_k is a basis of V. It coincides with ours only when $[n/2]$ is even. The reason behind our choice is that it makes the isomorphism $h : (\mathbb{C}^n_{\mathbb{R}}, \omega) \to (\mathbb{R}^{2n}, \text{can})$ orientation-preserving, where ω denotes the orientation of $\mathbb{C}^n_{\mathbb{R}}$ from Proposition 8.4, and can the canonical orientation of $\mathbb{R}^{2n}$.

We next look at isometric automorphisms of a Hermitian inner product space; i.e., automorphisms that preserve the Hermitian inner product. Since such a space is linearly isometric to $\mathbb{C}^n$ with the standard Hermitian inner product, we only need to study linear transformations $L : \mathbb{C}^n \to \mathbb{C}^n$ that satisfy $\langle Lv, Lw \rangle = \langle v, w \rangle$, v, $w \in \mathbb{C}^n$. Recall that the *adjoint* $L^* : \mathbb{C}^n \to \mathbb{C}^n$ of L is defined by $\langle L^* v, w \rangle = \langle v, Lw \rangle$ for v, w in $\mathbb{C}^n$. If v_k is an orthonormal basis of $\mathbb{C}^n$, then the matrix $[L^*]$ of L in this basis is the conjugate transpose of the matrix $[L]$ of L:

$$[L^*]_{ij} = \langle L^* v_j, v_i \rangle = \langle v_j, L v_i \rangle = \overline{\langle L v_i, v_j \rangle} = \overline{[L]}_{ji}.$$

Now, the transformation L preserves the Hermitian inner product iff $\langle Lv, Lw \rangle = \langle v, w \rangle$, iff $\langle L^* Lv, w \rangle = \langle v, w \rangle$ for all v and w in $\mathbb{C}^n$; equivalently, $L^* L = L L^* = 1_{\mathbb{C}^n}$. In terms of matrices, $[L] \overline{[L]}^t = \overline{[L]}^t [L] = I_n$.

DEFINITION 8.5. The *unitary group* $U(n)$ is the subgroup of $GL(n, \mathbb{C})$ that preserves the Hermitian inner product:

$$U(n) = \{M \in GL(n, \mathbb{C}) \mid \overline{M}^t M = M \overline{M}^t = I_n\}.$$

LEMMA 8.2. $h(U(n)) = h(GL(n, \mathbb{C})) \cap SO(2n)$.

PROOF. By Lemma 8.1, it suffices to show that $M \in U(n)$ iff $h(M) \in O(2n)$. But since $h(\overline{M}^t) = h(M)^t$, we have that $A \in U(n)$ iff $A \overline{A}^t = I_n$ iff $h(A) h(A)^t = I_{2n}$ iff $h(A) \in O(2n)$. $\qquad\square$

For example, $U(1)$ is the group of all complex numbers z such that $\langle zv, zw \rangle = \langle v, w \rangle$. Since $\langle zv, zw \rangle = zv\overline{zw} = z\overline{z}\langle v, w \rangle$, $U(1)$ is the group S^1 of all unit complex numbers, and

$$h(U(1)) = \{ \begin{pmatrix} a & -b \\ b & a \end{pmatrix} \mid a^2 + b^2 = 1 \}.$$

The exponential map $e : M_{n,n}(\mathbb{C}) \to GL(n, \mathbb{C})$ is defined as in the real case by

$$e^M := \sum_{k=0}^{\infty} \frac{M^k}{k!};$$

cf. Examples and Remarks 4.2(iv) in Chapter 4. Since $h(MN) = h(M)h(N)$, we have that $h(e^M) = e^{h(M)}$, and the diagram

$$
\begin{array}{ccc}
M_{n,n}(\mathbb{C}) & \xrightarrow{\ h\ } & M_{2n,2n}(\mathbb{R}) \\
e \downarrow & & \downarrow e \\
GL(n, \mathbb{C}) & \xrightarrow[\ h\ ]{} & GL(2n, \mathbb{R})
\end{array}
$$

commutes. In particular, e is one-to-one on a neighborhood V of $I_n \in M_{n,n}(\mathbb{C})$, so that given $A \in U(n) \cap e^V$, $A = e^M$ for a unique M. Then $I = A\overline{A}^t = e^M e^{\overline{M}^t}$, and $e^{\overline{M}^t} = (e^M)^{-1} = e^{-M}$; i.e., $M + \overline{M}^t = 0$. Conversely, if $M + \overline{M}^t = 0$, then $e^M \in U(n)$. This shows that $U(n)$ is an n^2-dimensional Lie subgroup of $GL(n, \mathbb{C})$ with Lie algebra $\mathfrak{u}(n)$ canonically isomorphic to

$$\{ M \in M_{n,n}(\mathbb{C}) \mid M + \overline{M}^t = 0 \} \cong \{ \begin{pmatrix} A & -B \\ B & A \end{pmatrix} \mid A + A^t = 0, B = B^t \},$$

a fact that also follows from Lemma 8.2.

PROPOSITION 8.5. *For any $M \in \mathfrak{u}(n)$, there exists $A \in U(n)$ such that*

$$AMA^{-1} = \begin{pmatrix} i\lambda_1 & & \\ & \ddots & \\ & & i\lambda_n \end{pmatrix}, \qquad \lambda_i \in \mathbb{R};$$

equivalently,

$$h(A)h(M)h(A)^{-1} = \begin{pmatrix} & & & -\lambda_1 & & \\ & & & & \ddots & \\ & & & & & -\lambda_n \\ \lambda_1 & & & & & \\ & \ddots & & & & \\ & & \lambda_n & & & \end{pmatrix}.$$

PROOF. Recall that an endomorphism L of $\mathbb{C}^n$ is *normal* if $LL^* = L^*L$. The spectral theorem asserts that a normal endomorphism of $\mathbb{C}^n$ has n orthonormal eigenvectors. The endomorphism $v \mapsto Lv := M \cdot v$ is skew-adjoint, hence normal, so that there exists a matrix $A \in GL(n, \mathbb{C})$ such that AMA^{-1} is diagonal. Since the eigenvectors are orthonormal, $A \in U(n)$. Furthermore, the conjugate transpose of

$$AM\overline{A}^t = \begin{pmatrix} \lambda_1 & & \\ & \ddots & \\ & & \lambda_n \end{pmatrix}$$

is $-AM\overline{A}^t$, so that $\lambda_i + \overline{\lambda}_i = 0$, and each λ_i is imaginary. ☐

A *polynomial* on $\mathfrak{u}(n)$ is a map $p : \mathfrak{u}(n) \to \mathbb{R}$ such that $p \circ h^{-1} : h(\mathfrak{u}(n)) \subset M_{2n,2n}(\mathbb{R}) \to \mathbb{R}$ is a polynomial in the usual sense. p is said to be *invariant* if it is invariant under the action of $U(n)$. For example, $f_{2k} \circ h$ and $\mathrm{Pf} \circ h$ are invariant polynomials, because $h(U(n)) \subset SO(2n)$. Notice that f_k can actually be defined on $M_{n,n}(\mathbb{C})$ as in Example 1.1, but is not, in general, real-valued. However, the polynomial f_k^i, where $f_k^i(M) = f_k(iM)$, is real-valued on $\mathfrak{u}(n)$:

$$\sum_{k=0}^{n} (-1)^k \overline{f_k^i}(M) x^{n-k} = \sum_{k=0}^{n} (-1)^k \overline{f_k(iM)} x^{n-k} = \overline{\det}(xI_n - iM)$$

$$= \det(xI_n + i\overline{M}^t) = \det(xI_n - iM)$$

$$= \sum_{k=0}^{n} (-1)^k f_k^i(M) x^{n-k}.$$

THEOREM 8.1. *Any invariant polynomial on the Lie algebra $\mathfrak{u}(n)$ is a polynomial in $f_1^i, \ldots, f_n^i$.*

PROOF. For $z_1, \ldots, z_n \in \mathbb{C}$, let $(z_1 \ldots z_n)$ denote the matrix

$$\begin{pmatrix} z_1 & & \\ & \ddots & \\ & & z_n \end{pmatrix}.$$

Given an invariant polynomial f on $\mathfrak{u}(n)$, it suffices to show that there exists a polynomial p such that

$$f(i\lambda_1 \ldots i\lambda_n) = p(f_1^i(i\lambda_1 \ldots i\lambda_n), \ldots, f_n^i(i\lambda_1 \ldots i\lambda_n))$$

for all $\lambda_i \in \mathbb{R}$. To see this, denote by q the polynomial given by $q(\lambda_1, \ldots, \lambda_n) = f(i\lambda_1 \ldots i\lambda_n)$. Since any pair (λ_k, λ_l) can be transposed when conjugating the matrix $(i\lambda_1 \ldots i\lambda_n)$ by an appropriate $A \in U(n)$, q is symmetric, so that

$$q(\lambda_1, \ldots, \lambda_n) = p(s_1(\lambda_1, \ldots, \lambda_n), \ldots, s_n(\lambda_1, \ldots, \lambda_n))$$

for some polynomial p. Then

$$f(i\lambda_1 \ldots i\lambda_n) = q(\lambda_1, \ldots, \lambda_n) = p(s_1(\lambda_1, \ldots, \lambda_n), \ldots, s_n(\lambda_1, \ldots, \lambda_n))$$

$$= p(f_1(\lambda_1 \ldots \lambda_n), \ldots, f_n(\lambda_1 \ldots \lambda_n)).$$

But $(\lambda_1 \ldots \lambda_n) = -i(i\lambda_1 \ldots i\lambda_n)$, so that $f_k(\lambda_1 \ldots \lambda_n) = (-1)^k f_k^i(i\lambda_1 \ldots i\lambda_n)$. Thus,

$$f(i\lambda_1 \ldots i\lambda_n) = p(-f_1^i(i\lambda_1 \ldots i\lambda_n), \ldots, (-1)^n f_n^i(i\lambda_1 \ldots i\lambda_n)),$$

as claimed. ☐

According to Theorem 8.1, $f_{2k} \circ h$ and $\mathrm{Pf} \circ h$ are polynomials in $f_1^i, \ldots, f_n^i$. These polynomials can be described explicitly:

PROPOSITION 8.6. $f_{2k} \circ h = (-1)^k \sum_{l=0}^{2k} (-1)^l f_l^i f_{2k-l}^i$, $\mathrm{Pf} \circ h = (-1)^{[n/2]} f_n^i$.

PROOF. By Lemma 8.1,

$$|\det(xI_n - M)|^2 = \det(h(xI_n - M)) = \det(xI_{2n} - h(M)) = \sum_{k=0}^{n} x^{2(n-k)} f_{2k} \circ h(M).$$

On the other hand,

$$
\begin{aligned}
|\det(xI_n - M)|^2 &= |\det(xI_n - i(-iM))|^2 = \left| \sum_{k=0}^{n} (-1)^k (-i)^k f_k^i(M) x^{n-k} \right|^2 \\
&= |x^n + i x^{n-1} f_1^i(M) - x^{n-2} f_2^i(M) - i x^{n-3} f_3^i(M) + \cdots|^2 \\
&= |(x^n - x^{n-2} f_2^i(M) + x^{n-4} f_4^i(M) \cdots) \\
&\quad + i(x^{n-1} f_1^i(M) - x^{n-3} f_3^i(M) + x^{n-5} f_5^i(M) \cdots)|^2 \\
&= (x^n - x^{n-2} f_2^i(M) + x^{n-4} f_4^i(M) \cdots)^2 \\
&\quad + (x^{n-1} f_1^i(M) - x^{n-3} f_3^i(M) + x^{n-5} f_5^i(M) \cdots)^2.
\end{aligned}
$$

The coefficient of x^{2n-2k} in the last equality is

$$\sum_{k-j \text{ even}} (-1)^{(k-j)/2} f_{k-j}^i(M)(-1)^{(k+j)/2} f_{k+j}^i(M)$$

$$+ \sum_{k-j \text{ odd}} (-1)^{(k-j+1)/2} f_{k-j}^i(M)(-1)^{(k+j+1)/2} f_{k+j}^i(M)$$

$$= (-1)^k [\sum_{k-j \text{ even}} f_{k-j}^i(M) f_{k+j}^i(M) - \sum_{k-j \text{ odd}} f_{k-j}^i(M) f_{k+j}^i(M)]$$

$$= (-1)^k \sum_{k-j} (-1)^{k-j} f_{k-j}^i(M) f_{k+j}^i(M)$$

$$= (-1)^k \sum_{l} (-1)^l f_l^i(M) f_{2k-l}^i(M).$$

This establishes the first identity in the proposition. For the one involving the Pfaffian, it suffices to check the formula in the case when $M = (i\lambda_1 \ldots i\lambda_n)$. Then

$$\mathrm{Pf}(h(M)) = \mathrm{Pf} \begin{pmatrix} & & & -\lambda_1 & & \\ & & & & \ddots & \\ & & & & & -\lambda_n \\ \lambda_1 & & & & & \\ & \ddots & & & & \\ & & \lambda_n & & & \end{pmatrix}$$

$$= \epsilon^{1(n+1)2(n+2)\ldots n(2n)} (-1)^n \lambda_1 \cdots \lambda_n$$

$$= (-1)^{[n/2]} (-1)^n \lambda_1 \cdots \lambda_n = (-1)^{[n/2]} \det iM = (-1)^{[n/2]} f_n^i(M).$$

□

EXERCISE 161. Show that any Hermitian inner product is determined by its norm function. Specifically,

$$\mathrm{Re}\langle v, w \rangle = \frac{1}{4}(|v + w|^2 - |v - w|^2), \qquad \mathrm{Im}\langle v, w \rangle = \frac{1}{4}(|v + iw|^2 - |v - iw|^2).$$

EXERCISE 162. Show that a symplectic form on V induces a Hermitian inner product on V, and that conversely, if $\langle, \rangle$ is a Hermitian inner product on V, then $\sigma(v, w) = -\mathrm{Im}\langle v, w \rangle$ defines a symplectic form on V.

EXERCISE 163. Fill in the details of the proof of Lemma 8.1.

9. Chern Classes

A *complex rank n vector bundle* is a fiber bundle with fiber $\mathbb{C}^n$ and structure group $GL(n, \mathbb{C})$. Thus, the fiber over each point inherits a complex vector space structure. The realification $\xi_{\mathbb{R}}$ of a complex bundle ξ and the complexification $\xi_{\mathbb{C}}$ of a real bundle ξ are defined in the same way as for vector spaces. In particular, $\xi_{\mathbb{R}}$ is orientable, with a canonical orientation.

A *Hermitian metric* on a complex vector bundle $\xi = \pi : E \to M$ is a section of the bundle $\mathrm{Hom}(\xi \otimes \xi, \mathbb{C})$ which is a Hermitian inner product on each fiber. Such a metric always exists, since one can choose a Euclidean metric on $\xi_{\mathbb{R}}$, and this metric induces, by Exercise 161, a Hermitian one on ξ. A *Hermitian connection* ∇ on ξ is one for which the metric is parallel. In this case,

$$X\langle U, V \rangle = \langle \nabla_X U, V \rangle + \langle U, \nabla_X V \rangle, \qquad X \in \mathfrak{X}M, \quad U, V \in \Gamma\xi.$$

Just as in the Riemannian case, the curvature tensor R of a Hermitian connection is skew-adjoint:

$$\langle R(X, Y)U, V \rangle = -\langle U, R(X, Y)V \rangle.$$

Thus, given $p \in M$, and an orthonormal basis $b : \mathbb{C}^n \to E_p$, $b^{-1} \circ R(x, y) \circ b \in \mathfrak{u}(n)$ for any $x, y \in M_p$.

Let g_k^i denote the polarization of the polynomial f_k^i from the previous section. By Proposition 1.1, g_k^i induces a parallel section $\bar{g}_k^i$ of $\mathrm{End}_k(\xi)^*$, and $\bar{g}_k^i(R^k)$ is a $2k$-form on M. By Theorem 1.1, this form is closed, and its cohomology class is independent of the choice of connection.

DEFINITION 9.1. The *k-th Chern class* $c_k(\xi) \in H^{2k}(M)$ of ξ is the class determined by the $2k$-form

$$c_k = \frac{1}{(2\pi)^k} \bar{g}_k^i(R^k).$$

c_k is called the *k-th Chern form* (of the connection). The *total Chern class* of ξ is

$$c(\xi) = c_0(\xi) + c_1(\xi) + \cdots + c_n(\xi),$$

where $c_0(\xi)$ denotes the class containing the constant function 1.

EXAMPLE 9.1. A complex line bundle (or, more accurately, its realification) is equivalent to an oriented real plane bundle: To see this, it suffices to exhibit a complex structure J on an oriented plane bundle $\xi = \pi : E \to M$. Choose a Euclidean metric on ξ, and for nonzero u in E, define Ju to be the unique vector of norm equal to that of u, such that u, Ju is a positively oriented orthogonal basis of $E_{\pi(u)}$. J is then a complex structure on ξ, and it makes sense to talk about the first Chern class $c_1(\xi)$ of ξ. Given a Hermitian connection on ξ, the Chern form c_1 at $p \in M$ is given by

$$c_1(x, y) = \frac{1}{2\pi} \operatorname{tr} iR(x, y) = \frac{1}{2\pi} \langle iR(x, y)u, u \rangle = \frac{1}{2\pi} \langle R(x, y)u, -iu \rangle$$

$$= \frac{1}{2\pi} \langle R(x, y)iu, u \rangle \in \mathbb{R},$$

for unit u in E_p. In terms of the underlying real plane bundle,

$$c_1(x, y) = \frac{1}{2\pi} \langle R(x, y)Ju, u \rangle,$$

where $\langle , \rangle$ now denotes the Euclidean metric on $\xi_{\mathbb{R}}$ induced by the real part of the Hermitian metric on ξ. By Examples and Remarks 3.1(i), the first Chern class of a complex line bundle equals the Euler class of its realification.

More generally, consider a complex rank n bundle $\xi = \pi : E \to M$ with Hermitian connection ∇. The real part of the Hermitian metric is a Euclidean metric which is parallel under ∇. Thus, ∇ induces a Riemannian connection $\tilde{\nabla}$ on $\xi_{\mathbb{R}}$. Since iU is parallel along a curve whenever U is, the complex structure J is parallel.

A Hermitian orthonormal basis $b : \mathbb{C}^n \to E_p$ induces an isomorphism $B : \mathfrak{u}(E_p) \to \mathfrak{u}(n)$. There is a corresponding Euclidean orthonormal basis $b \circ h^{-1} : \mathbb{R}^{2n} \to E_p$ that induces an isomorphism $\tilde{B} : \mathfrak{o}(E_p) \to \mathfrak{o}(2n)$. Denote by $\tilde{h}$ the corresponding homomorphism $\tilde{B}^{-1} \circ h \circ B : \mathfrak{u}(E_p) \to \mathfrak{o}(E_p)$. If $R, \tilde{R}$ denote the curvature tensors of ∇ and $\tilde{\nabla}$, then $\tilde{R} = \tilde{h} \circ R$. Thus,

$$\tilde{B}\tilde{R} = \tilde{B} \circ \tilde{h} \circ R = \tilde{B} \circ \tilde{B}^{-1} \circ h \circ B \circ R = h(BR),$$

and by Proposition 8.6,

$$\bar{g}_{2k}(\tilde{R}^{2k}) = f_{2k}(\tilde{B}\tilde{R}) = f_{2k} \circ h(BR) = (-1)^k \sum_{l=0}^{2k} (-1)^l f_l^i(BR) f_{2k-l}^i(BR)$$

$$= (-1)^k \sum_{l=0}^{2k} (-1)^l \bar{g}_l^i(R^l) \wedge \bar{g}_{2k-l}^i(R^{2k-l}).$$

Similarly,

$$\bar{\mathrm{pf}}(\tilde{R}^n) = \mathrm{Pf}(\tilde{B}\tilde{R}) = \mathrm{Pf} \circ h(BR) = (-1)^{[n/2]} f_n^i(BR) = (-1)^{[n/2]} \bar{g}_n^i(R^n).$$

Summarizing, we have proved the following:

THEOREM 9.1. *If ξ is a complex rank n bundle, then*

$$p_k(\xi_{\mathbb{R}}) = (-1)^k \sum_{l=0}^{2k} (-1)^l c_l(\xi) \cup c_{2k-l}(\xi), \qquad k = 1, \ldots, n,$$

and

$$e(\xi_{\mathbb{R}}) = (-1)^{[n/2]} c_n(\xi).$$

In many references, one finds instead $e(\xi_{\mathbb{R}}) = c_n(\xi)$. The sign in Theorem 9.1 stems from our choice of imbedding $h : \mathbb{C}_{\mathbb{R}}^n \to \mathbb{R}^{2n}$ and the resulting orientation on $\xi_{\mathbb{R}}$.

Instead of looking at the Pontrjagin classes of the realification of a complex bundle ξ, one can instead begin with a real bundle ξ, and look at the Chern classes of its complexification $\xi_{\mathbb{C}} = (\xi \oplus \xi, J)$, where $J(u, v) = (-v, u)$.

THEOREM 9.2. *If ξ is a real vector bundle, then $c_{2k}(\xi_{\mathbb{C}}) = (-1)^k p_k(\xi)$.*

PROOF. Consider a Euclidean metric $\langle , \rangle$ on ξ, and denote by $\langle , \rangle_{\mathbb{C}}$ the Hermitian metric on $\xi_{\mathbb{C}}$ the real part of which is $\langle , \rangle$. Then

$$\langle (U_1, U_2), (V_1, V_2) \rangle_{\mathbb{C}} = \langle U_1, V_1 \rangle + \langle U_2, V_2 \rangle + i(\langle U_2, V_1 \rangle - \langle U_1, V_2 \rangle),$$

for $U_i, V_i \in \Gamma\xi$; cf. Exercise 164. A Riemannian connection ∇ on ξ induces one on $\xi \oplus \xi$, with

$$\tilde{\nabla}_x(U_1, U_2) = (\nabla_x U_1, \nabla_x U_2).$$

If (U_1, U_2) is parallel along a curve, then so is $J(U_1, U_2) = (-U_2, U_1)$, implying that J is parallel. Furthermore, if (V_1, V_2) is also parallel, then the function $\langle (U_1, U_2), (V_1, V_2) \rangle_{\mathbb{C}}$ is constant. Thus, $\tilde{\nabla}$ is a Hermitian connection, with curvature tensor

$$\tilde{R}(x, y)(U_1, U_2)(p) = (R(x, y)U_1(p), R(x, y)U_2(p)), \qquad x, y \in M_p, \quad U_i \in \Gamma\xi.$$

Denoting by $[R] \in \mathfrak{o}(n)$ the matrix of $R(x, y)$ in an orthonormal basis $b : \mathbb{R}^n \to E_p$ of E_p, we have that the matrix of $\tilde{R}(x, y)$ in the basis (b, b) of $E_p \oplus E_p$ is given by

$$\begin{pmatrix} [R] & 0 \\ 0 & [R] \end{pmatrix}.$$

In the corresponding Hermitian basis $(b, b) \circ h$, this matrix is just the original $[R]$. In other words, if $B : \mathfrak{o}(E_p) \to \mathfrak{o}(n)$ is the isomorphism induced by b, and $\tilde{B} : \mathfrak{u}(E_p \oplus E_p) \to \mathfrak{u}(n)$ the one induced by $(b, b) \circ h$, then $\tilde{B}\tilde{R} = BR$. Thus,

$$\bar{g}_{2k}^i(\tilde{R}^{2k}) = f_{2k}^i(\tilde{B}\tilde{R}) = f_{2k}^i(BR) = (-1)^k f_{2k}(BR) = (-1)^k \bar{g}_{2k}(R^{2k}),$$

which establishes the claim. □

To account for the odd Chern classes that are missing in the above theorem, define the *conjugate bundle* $\bar{\xi}$ of a complex bundle ξ to be the (complex) bundle with the same underlying total space and addition, but with scalar multiplication $\bullet$ given by $\alpha \bullet u = \bar{\alpha}u$, where the right side is the usual scalar multiplication in ξ. Although the identity is a *real* bundle equivalence, ξ and its conjugate need not be equivalent as complex bundles; i.e., there may not be an equivalence $h : \xi \to \bar{\xi}$ satisfying $h(\alpha u) = \alpha \bullet h(u) = \bar{\alpha}h(u)$. Such an h does, however, exist when ξ is the complexification $\eta_{\mathbb{C}}$ of a real bundle η: It is straightforward to verify that the formula $h(u, v) = (u, -v)$ defines such an equivalence.

PROPOSITION 9.1. *If ξ is a complex bundle, then the total Chern class of its conjugate is given by*

$$c(\bar{\xi}) = 1 - c_1(\xi) + c_2(\xi) - c_3(\xi) + \cdots$$

PROOF. A Hermitian inner product $\langle , \rangle$ on ξ induces a Hermitian inner product $\overline{\langle , \rangle}$ on $\overline{\xi}$ given by

$$\overline{\langle U, V \rangle} := \overline{\langle U, V \rangle} = \langle V, U \rangle, \qquad U, V \in \Gamma\xi.$$

A Hermitian connection ∇ on ξ then becomes also a Hermitian connection $\overline{\nabla}$ on the conjugate bundle, and their curvature tensors are related by

$$\overline{\langle \overline{R}(x,y)u, v \rangle} = \langle v, R(x,y)u \rangle = \overline{\langle R(x,y)u, v \rangle}.$$

Since the eigenvalues of R and $\overline{R}$ are imaginary, $\overline{R}(x,y) = -R(x,y)$. Thus,

$$\overline{g}_k^i(\overline{R}) = \overline{g}_k^i(-R) = (-1)^k \overline{g}_k^i(R),$$

which establishes the claim. $\qquad\qquad\qquad\qquad\qquad\qquad\qquad\qquad\qquad\square$

We have seen that given a real bundle ξ, its complexification $\xi_{\mathbb{C}}$ is equivalent, in the complex sense, to the conjugate bundle $\overline{\xi}_{\mathbb{C}}$. Proposition 9.1 then implies the following:

COROLLARY 9.1. *If ξ is a real bundle, then the odd Chern classes of its complexification are zero.*

THEOREM 9.3. *For complex bundles ξ and η, $c(\xi \oplus \eta) = c(\xi) \cup c(\eta)$.*

PROOF. Notice that for complex matrices M, N,

$$f_k^i(A \circledast B) = \sum_{l=0}^{k} f_l^i(A) f_{k-l}^i(B).$$

The statement now follows by an argument similar to that in Theorem 4.2. $\quad\square$

EXAMPLE 9.2. Consider an oriented rank 4 bundle ξ_0, and suppose its structure group reduces to $S_+^3 \subset SO(4)$; cf. Section 5. Thus, if P denotes the total space of the corresponding principal S^3-bundle, then $\xi_0 = \pi : P \times_{S_+^3} \mathbb{H} \to P/S_+^3$, with S_+^3 acting on $\mathbb{H} = \mathbb{R}^4$ by left multiplication. Any quaternion $q = a + bi + cj + dk$ can be written as $(a + bi) + j(c - di) = z_1 + jz_2$ for some complex numbers z_1, z_2. The map

$$\overline{h} : \mathbb{H} \longrightarrow \mathbb{C}^2,$$

$$z_1 + jz_2 \longmapsto (z_1, z_2), \qquad z_i \in \mathbb{C}$$

becomes a complex isomorphism if we define scalar multiplication in $\mathbb{H}$ by $\alpha(z_1 + jz_2) := (z_1 + jz_2)\alpha = z_1\alpha + jz_2\alpha$.

The map $\overline{h}$ in turn induces a homomorphism $\overline{h} : GL(1, \mathbb{H}) \to GL(2, \mathbb{C})$ determined by

$$\overline{h}(qu) = \overline{h}(q)\overline{h}(u), \qquad q \in \mathbb{H} \setminus \{0\}, \quad u \in \mathbb{H}.$$

Given $q = z_1 + jz_2 \in S^3$ and $u = w_1 + jw_2 \in \mathbb{H}$,

$$qu = (z_1 + jz_2)(w_1 + jw_2) = (z_1 w_1 - \overline{z_2} w_2) + j(z_2 w_1 + \overline{z_1} w_2).$$

Recalling that $z_1 \overline{z_1} + z_2 \overline{z_2} = 1$, we conclude that

$$\overline{h}(z_1 + jz_2) = \begin{pmatrix} z_1 & -\overline{z_2} \\ z_2 & \overline{z_1} \end{pmatrix} \in U(2).$$

This exhibits ξ_0 as the realification of a complex bundle ξ with group $U(2)$. By Theorem 9.1,

$$p_1(\xi_0) = -(2c_2(\xi) - c_1(\xi) \cup c_1(\xi)) = 2e(\xi_0) + c_1^2(\xi).$$

Consider the map $L : \mathbb{H} \to \mathbb{H}$ that sends $q \in \mathbb{H}$ to qj. L preserves addition, and given $\alpha \in \mathbb{C}$, $q = z_1 + jz_2 \in \mathbb{H}$,

$$L(\alpha q) = L(z_1\alpha + jz_2\alpha) = (z_1\alpha + jz_2\alpha)j = z_1 j\overline{\alpha} + jz_2 j\overline{\alpha} = (z_1 + jz_2)j\overline{\alpha}$$
$$= \overline{\alpha} L q.$$

Thus, L induces a complex equivalence $\xi \cong \overline{\xi}$, so that $c_1(\xi) = 0$ by Proposition 9.1, and

$$p_1(\xi_0) = 2e(\xi_0),$$

a property already observed earlier in the special case that the base is a 4-sphere, cf. Corollary 5.1.

EXERCISE 164. Let ξ be a real vector bundle with complexification $\xi_{\mathbb{C}} = (\xi \oplus \xi, J)$, $J(u, v) = (-v, u)$. A Euclidean metric on ξ extends naturally to $\xi \oplus \xi$ by setting

$$\langle (U_1, U_2), (V_1, V_2) \rangle = \langle U_1, V_1 \rangle + \langle U_2, V_2 \rangle, \qquad U_i, V_i \in \Gamma\xi.$$

By Exercise 161, there exists a unique Hermitian metric $\langle, \rangle_{\mathbb{C}}$ on $\xi_{\mathbb{C}}$ the norm function of which equals that of the Euclidean metric. Prove that

$$\langle (U_1, U_2), (V_1, V_2) \rangle_{\mathbb{C}} = \langle U_1, V_1 \rangle + \langle U_2, V_2 \rangle + i(\langle U_2, V_1 \rangle - \langle U_1, V_2 \rangle).$$

EXERCISE 165. Determine the total Chern class of $\gamma_{1,1}^{\mathbb{C}}$ (observe that $G_{1,1}^{\mathbb{C}}$ is just $\mathbb{C}P^1 = S^2$).

Bibliography

[1] W. Ballmann, *Spaces of Nonpositive Curvature*, Birkhäuser, Basel 1995.

[2] W. Ballmann, V. Schroeder, M. Gromov, *Manifolds of Nonpositive Curvature*, Birkhäuser, Boston 1985.

[3] M. Berger, B. Gostiaux, *Géométrie différentielle*, Armand Colin, Paris 1972.

[4] A. Besse, *Einstein Manifolds*, Springer-Verlag, Berlin Heidelberg 1987.

[5] R. Bott, L. W. Tu, *Differential Forms in Algebraic Topology*, Springer-Verlag, New York 1982.

[6] J.-P. Bourguignon, H. B. Lawson, Jr., *Stability and isolation phenomena for Yang-Mills theory*, Comm. Math. Phys. **79** (1982), 189–230.

[7] J.-P. Bourguignon, H. B. Lawson, Jr., J. Simons, *Stability and gap phenomena for Yang-Mills fields*, Proc. Nat. Acad. Sci. U.S.A. **76** (1979), 1550 1553.

[8] G. E. Bredon, *Introduction to Compact Transformation Groups*, Academic Press, New York 1972.

[9] J. Cheeger, *Some examples of manifolds of nonnegative curvature*, J. Diff. Geom. **8** (1973), 623–628.

[10] J. Cheeger, D. Ebin, *Comparison Theorems in Riemannian Geometry*, North Holland, New York 1975.

[11] J. Cheeger, D. Gromoll, *On the structure of complete manifolds of nonnegative curvature*, Ann. of Math. **96** (1972), 413 443.

[12] M. Do Carmo, *Differential Forms and Applications*, Springer-Verlag, Berlin Heidelberg 1994.

[13] ———, *Riemannian Geometry*, Birkhäuser, Boston 1992.

[14] S. Gallot, D. Hulin, J. Lafontaine, *Riemannian Geometry* (2nd edition), Springer-Verlag, Berlin Heidelberg 1990.

[15] D. Gromoll, W. Klingenberg, W. Meyer, *Riemannsche Geometrie im Großen* (2nd edition), Springer-Verlag, Berlin Heidelberg 1975.

[16] M. Gromov, J. Lafontaine, P. Pansu, *Structures métriques pour les variétés Riemanniennes*, Cedic/Fernand Nathan, Paris 1981.

[17] S. Helgason, *Differential Geometry, Lie Groups and Symmetric Spaces*, Academic Press, New York 1962.

[18] D. Husemoller, *Fiber Bundles* (3rd edition), Springer-Verlag, New York 1994.

[19] J. Jost, *Riemannian Geometry and Geometric Analysis*, Springer, Berlin Heidelberg 1995.

[20] S. Kobayashi, *Differential Geometry of Complex Vector Bundles*, Iwanami Shoten and Princeton University Press, Princeton 1987.

[21] S. Kobayashi, K. Nomizu, *Foundations of Differential Geometry*, John Wiley & Sons, New York 1963.

[22] H. B. Lawson, Jr., *The theory of Gauge fields in four dimensions*, Amer. Math. Soc, CBMS **58**, Providence 1985.

[23] H. B. Lawson, Jr., M.-L. Michelson, *Spin Geometry*, Princeton University Press, Princeton 1989.

[24] J. Milnor, *Morse Theory*, Princeton University Press, Princeton 1963.

[25] ———, *Topology from the Differentiable Viewpoint*, University Press of Virginia, Charlottesville 1965.

[26] J. Milnor, J. Stasheff, *Characteristic Classes*, Princeton University Press, Princeton 1974.

[27] B. O'Neill, *The fundamental equations of a submersion*, Michigan Math. J. **13** (1966), 459–469.

[28] ———, *Semi-Riemannian Geometry*, Academic Press, New York 1983.

[29] M. Özaydın, G. Walschap, *Vector bundles with no soul*, Proc. Amer. Math. Soc. **120** (1994), 565–567.

[30] G. Perelman, *Proof of the soul conjecture of Cheeger and Gromoll*, J. Differential Geom. **40** (1994), 209–212.

[31] P. Petersen, *Riemannian Geometry*, Springer, New York 1998.

[32] W. A. Poor, *Differential Geometric Structures*, McGraw-Hill, New York 1981.

[33] A. Rigas, *Some bundles of nonnegative curvature*, Math. Ann. **232** (1978), 187–193.

[34] M. Spivak, *A Comprehensive Introduction to Differential Geometry*, Publish or Perish, Inc., Berkeley 1979.

[35] N. Steenrod, *The Topology of Fiber Bundles*, Princeton University Press, Princeton 1951.

[36] F. W. Warner, *Foundations of Differentiable Manifolds and Lie Groups*, Springer-Verlag, New York 1983.

[37] G. Whitehead, *Elements of Homotopy Theory*, Springer-Verlag, New York 1978.

Index

Graduate Texts in Mathematics

(continued from page ii)